REDISCOVERING
TEILHARD'S
FIRE

REDISCOVERING TEILHARD'S FIRE

EDITED BY

KATHLEEN DUFFY, S.S.J.

SAINT JOSEPH'S UNIVERSITY PRESS
PHILADELPHIA

This publication was supported by a grant from
the American Teilhard Association.

Book design by Kory Klyman
Cover design by Maria Taffera Lewis

Library of Congress Cataloging-in-Publication Data

Rediscovering Teilhard's fire / edited by Kathleen Duffy.
    p. cm.
Includes bibliographical references (p.) and index.
    ISBN 978-0-916101-65-7 (alk. paper)
1. Teilhard de Chardin, Pierre. I. Duffy, Kathleen, 1941-
B2430.T374R38 2010
194--dc22

                        2009047901

Published by Saint Joseph's University Press
5600 City Avenue, Philadelphia, Pennsylvania 19131-1395, www.sjupress.com

Throughout my life,
by means of my life,
the world has
little by little
caught fire in my sight,
until aflame all around me,
it has become
wholly luminous from within.
Such has been my experience
in contact with the Earth.
The diaphany of the Divine
at the heart
of the universe on fire.

—Pierre Teilhard de Chardin
The Heart of Matter

CONTENTS

ACKNOWLEDGEMENTS

The writings of Pierre Teilhard de Chardin have always inspired me. They have helped to reassure me that the content of the fields of science and religion, which at one time seemed worlds apart, are actually interconnected. Yet it has only been in the last ten years that I have had the leisure to pursue Teilhard's thought more intensely and to understand his work more deeply. Many things have made this possible. Among the most important is the support of Chestnut Hill College, the Metanexus Institute for Religion and Science, and the American Teilhard Association. I am grateful to staff and board members at Metanexus, to co-faculty and students in the science and religion courses that I team-teach in the Interdisciplinary Honors Program at Chestnut Hill College, and to members of the American Teilhard Association. I must especially thank John Haught, Ursula King, Thomas King, S.J., John Grim, and Mary Evelyn Tucker who have continued to inspire and to encourage my scholarship in this area.

Perhaps the most uplifting experience of the past few years occurred in 2005 when I joined with thousands of people around the world who, on the anniversary of Teilhard's death, chose to celebrate, in a variety of ways, his legacy. His supporters gathered at Marist College and at Teilhard's gravesite in Pough-keepsie, NY, at the United Nations, Fordham University, and the Cathedral of St. John the Divine in New York City where he lived the last five years of his life, at Georgetown University in Washington, DC, at a conference center in Lonavla, India, at the Ateneo de Manila University in the Philippines, but, most wonderfully for me, at my own Chestnut Hill College where people from far and wide celebrated Teilhard's contributions and shared their insights regarding his legacy. These events have stimulated a renewed interest in Teilhard's life and work that continues to deepen with time. It is from the reflections of Teilhard scholars during this anniversary year that the present set of essays has emerged.

Besides thanking the authors of the essays in this volume who have so generously shared their material, I also wish to thank the administrators of Chestnut Hill College who were kind enough to provide me with release time to edit this manuscript. I am extremely grateful to Carmen R. Croce, Director, and Rev. Joseph F. Chorpenning, O.S.F.S., Editorial Director, both of Saint Joseph's University Press, for their encouragement and gracious assistance with this volume. I also want to thank the many Sisters of St. Joseph who have supported this work in so many ways, my brother, Joe, and my sister-in-law, Jane, who often provide me with a place to work in beauty and in quiet just when I need it, and all those who have looked over a passage, given technical assistance, or helped to translate a passage, among them Arthur Fabel, James Salmon, S.J., Mary Helen Kashuba, S.S.J., Aida Beaupied, David Contosta, Robert Meyer, and Rosemary Parkinson.

But, most of all, I am grateful to Teilhard for his vision. Without it, I feel that I would be so much less rich. Instead, the more and more deeply I delve into his work, the more my own life is set on fire.

INTRODUCTION

More than fifty years have passed since the death on April 10, 1955 of Jesuit paleontologist Pierre Teilhard de Chardin, a man who was at once priest, scientist, mystic, prophet, and lover of life. More than fifty years have also passed since his religious essays began to trickle out, first in French and then in English, to crowds of believers throughout the world who were hungering for his words. Published posthumously in thirteen volumes, these essays present a vibrant synthesis of evolution and Christology that many people continue to find inspiring and full of meaning. The first of these volumes contains his major opus, *Le phénomène humain*. It is for this treatise that he is perhaps best known. The collection of essays presented here, however, examines not only the many writings that are his legacy but also aspects of his life and work that shed light on his meaning.

Teilhard's legacy is remarkable. Broad enough to encompass science, theology, philosophy, art, and social thought, his essays were his attempt to update a Christology that had lost meaning in the light of evolutionary theory. His synthesis required a major shift in the understanding of both science and religion as they were practiced in the early twentieth century. It attempted to distill the truly significant features both from a belief system that had lost its vitality and ability to inspire and from a science that could no longer see beneath the surface of the phenomenon. Teilhard broke through to the core of his faith and his science to bestow on them a new vitality. Once he achieved this for himself, he yearned to share it with others. His love for the church and its potential to be a light in the darkness motivated him to continue his work even in the midst of painful rejection.

Teilhard was a man of passion. He was passionate about his science—so much so that he found himself working at the heart of a major paleontological find, the famous "Peking Man." He was passionate about his inner life—so

much so that he spent a lifetime developing and living out a vibrant spirituality—one that was rejected by the official church until well after his death. He
was also passionate about people—even allowing himself to fall in love with
several women despite the difficulties of maintaining these as celibate relationships. He was passionate about the evolutionary cosmos—so much so that it
became the framework for all of his writings. Yet the fire of his passion burned
most brightly when he was able to integrate these individual passions into a life of
meaning and purpose.

Perhaps this is why Teilhard believed so strongly that the universe has a
direction. Convinced that the direction of his own life was significant, he interpreted the fruitfulness of the universe as evidence for its continued progress
towards a meaningful goal. Many scientists—particularly biologists—disagree
with this. But Teilhard would ask us to look at the world with our hearts as well
as with our eyes. In order to see where evolution is leading, he would say, it is
necessary to see the cosmos as it is, to learn all we can about the workings of
nature, its intricacies, its vastness, its bounty, its evolutionary process, and to
experience our connectedness to nature. This is what makes Teilhard's mysticism
unique. For a person like Teilhard who is capable of doing this, direction in the
cosmos becomes obvious.

It is crucial to revisit Teilhard's synthesis in our day when we are surrounded
by so many voices that broadcast the impossibility of any connection between
science and religion. On the right, creationists and proponents of Intelligent
Design such as Philip Johnson, William Dembski, and Michael Behe find only
dissonance between their literal reading of scripture and the science of evolution.
On the left, "the new atheists" such as Richard Dawkins, Sam Harris, and
Christopher Hitchens proclaim that science, and in particular evolutionary
biology, rules out the very existence of God. Neither of these extreme camps
seems interested in testing out a more nuanced synthesis based on unbiased
science and mainstream theology. Rather, each side pursues superficial analyses
and fundamentalist interpretations of the other's field.[1] It was this sort of literal
interpretation of scripture that Teilhard found so debilitating in the religion of
his day and part of the reason he felt an obligation to reinvigorate the Christian
message with his synthesis. Fundamentalism, whether it appears as creationism
or scientism, misses the mark. It holds the mind captive rather than letting it
soar. Teilhard was one of the first to provide a viable alternative. Reading the
Word as metaphor allowed him deeper insight into the heart of a God who

loves without bound; seeing the cosmos as a place of ongoing creation allowed him deeper insight into the mind of a God who is unknowable.

Teilhard's profound understanding of our interconnectedness with one another and with our Earth provides another important motivation for probing his writings. His spirituality is so firmly rooted in a deep understanding of our place as humans within the cosmic becoming. The dynamic nature of the cosmos as a whole and its inherent creativity, diversity, and unity revealed to him the heart, mind, and action of the Cosmic Christ at work within every fiber. His reflections on these aspects of the cosmos encourage us to develop our creativity, to participate in a world that celebrates differences as a critical ingredient for forming a healthy whole, to care for our planet with deep passion, and to courageously confront the powers that are driving us apart. He teaches us how the remarkable beauty and diversity of nature as well as its amazing history can stir up in us the courage and creativity we need to survive the global ecological and social problems that we now face.

The present collection of scholarly essays gathers the fruit of recent reflection on Teilhard's legacy. Most of these essays were presented at conferences, symposia, and lecture series scheduled around the world to honor Teilhard's memory on the fiftieth anniversary of his death and to celebrate the fiftieth anniversary of the publication of *Le phénomène humain*. They examine, critique, and expand Teilhard's fascinating worldview, a worldview shaped as much by the theory of evolution and the Christian message as by his open mind, his loving heart, and his free and adventurous spirit, a worldview that is the culmination of a life in search of consistence. They provide fresh insight into the life, work, and thought of this most amazing individual. Although each section focuses on a single aspect, it is impossible to isolate that aspect from a life so integrated.

Section I provides an introduction to Teilhard's thought and spirituality. John Grim begins with a description of Teilhard's evolutionary worldview, while Ursula King discusses his cosmic spirituality. Reflecting on Teilhard's love for Earth and influenced by the writings of Thomas Berry, Mary Evelyn Tucker focuses on the ecological implications of Teilhard's spirituality while John Haught discusses Teilhard's approach to the theodicy problem, the difficult theological question of why there is suffering and evil in a world created by a good God. Donald Viney concludes the section by exploring the difficulties Teilhard had with the church and how these affected his struggle to articulate a relevant metaphysics. These essays set the stage for the analysis of Teilhard's thought that follows.

Since the poetic quality of Teilhard's work is a major part of its allure, the essays in Section II are devoted to Teilhard's aesthetics. Thomas King, S.J., introduces this section with new insights about Teilhard's primary motivation: drawing others outside of themselves into an experience of Divine Beauty. The next three essays explore more deeply how Teilhard's poetry enhances his meaning. John Ryan explores the importance and role of Teilhard's poetic language in articulating religious truth; Kathleen Duffy, S.S.J., discusses Teilhard's use of scientific imagery; and William Falla compares Teilhard's aesthetic theology to that of Erich Przywara, John de Gruchy, Hans Urs von Balthasar, and Karl Rahner.

Although Teilhard was unable to publish his theological and philosophical writings during his lifetime, his singularly creative contribution to these fields has had tremendous impact on present-day thinking. Since issues that he dealt with continue to confront theologians and philosophers today, a review of Teilhard's solutions and viewpoints provide new ways of responding to these difficulties. In Section III, authors contrast Teilhard's theological and philosophical work with that of other scholars. Gloria Schaab, S.S.J., compares Teilhard's idea of God's action in an evolutionary world with that of theologian and biologist Arthur Peacocke; Hugh McElwain notes the similarities between Teilhard's view of teleology, the belief that evolution has a direction, and that of evolutionary theorist John Stewart; Joseph Bracken, S.J., discusses how both Teilhard and Alfred North Whitehead might benefit from developing more fully their metaphysics of intersubjectivity.

Teilhard was a well-respected scientist who contributed several volumes of scientific papers to the fields of geology and paleontology. However, it was the extension of his religious ideas into science that have often been criticized by scientists who claim that his teleology is scientifically unfounded. James Salmon, S.J., begins Section IV by considering some of these critiques. He also discusses Teilhard's controversial conjectures about radial energy in the light of recent findings from thermodynamics and information theory that lend support to Teilhard's ideas. Daryl Domning criticizes Teilhard's failure to address the mechanism of natural selection more fully in his evolutionary scheme, and Ludovico Galleni traces Teilhard's attempt to broaden the definition of biology to include not only the biosphere but also the noosphere. James Skehan, S.J., discusses Teilhard's life as both geologist and mystic. Finally, in light of Teilhard's view of the evolutionary progress of humanity, Ronald Cole-Turner explores ethical considerations regarding recent developments in genetic engineering.

This volume should be of interest and importance to the many people who continue to find Teilhard's life and thought an inspiration and a challenge. It serves as well to introduce Teilhard to those who know him only by name. In it, all will find comfort with the sense of meaning that Teilhard's vision provides even as it challenges us to take responsibility for our evolutionary future.

After more than fifty years of scholarship regarding Teilhard's work, we look back on his legacy with new eyes to discover what can truly inspire us, what can truly lead us to a more profound understanding of our cosmos and our God. What emerges is not only deeper insight into Teilhard's life, work, and thought but also the impact that his thought has had and can have on our religious, scientific, and social thought. Today more than ever, when we are in need of better ways of connecting rapidly changing scientific understandings of our world with our traditional religious beliefs, Teilhard's attempt at integration is invaluable. We rediscover the passion of a man whom, in his own words, "the Lord had drawn to follow the road of fire."[2]

Kathleen Duffy, S.S.J.

Notes

1. See John F. Haught, *God and the New Atheism: A Critical Response to Dawkins, Harris, and Hitchens* (Louisville, KY: Westminster John Knox Press, 2008) for a thorough rebuttal of the arguments of "the new atheists."

2. Pierre Teilhard de Chardin, *Human Energy*, trans. J. M. Cohen (New York: Harcourt Brace Jovanovich, 1969), 67.

I

TEILHARD

VISIONARY, MYSTIC,
THEOLOGIAN,
AND
PHILOSOPHER

TEILHARD'S EVOLUTIONARY VISION

Born into a Catholic Family in the Auvergne region of southern France in 1881, Teilhard entered the Jesuit religious order in 1899 where, along with theological studies, he undertook the study of early life forms or paleontology. His readings in evolutionary thought and his field studies of fossils brought him to explore new understandings of cosmology. In the field, Teilhard experienced a deep resonance with the concept of evolution as he studied Earth's physical layers and came to the realization that not only life on Earth, but also the Earth itself and the universe were all emerging processes that had radically changed over time. The fossil rich chalk cliffs of Hastings in England literally vibrated for him with a deep story of time and the emergence of life. The layers of the rocks and minerals in the Earth, or lithosphere, the water layer of hydrosphere, and the layers of life, or biosphere, became for him a palpable cosmology.

Contemplation of the curvature of these layers of Earth emergence gradually brought him to a vision of the human layer, or noosphere, and the florescence of human consciousness around the Earth. As a stretcher-bearer during many of the major battles of World War I, Teilhard struggled to harmonize the new scientific story of an emerging world with his chosen religious path. As he wrote then, he knew of a "communion with God, and a communion with the Earth." Instead, he sought "a communion with God through the Earth."[2]

One challenge that Teilhard undertook was to bring Christianity and evolution into a mutually enhancing relationship with one another. What was needed for this rapport was first to awaken to the immense dimensions of time that evolution opened up. Teilhard says,

> For our age, to have become conscious of evolution means something very different from and much more than having discovered one further fact.... It means (as happens with a child when he acquires the sense of perspective) that we have become alive to a new dimension.[3]

This new dimension, namely, the place of the human in the larger emergent process of planet Earth and the cosmos, is what characterizes Teilhard's vision of evolution. In fact, his is a vision still immensely challenging to both religious and scientific perspectives.

Scientific perspectives tend to reduce the cosmos to analyses of material processes void of direction or spiritual meaning. From the standpoint of the empirical sciences, consciousness appears as an emergence phenomenon having come from nothing but inert, non-conscious randomly mutating matter that composes the known universe. Teilhard presented a vision of human consciousness that challenges this materialist perspective in that he saw consciousness as resulting from the self-organizing processes within evolution itself.

Religious-oriented thinkers have often framed their inquiry into human consciousness in terms of divine and human interactions. That is, a divine mediation is seen as having broken into the created worlds that bestowed consciousness on the human. Consciousness is imaged as having been extended from the divine realm to the human as if God reached across space to impart psychic vitality to the languid body of Adam.

Secular humanistic thinkers have emphasized a purely human mediation by highlighting the significance of personal experience and interactions with other humans. Human agency is considered primary and divine agency is discounted. In these anthropocentric perspectives, matter in the non-human life-world may be acknowledged as evolving, but it is seen as subservient and as a resource for humans. Directly centered in the controversial ground of these perspectives is the human dimension of consciousness.

From a scientific standpoint, human consciousness is often seen as an anomaly or aberration, a side eddy in the enormous flood of evolution. From a traditional religious perspective, human consciousness is lifted out of the surrounding creation as a separate and special image of a transcendent Creator, or as a result of karmic forces, or a human ancestral inheritance. In secular worldviews matter and spirit are marginalized or eliminated, and human consciousness is both alienated and aggrandized.

Teilhard took a different approach. He offered a more holistic vision by situating human consciousness as integral to the emerging universe; that is, a form of consciousness must have been in the process from the beginning. Teilhard proposed that the increasing complexity and consciousness of evolution in the universe manifested that differentiating consciousness. The emergence of galaxies from the initial flaring forth of radiance and proto-particles as well as the solar systems formed within those galaxies give indication of increasing organization and complexity that, for Teilhard, directly relate to the eventual appearance of humans.

Complexity-consciousness, for Teilhard, emerges in evolution from the interaction of matter with spirit. Teilhard did not separate matter and spirit but spoke of them as forms of energy, namely, tangential and radial energies that are dimensions of a unity. Radial describes that energy within that draws matter forward. Tangential refers to that energy directed without, that attaches matter to other forms of matter. For Teilhard this increasing differentiation results in the plurality of beings in the universe. However, this massive plurality and effulgence of the universe could also draw matter back into entropy. In Teilhard's thought both energy and entropy are necessary for increasing complexity-consciousness in the universe process.

Radial energy, or the "Christic" as Teilhard called it, draws matter forward into increased centration and complexity-consciousness. Tangential energy gives rise to connections and plurality of matter manifestations and eventually to fragmentation and entropy. Thus, for Teilhard, the cosmos also contains a dimension of evil that could collapse into a random plurality of matter. Even as the cosmos becomes conscious of itself in humans, the possibility of falling back into the chaos of entropy remains an ongoing challenge. The work of the human as a manifestation of Earth's spirit-matter is for Teilhard a co-creative act. That is, the human, through the daily work of cultural activity, can directly participate in cosmogenesis, the ongoing creation of the cosmos.

Using the phrase, "the spirit of the Earth," Teilhard focused on the quantum of matter that successively evolves into the layered envelopes encircling the planet from the lithosphere of rock, the hydrosphere of water, and the biosphere of life. This "spirit of Earth" subsequently evolves into the conscious-ness humankind now displays in the thought sphere or noosphere surrounding the globe. Unwilling to separate matter and spirit, he understood these linked spheres as differential and interrelated dynamics operative within the same emergent reality. For Teilhard, the plural, diverse matter of the universe in the process of evolutionary change is ultimately pulled forward by the unifying dynamics of spirit. This hope in the ultimate unity of the cosmos is the under-lying source of Teilhard's deep zest for life.

Teilhard dedicated his life work to fostering an active realization by humans of their evolutionary roles in relation to emerging matter-spirit. This is what he envisioned as seeing. He was aware of the incompleteness of his thought, since he did not teach in an academic setting where his ideas could be challenged and developed. Yet, he struggled to articulate his vision of a union of matter-spirit that would provide the human with a hope centered on the human person as participating in the ongoing cosmogenesis.

Teilhard's sense of "the formation of the noosphere" and of "the planeti-sation of humanity" has major contemporary political, ecological, and spiritual implications. He directs us to consider the process of globalization as planetary and cosmological. Teilhard's thought encourages us to consider our political interconnectedness and global activity as planetary responsibility that has both social and environmental components. Teilhard challenges us to think of the world in its many–layered parts as an interacting whole that we can now identify as ecological. Finally, his legacy challenges us to a deep spirituality in which humans realize in all their diversity that the health and well–being of all life forms, of the Earth itself, is now dependent upon us.

This vision of evolution is the communion with God through the Earth that Teilhard sought so many years ago. Now, we are called to "build the Earth" in our times in ways that Teilhard himself could not have anticipated. Our duty is to acknowledge and encourage the extraordinary contributions of science in widening our understanding of the world, yet to resist its reduction to a purposeless, machine-like materialism. Our duty is to credit the roles of the nation states, yet to resist their unbridled militarism and unilateral domino of power as we aspire to planetary citizenship. Our duty is to realize that the religions are necessary for any transformation into mutually enhancing human-Earth relations, yet to realize they are not sufficient in themselves for understanding the technical, environmental crises we have created.

What Teilhard has provided is the beginning of a vision of evolution that both we and future generations will need to think through again and again as we make our way forward. Significantly, Teilhard's life also models for us the zest for life that sustained him through difficult times. As he wrote,

> For the human . . . the *initial* basis of obligation is the fact of being born and developing *as a function of a cosmic stream.* We must act, and in a certain way, because our individual destinies are dependent on a universal destiny. Duty, in its origins, is nothing but the reflection of the universe in the atom.[4]

Notes

1. Senior Lecturer and Research Scholar, Yale School of Forestry and Environmental Studies and Yale Divinity School; Environmental Ethicist-in-Residence, Interdisciplinary Center for Bioethics, Yale University, New Haven, CN 06520; President, American Teilhard Association.
2. Pierre Teilhard de Chardin, *Writings in Time of War*, trans. René Hague (London: William Collins Sons & Co, 1968), 14.
3. Pierre Teilhard de Chardin, *Science and Christ*, trans. René Hague (New York: Harper & Row, Publishers, 1968), 193.
4. Pierre Teilhard de Chardin, *Human Energy,* trans. J. M. Cohen (New York: Harcourt Brace Jovanovich, 1969), 29.

SPIRIT OF FIRE:
TEILHARD'S COSMIC SPIRITUALITY[1]

URSULA KING[2]

AT THE HEART OF MATTER
A WORLD-HEART
THE HEART OF A GOD.[3]

Pierre Teilhard de Chardin was not only a French Jesuit, but also a distinguished scientist who studied human origins and geology and who spent over twenty years of his life in China, traveling between East and West. Born in the volcanic region of the Auvergne in central France, he belonged to an old aristocratic family, which, through his mother's line, was distantly related to Voltaire, the famous eighteenth–century French philosopher and rationalist. Teilhard possessed a sharp intellect and achieved the highest academic and professional distinctions, but his deeply religious soul had more in common with Pascal than with Voltaire, with that great Auvergnat of the seventeenth century who, like Teilhard himself, was philosopher, scientist, and mystic.[4]

Too many writers on spirituality still tend to see the spiritual quest as largely an individual, inward search for personal transformation that is unconnected to the world at large. Christian spirituality can still remain too ascetic, too world- and body-denying without being linked to outward social transformation and an integral view of the whole of life. But for Teilhard spirituality is never separate, over, above, and apart from our daily tasks and calling. Instead, it is fully embedded in life and action itself. It is a divine dynamic that motivates, empowers, and transforms. His is a spirituality of transfiguration. It is no accident, then, that the Christian feast of the Transfiguration was so dear to him, second only to the joy of the Resurrection event that

Christians celebrate at Easter. It is this extraordinary strength of the inter-weaving of the spiritual and the concretely material in a truly incarnational sense that Teilhard can contribute to contemporary studies on spirituality. Here is a vivid writer who lived, breathed, and reflected on Christian spirituality throughout an unusually rich and difficult life. Towards its end he acknowledged that his deeply mystical vision of God, the world, and human beings emerged to its full maturity through his two most formative experiences, his life in the trenches of the First World War, which was for him a true crucible of fire, and his encounters onwards from 1923 with the living world of Asia.

Most think of Teilhard as a man of ideas and, what is more, ideas that are difficult to understand. But he was also a man of extraordinary passion and sensitivity, one who displayed a unity of heart and mind that is rare. His deepest desire was to see the essence of things, to find their heart and to probe the mystery of life, its origin, and its goal. In the rhythm of life and its evolution, at the center of the cosmos and the world, he saw a divine center, a living heart animated by the fiery energies of love and compassion. Although the heart is a fleshly reality, the image of this very flesh, this concentration of living, breathing matter, came to symbolize for Teilhard the very core of the spirit.

His entire outlook on life was profoundly mystical, but his mysticism was firmly grounded in contemporary scientific research that has so greatly expanded the frontiers of human knowledge and self-understanding. For Teilhard, the mystic seer and believer, the immense research effort of humanity and the advances of contemporary science, notwithstanding their negative side effects and the new ethical problems they create, ultimately lead to the adoration and worship of something greater than ourselves, to the celebration of and surrender to a heart and soul of the world.

Teilhard intended above all to communicate this vision to others; he wanted to make other people *see* and *feel* as deeply about God and the world as he had. Over the years he made several attempts to describe and sum up this vision in succinct essays with titles such as "My Universe,"[5] "How I Believe,"[6] and "My Fundamental Vision."[7] Written at different times in his life, each essay not only reaffirms, but also subtly nuances his profoundly spiritual outlook.

There are many ways of discussing Teilhard's understanding of spirituality. One could consider his mystical experiences and long spiritual practice, or his numerous references and explicit writings on spirituality and mysticism, as I have done elsewhere,[8] or one could compare his views on spirituality to those of others. Instead, I have chosen to look at the three components that, when retracing his inner development in 1950 near the end of his life, he singled out as the defining characteristics of his spirituality. In this most autobiographical piece of his writings called "The Heart of Matter," Teilhard developed a systematic account of his mystical vision.[9] This essay provides the best interpretative key to his spiritual experience and thought, and is prefaced by the motto quoted at the beginning of this article. Here, Teilhard sums up his spiritual vision as a divine "diaphany," a "shining through," a luminous transparency of divine presence, energy, and power in all living things. He writes: "The Diaphany of the Divine at the heart of a glowing Universe . . . experienced . . . through contact with the Earth—the Divine radiating from the depths of a blazing Matter. . . ."[10] The three components which form this spiritual vision are named as follows:

1. *The cosmic, or the evolutive:* this includes the overwhelming appeal of matter, of the tangible, the haunting beauty of the natural world, the immensity of cosmic evolution, the exhilarating dynamism of the forces of life;

2. *The human, or the convergent:* this acknowledges the human phenomenon as an integral part of the evolution of all lifeforms, but also as reaching a new experience of union and communion through the emergence of the "*noosphere*," understood as a specifically human web of interlinked knowing, loving, and acting together;

3. *The Christic, or centric:* this expresses a particular perception of the Divine which focuses on a Christic element as an energizing divine presence or center, "a fire"[11] in all things which he described as both a "heart" and a "divine milieu," a center and an all-pervading environment.

These three elements, "cosmic-human-divine," represent a great cosmotheandric vision which first irrupted in the trenches. I will discuss each element separately, although all three are closely interlinked and interdependent.

THE COSMIC

Teilhard often referred to himself as a naturally pantheistic soul who since early childhood was drawn toward the earth, to rocks, stones, and bones, through which he could unravel the history of living forms. He was magically entranced by the power and beauty of nature, which overwhelmed him; he celebrated the dynamism of life, discovered more than anywhere else in the cosmic process of evolution. The realism of this monistic sense of oneness, so strongly expressed in the collection of essays written in the trenches during the First World War and published as *Writings in Time of War*,[12] shocked some of his Christian friends and was criticized by his correspondents.[13] Teilhard expressed deep regret about the lack of a cosmic sense that he found in the Christian mystics and felt that Christian spirituality urgently needed a strong "new blood transfusion from matter," so as not to lose its vigor and become lost in the clouds.[14] Teilhard's cosmic consciousness, his "passion for the whole," for an all-embracing unity and union, made him argue for a legitimate place for pantheism in Christianity.[15]

While the development of Teilhard's "cosmic sense" was grounded in childhood experiences, his sense of the living "Mother Earth" or *Terra Mater*[16] developed in early adulthood. It found its full expression through his encounter with the forces of the sea, especially while staying on the Channel island of Jersey (1902-5), through his excursions into the desert, first in Egypt (1905-8) and later during his expeditions in China, and through his exploration of the living forms of hills and quarries during his theological studies in Hastings (1908-12) in the South of England, where he read Bergson's influential book *Creative Evolution*. Of great importance, too, was his life in the open on his expeditions as a geologist; even during life in the trenches he was able to build up a fossil collection sufficient for his doctoral research after the war.

From a young age he had been aware of a strong attraction to nature, of seeking and finding a sense of plenitude, a sense of the whole, in his discovery of the wonders of the earth, but also a sense of well–being, of wholeness of body, mind, and spirit. A key experience was his encounter with evolution, which led his creative mind in new directions. Understanding the dynamics of evolution, the rhythm and meaning of transformative change in myriad living forms expanded his sense of plenitude, making him feel part of a much larger reality, a greater whole. Studying the "without" of things, their outer appearance and composition, he was led to perceive their "within," their heart and soul.

The discovery of evolution—not as an outward mechanical process, but as a dynamic, living pattern in an evolutively unfolding universe—brought a tremendous breakthrough in his psychological, intellectual, and religious life. It tore apart the rigid divisions of the traditional dualism between matter and spirit by making him realize that these were not two separate realities, but two aspects of one and the same reality, blazing matter disclosing the fire of spirit. This gave him an immense sense of release, a great thrill and feeling of inner expansion.

These nature experiences strongly reverberate through his first essay "Cosmic Life" (1916) which bears the motto, "There is a communion with God, and a communion with earth, and a communion with God through earth."[17] This essay describes his awakening to the cosmos, the mystical experience of nature as a sense of oneness which he described as the "temptation of matter," an enticing allurement to merge with nature by abandoning the world and its responsibilities. Temporarily passing through this phase he eventually discovered, through his searching and wrestling, the presence of God and the formation of Christ's body in all of nature. Composed during Easter week of 1916, and signed at Dunkirk amidst the terrible battles of war, this essay opens with the extraordinary affirmation that it is written "from an exuberance of life and a yearning to live,"[18] and it closes with a moving, deeply personal and mystical prayer to Christ:

> Lord Jesus Christ, you truly contain within your gentleness, within your humanity, all the unyielding immensity and grandeur of the world. . . .

> Lord Jesus, you who are as gentle as the human heart, as fiery as the forces of nature, as intimate as life itself, you in whom I can melt away and with whom I must have mastery and freedom: I love you as a world, as *this* world which has captivated my heart; and it is you, I now realize, that my brother-men, even those who do not believe, sense and seek throughout the magic immensities of the cosmos. . . .

> To live the cosmic life is to live dominated by the consciousness that one is an atom in the body of the mystical and cosmic Christ. . . .[19]

With extraordinary insight, sensitivity, and great poetic gift, he celebrated the spiritual power of matter, source of all energy, and crucible of spirit. His powerful attraction to matter—matter ensouled, divinized, and holy—

culminates in a hymn of praise to "The Spiritual Power of Matter" and ends in a "Hymn to Matter"[20] wherein matter calls to all human beings:

> steep yourself in the sea of matter, bathe in its fiery waters, for it is the source of your life and your youthfulness.

> You thought you could do without it because the power of thought has been kindled in you? You hoped that the more thoroughly you rejected the tangible, the closer you would be to spirit. . . . all abstract knowledge is only a faded reality; this is because to understand the world, knowledge is not enough, you must see it, touch it, live in its presence and drink the vital heat in the very heart of reality. . . .[21]

The heart of matter, the heart of reality is infused with divine power and presence, it is "the hand of God, the flesh of Christ,"[22] and that is why Teilhard can embrace the universe in an act of communion and union, praising matter in a hymn of exultation as the matrix of spirit: "I bless you, matter. . . . I acclaim you as the divine *milieu*, charged with creative power, as the ocean stirred by the Spirit, as the clay molded and infused with life by the incarnate Word."[23]

The concrete tangibility of the earth, the fragility of the living world, the haunting beauty of nature—all these were for Teilhard potential means for divine disclosure. The human experience of the senses—of seeing, touching, and feeling—could reveal a path leading to the "heart of reality," to God. Teilhard possessed an extraordinary sense of physical concreteness, of the strength and revelatory power of all created things in this world. Both science and religion helped him in this and, in their combined effect, made him see things differently. To see more and to feel more means to be more, to live a fuller, richer life, a life of plenitude and wholeness. "See or perish. This is the situation imposed on every element of the universe by the mysterious gift of existence," he wrote in the Prologue of his book *The Human Phenomenon* which in its first, inaccurate translation became widely known as *The Phenomenon of Man*.[24] Teilhard's particular way of seeing everything in an interconnected, holistic, and all-embracing, unifying vision provided him with deep mystical insight and wisdom. He wished above all to communicate his vision of the splendor of the spirit and of a living divine presence to his fellow human beings.

Few contemporaries have so palpably experienced both the "temptation of matter" and the strength of communion with the earth, our great mother. Again and again, Teilhard expressed not only the ecstasy of the experience but also the struggle and passivities endured in being part of a larger life. He spoke of hallowed matter and hallowed life, even of the holiness of evolution at a time when the Roman Catholic Church still officially rejected evolutionary theory. Teilhard's faith made him see the evolutionary stream of becoming as God's creative action of which we are an integral part and co-creators, allowing us to find and commune with God through the earth and through life. In 1916 he wrote in "Cosmic Life" about his conviction that "*life is never mistaken*, either about its road or its destination."[25] More than twenty years later, in 1939, he assured one of his friends: "Just trust Life: Life will bring you high, if only you are careful in selecting, in the maze of events, those influences or those paths which can bring you each time a little more upward. Life has to be discovered and built step by step: a great charm, if only one is convinced (by faith and experience) that the world is going somewhere."[26]

Much could be said about Teilhard's attitude to the living world, his reverence for nature, and the immense grandeur of the universe. All of these are closely interconnected with his perception of the power and presence of the living spirit of God to which I will return after discussing the significance of the human in Teilhard's spiritual worldview.

THE HUMAN

Together with his cosmic sense Teilhard developed a strong sense of the human, equally important for the understanding of his spirituality. This sense first emerged in full during his experience of the 1914-18 war, when he lived amidst people drawn from diverse cultures and widely different classes. His grasp of the "human phenomenon" on earth was subsequently greatly enhanced through his life in China and his travels around the world. It was soon after the First World War that, in analogy to the term "biosphere," he coined the word "*noosphere*" in collaboration with the philosopher Édouard Le Roy. This concept, derived from the Greek word for mind (*nous*), points to an important spiritual reality: it describes a layer of interactive thinking and interdependent action, and ultimately of collaborative love among people and human groups around the globe. It is an invisible, yet real layer enveloping our planet like the living forms of the biosphere or the atmosphere in which we live and breathe.

According to Teilhard, an accelerating movement towards greater unification is spreading across the earth like an invisible spiritual membrane. This is an insight that in itself has important implications for our understanding of spirituality. This great vision of the oneness of humanity around the earth first dawned on him at the front, when at night he silently contemplated the fullness of the moon suspended above the earth, shining over the trenches of soldiers. He then realized that, in spite of the turmoil of war, humankind is drawing more closely together within the ongoing process of evolutionary becoming to form a new, greater unity. To explain how this is going to happen, he developed his theory of "creative union" which tries to set out how the many can become one, not through fusion and loss of identity, but through a higher form of union which enhances individual elements as it unites them at a deeper level. This is a new, complex synthesis of a higher order which produces something new, and whose ultimate outcome or spiritual summit Teilhard calls "Omega."[27]

Teilhard wrote extensively on the significance of the human phenomenon, not only in his magnum opus *The Human Phenomenon* (1938-40), but also in two earlier essays of the same title and in many other passages throughout his works. These express the significance of the human being within the overall development of the universe. He was much concerned with the urgent problem of human action and with the kind of choices humanity faces, as also with the question of what energy resources are needed for maintaining and developing the dynamics of the noosphere. He often pointed out the need to feed the zest or ardor for life, and for developing an appropriate human energetics to do so.

His thoughts about the human phenomenon are a fine example of contemporary reflection on the age-old philosophical problem of the one and the many. He understood the individual human being as part of the whole of humanity or, at another level, as "an atom in the body of the mystical and cosmic Christ,"[28] and humanity as part of the stream of life within an evolving world and cosmos. In many ways his thought is very ecological, for he could not see the human being except as part of nature. To interpret the significance of the human phenomenon in relation to humankind, and humankind in relation to life, and life in relation to the universe, is the basic plan of *The Human Phenomenon*, which deals with the emergence of "Pre-Life," "Life," and "Thought" in the past, followed by a discussion of the next stage in human evolution, that of "*Superlife*."[29] In this vision the human being is not a static center, but the axis and leading shoot of evolution. The continuing dynamic of the evolutionary process is an immense movement through time, from the development of the atom to the molecule and cell, to different forms of life, to human beings with their great diversity and wealth of social organisations.

Given our modern scientific and technological developments, especially in electronic information technology, one can see that the idea of the *noosphere* as an interactive web of human influence, interthinking, and reciprocal sphere of love connecting people around the globe, represents a new stage in human development. This idea provides us also with an inspiring new image of humanity for which so many are looking today.[30] The concept of the noosphere, together with the idea of the ongoing convergence of humanity, furnished Teilhard de Chardin with a particularly helpful perspective for interpreting racial, cultural, and religious pluralism within the new context of our global complexities.

However, the rise of self-reflective thought or consciousness is not a simple by-product of evolution; it is the very key for understanding evolution itself. Any further development of evolution is linked to the further advance of thought. That is why research has such a central function in Teilhard's work, for it is essential for the further social and cultural evolution of humankind, which follows its biological evolution and consists of the further expansion and growth of the *noosphere*. Teilhard foresaw a world civilization, neither in the sense of dominant uniformity nor in the fragmented manner of postmodernity, but through both enhancing and yet correlating the rich ethnic, cultural, and religious diversities of humankind. In relation to these developments he reflected on the future of work and leisure, the future of morality and ethics, the future of spirituality, and the future of humanity and our planet, for which we all bear responsibility together.[31]

This development is not automatic; it involves human participation and co-creativity. Thus Teilhard's mind was much exercised by the moral and ethical responsibilities for shaping the future of humanity and the life of the planet, but also for advancing the life of the spirit. He enquired into the spiritual energy resources needed to create a better quality of life, greater human integration, and a more peaceful and just world. Well aware that there are thousands of engineers calculating the material energy resources of the planet, he was fond of asking where are the "technicians of the spirit" who pay attention to the preservation and transmission of our spiritual energy resources which nurture and sustain the life of individuals and communities, and feed the human spirit and our hunger for transcendence? To answer this, he insists that the spiritual heritage of the different world faiths is most important, for they provide us with the most precious reservoir of spiritual energy resources, although they are not the only ones to offer the necessary wisdom for guiding our life and future.

In Teilhard's spiritual and scientific perspective human beings are responsible for their further self-evolution, but ultimately, the goals of a higher social and cultural development, and of a greater unity of the human community, are only achievable by combining spiritual and material resources, not through material resources alone. The greatest spiritual resource is represented by the powers of love, understood in a deeply Christian incarnational sense. Using the organic metaphor of "phylum" drawn from the animal kingdom, Teilhard speaks of Christianity as a "phylum of love." He thus understands Christianity as a channel for the unifying powers of all-transforming love that is needed to bring human beings more closely together. The theme of love, also linked to the unitive element of the feminine mentioned as another important aspect of his thinking in "The Heart of Matter," is so central in his thought that his entire work can be rightly called a metaphysic and mysticism of love.

Teilhard de Chardin was convinced that we must study the powers of love as the most sacred spiritual energy resource in the same way that we study and research everything else in the world. As he wrote in 1934: "The day will come when, after harnessing the ether, the winds, the tides, gravitation, we shall harness for God the energies of love. And, on that day, for the second time in the history of the world, man will have discovered fire."[32] Teilhard de Chardin's vision of the world and the human being was grounded in a vision of love; it was a spirituality that celebrates the wonders of creation, a spirituality "that acknowledges love as the clearest understanding we have of God, of ourselves, of history, and the cosmos," as David Tracy has commented.[33]

Since Teilhard understood evolution as an increasing process of spiritualization, he was particularly interested in the awakening and rise of the spirit in the world. Since the earth is in a state of growth where we can witness the birth of spiritual realities amidst much turmoil and tension, this involves a fundamental change in human awareness and consciousness. It also involves the nurturing of a spirituality that feeds and strengthens the taste and zest for life. For this, physical, mental, and spiritual energies are needed. Teilhard compares the "building of the earth" to the tending of a garden with numerous plants and diverse soil, or to the construction of a house with many materials brought by different laborers. At a deeper level, from a religious and mystical perspective, he understands the awakening and growth of the spirit as an increase in the reality and consistence of the incarnate Word becoming flesh in the world.

Numerous are the passages where these ideas are simply mentioned or developed at some length. From his long experience as a researcher and traveller mixing with different social groups and creeds, Teilhard was acutely aware that the modern ideal of the Divine and the nature of human religiosity were undergoing radical changes. Contemporary spiritual sensibility is closely linked to the scientific understanding of life in the universe, to the importance of human efforts, to the responsibility for our environment and planet. The most sincere and passionate human aspirations must thus be integrally linked with our understanding of God. Yet Christians often fail to comprehend and respond to the desires and anxieties of the earth. According to Teilhard, the Church needs to link the gospel of Christ to the gospel of human effort so that its message is presented in a way that relates to people's experience and feelings. Teilhard de Chardin was more aware than most that we are standing at the threshold of a new era, living in a new kind of society, globally interlinked, our former geocentric, anthropocentric, and national viewpoints being replaced by a new, much larger, more complex vision of the world. Few perceived this radical shift in human consciousness so acutely and so early in the twentieth century.

One of the finest visions of his dream of a united human community is found in the essay "The Spirit of the Earth" (1931)[34] which celebrates God as spiritual and personal center of cosmic evolution. It also praises the dynamics of human unification, initially most visible in the numerous material links now increasingly being forged between different groups and societies around the globe. This material network is in advance of what Teilhard calls the "soul-making" that is needed to create a stronger community among the human family. Such bonds, however, cannot be created nor strengthened without the participation of the different world faiths, for they possess an ocean of energy reserves able to help solve the problems of human action. What interested Teilhard most were the spiritual energy reserves found in the still active currents of faith in the world today. What can the world faiths contribute to the solution of contemporary problems such as attitudes towards money, unemployment, poverty, or war? What ethical insights do they possess to guide human action? What vision of God do they convey to draw us to higher spiritual ideals?

Such were some of the questions he reflected upon in "The Zest for Living" (1950),[35] one of the talks he gave to an interfaith group in post-Second World War Paris. In a quiet but sustained way, Teilhard was a great supporter of ecumenical and interfaith ideas[36] while always emphasizing the transformative power of the Christian faith, its action-oriented and activating potential, due to its incarnational rootedness in the world. This power of spiritual transformation is celebrated in many of his writings; it is visible in his approach to the spiritual significance of suffering and the experience of true happiness, in his reflections on the energies of sexual attraction and embodied love, and in his description of the feminine as an element of union.

Teilhard celebrated the powers of love, love for the cosmos, love between woman and man, love between different members of the human family. He saw love and union as central to Christianity. The Christian God is above all a God of love who can ultimately only be reached through love. Teilhard dreamt of a humanity that forms one single body animated by one single heart. A great visionary of human unity, he ultimately saw the building of the human community as a spiritual task leading human hearts to the heart of God, a heart burning like a blaze of fire in the midst of matter, radiating energy through the entire universe, consecrated and made holy by the powers of love and creative union.

THE DIVINE

For Teilhard, God's creative action takes place through the immense evolutionary process in the universe. Human beings are an integral part of this process, shaped and molded by universal energies, but in turn they themselves also contribute and help to shape the direction of this process. Human efforts assist in building up the body of God, the divine kingdom. The struggles of the universe reach into the most hidden parts of our being so that, given the power to see, we can recognize God's action through all events in our lives. Thus life becomes for the believer one long act of living communion with the incarnate Word and with God's creative action.

Teilhard's image of God is commensurate with the greatness of the universe, with the dimensions of the cosmos discovered by modern science. He felt that much of traditional theology works with an image of God that remains far too small in comparison to our knowledge of the world around us. He shared this deep dissatisfaction with many contemporary critics of religion, but understood their atheism to be at root a deeply "dissatisfied theism." Teilhard's experience of the Divine is closely linked to the cosmos and centered on the cosmic Christ, incarnate as heart and center of every element and reality in the universe. Christ is a "God with us,"[37] described in a 1918 essay as "The Soul of the World."[38] Much has been written on Teilhard's Christology,[39] and I have dealt with his pan-Christic mysticism elsewhere.[40] Here I can only summarize Teilhard's understanding of spirituality as informed by his powerful perception of the pervasive, immanent presence of the Divine within the universe, as described in his book *The Divine Milieu*, originally written in 1927 "For those who love the world." This book was widely circulated among friends in manuscript form, but only published in France in 1957, and in English translation, in 1963.[41]

It troubled Teilhard immensely that while science has revealed to us the immensity and unity of the world, the implications of our tremendously changed understanding of the universe, the earth, and all of life have not yet been fully incorporated into theology and spiritual practice. More theologians may be concerned with the relationship between science and religion today than during Teilhard's own lifetime, but there is no one else who has so radically thought through the ramifications of the contemporary scientific and ecological worldview for Christian spirituality. Teilhard wrote *The Divine Milieu* as someone "who believes himself to feel deeply in tune with his own times," and someone who sought "to teach how to see God everywhere, to see him in all that is most hidden, most solid, and most ultimate in the world."[42] He conceived of his book as an essay "on life or on inward vision," which was "not specifically addressed to Christians who are firmly established in their faith," but to those who primarily listen "to the voices of the earth" and "to the waverers" both inside and outside the Church.[43]

The "divine milieu" is an expression that attempts to capture the meaning of two different experiences. On one hand it refers to "milieu" as an environment, like the atmosphere that surrounds us and the air we breathe. On the other hand "milieu" also means a central point, a center where all realities come together, meet, and converge. The divine presence in the world is this mysterious "milieu" radiating like an "atmosphere" throughout all levels of the universe, through matter, life, and human experience. We are immersed in this milieu; it can invade our whole being and transform us, if we but let it. Teilhard called it also a "mystical milieu" and a "divine ocean" in which our soul may be swept away and divinized. All realities, all experiences, all our activities, all our joys and suffering, have this potential for divinization, for being set on fire through the outpouring of divine love.

Elsewhere Teilhard refers to the image of "the burning bush," drawn from the Hebrew Bible, to convey something of this great fire of the spirit pervading the world. In *The Divine Milieu* another image from the same biblical source is called upon, the struggle of Jacob wrestling with the angel. This is a metaphor for the struggle of human life, its advances and diminishments. For Teilhard the essence of spiritual practice is to establish ourselves in the divine milieu, to become part of it, to live and die in it. Thus we can find plenitude, fullness of being, which leads us to the Omega point, identified with "Christ-Omega," the incarnate flesh of Christ in matter.

To be surrounded by and live in the divine milieu, to experience it as if it were like an ocean in which we are immersed or like the air that we breathe, is celebrated in the hymn-like offering of all human experiences, of toil and pain, and of the earth itself, in "The Mass on the World."[44] To say "a Mass on all things" had been Teilhard's prayerful meditation practice in the trenches when he was unable to celebrate the customary Christian liturgy of the Mass, offering bread and wine on the altar of a church. He first wrote about this practice in 1918 in his essay "The Priest."[45] In 1923, when he was on an expedition on the Yellow River in China, he was in a similar situation. Instead of saying Mass in a church, he symbolically offered the entire cosmos to God at the moment of sunrise and left us his great visionary and inspirational piece, "The Mass on the World." This celebrates the magnificent grandeur, power, and beauty of the divine milieu, the milieu that Teilhard loved so intensely, the ambience in which he lived, worked, and died.

His deep, Christ-centered spirituality is already vividly expressed in an early, intensely lyrical essay written in 1916 and entitled "Christ in the World of Matter."[47] On the walls of a church where he had gone to pray, Teilhard saw a picture representing "Christ offering his heart." Suddenly the outlines of this isolated, individual figure of the human Jesus shown in the painting were melting away, radiating outwards towards infinity so that the entire universe was vibrant with movement, energy, and life: "All this movement seemed to emanate from Christ, and above all from his heart."[48] Teilhard describes Christ's garments and gaze, the beauty of his eyes, their expression of both immense joy and suffering. And then he moves on to the Eucharistic host and its mysterious expansion so that "the whole world had become incandescent, had itself become like a single giant host."[49] He describes the act of communion, the receiving of the host, yet the center of the host was receding from him as it drew him on. He writes, "I will not dwell on the feeling of rapture produced in me by this revelation of the universe placed between Christ and myself. . . . I live at the heart of a single, unique Element, the center of the universe and present in each part of it: personal Love and cosmic Power." It is God who is "the heart of everything" and that is "why even war does not disconcert me."[50]

Similar mystical experiences echo through the lines of the essays "The Mystical Milieu" (1917),[51] "The Soul of the World" (1918),[52] "The Priest" (1918),[53] and "Forma Christi" (1918).[54] Each of these is like a variation on the same theme while containing a note of its own. It is impossible to provide a detailed textual analysis of these important writings here[55] or to give an exhaustive account of Teilhard's cosmic Christology that is at the heart of his pan-Christic mysticism. Instead, I illustrate these with another passage from "The Mystical Milieu" which contains a prayer addressed to the person of Jesus:

> His presence impregnated and sustained all things. His power animated all energy. His mastering life ate into every other life, to assimilate it to himself. . . . You, the Ocean of Life, the life that penetrates and quickens us. Since first, Lord, you said, "Hoc est corpus meum," not only the bread on the altar, but (to some degree) everything in the universe that nourishes the soul for the life of Spirit and Grace, has become yours and has become divine—it is divinized, divinizing, and divinizable. Every presence makes me feel that you are near me; every touch is the touch of your hand; every necessity transmits to me a pulsation of your will. And so true is this, that everything around me . . . has become for me . . . in some way, the substance of your heart: Jesus![56]

In "The Mass on the World," Teilhard returns to his vision of the figure of Christ, first described in "Christ in the World of Matter." Christ's central position in the cosmos is again expressed through the image of the heart. Alluding to the Church's devotion to the Sacred Heart of Jesus, Teilhard understands the main purpose of this devotion as escaping "from the constrictions of the too narrow, too precise, too limited image" we have fashioned for ourselves of Jesus. Teilhard expresses this with great power and beauty:

> What I discern in your breast is simply a furnace of fire; and the more I fix my gaze on its ardency the more it seems to me that all around it the contours of your body melt away and become enlarged beyond all measure, till the only features I can distinguish in you are those of the face of a world which has burst into flame.

> Glorious Lord Christ: the divine influence secretly diffused and active in the depths of matter, and the dazzling centre where all the innumerable fibres of the manifold meet; power as implacable as the world and as warm as life; you

whose forehead is of the whiteness of snow, whose eyes are of fire, and whose feet are brighter than molten gold; you whose hands imprison the stars; you who are the first and the last, the living and the dead and the risen again; you who gather into your exuberant unity every beauty, every affinity, every energy, every mode of existence; it is you to whom my being cried out with a desire as vast as the universe, "In truth, you are my Lord and my God."[57]

This heart and fire mysticism was underwritten by Teilhard's life, as he expresses so clearly at the end of "The Mass on the World": "For me, my God, all joy and all achievement, the very purpose of my being and all my love of life, all depend on this one basic vision of the union between yourself and the universe."[58]

CONCLUDING REFLECTIONS

Whenever I re-read Teilhard's works, particularly his early seminal essays in *Writings in Time of War* and now the renewed, much better translation of *The Human Phenomenon*, I discover new insights and striking parallels to contemporary concerns. But from the perspective of today there are also a number of troubling questions that arise. Some people detect a rather overconfident, even naive attitude to science in Teilhard, especially in his expectations of its practical, technological developments. They also accuse him of a rather optimistic worldview when his views are in fact grounded in a deep Christian sense of hope rather than a facile optimism. Traditional Christians, too, can misread his spirituality as too world-oriented, too influenced by matter and science rather than shaped by a supernaturalist approach to God, whereas perennialist writers on spirituality miss in Teilhard the privileging of transcendence over immanence, the distinct separation of spirit from matter.[59] However, many such criticisms are due to a misunderstanding of his texts or an incomplete knowledge of the total context of Teilhard's thinking which, in a true evolutionary sense, is always open to further development.

The real, cohesive strength of Teilhard de Chardin's spiritual vision lies in his close, but open-ended and dynamic integration (not fusion) of the cosmic, human, and divine elements not found in the Christian tradition before, although earlier parallels and intimations exist. The cosmic and divine elements are perhaps less problematic and present fewer difficulties for us than some aspects of the human. Teilhard sensed so vividly the great story of the universe, more fully revealed and known to us today. He perceived the earth as a living planet and expressed his wonder at the beauty of the world around us, which he celebrated as a powerful diaphany, "the divine welling up and showing through"[60] in and across all things. "By means of all created things, without exception, the divine assails us, penetrates us, and molds us. We imagined it as distant and inaccessible, whereas in fact we live steeped in its burning layers." That is the way Teilhard de Chardin expressed his view to a young listener in the mid-1950s.[61] More recently, Brian Swimme has described the unfolding of these cosmic mysteries in an illuminating way in his book *The Hidden Heart of the Cosmos*.[62] Teilhard, the believer, knew and loved this heart at the center of the world as the heart of God. For Teilhard de Chardin, God was the most intimate presence whose insertion into the world through the incarnation meant that the Divine runs through all of matter and life.

Some contemporary cosmologists are prepared to acknowledge a spiritual presence and power in the universe, but only in impersonal form, whereas for Teilhard the highest form of the spiritual is always a special form of the personal. He is a theist through and through, and an incarnational, Trinitarian theist at that. The Divine runs like a fire through all things, but this ubiquitous presence of the spirit is perceived as a person, as the fibers of the cosmic Christ, as the triune God, a real person, with whom he could speak and to whom he could communicate his innermost thoughts and doubts. God was his mother and father, his most intimate friend, someone he could love, embrace, and worship with all the powers of his heart.

Contemporary discussions on religion and science often bypass Teilhard's work because many of the theologians and philosophers involved are not sufficiently familiar with his ideas. A notable exception is Ian Barbour who, through his geologist father's collaboration and close personal friendship with Teilhard de Chardin, has had much more access to and contact with his thinking. In his study, *Religion and Science*,[63] Barbour describes Teilhard's book *The Human Phenomenon* as an evolutionary theology of nature, a synthesis based on ideas drawn from evolutionary biology and from Christian tradition and experience. According to him, we can learn much from this, despite the problems with Teilhard's style of writing.[64] Barbour does not comment, however, about how such a modern theology of nature can inform contemporary Christian spirituality and attitudes to nature. Beyond doubt, Teilhard's perspective can affirm and enhance a reverential attitude to all of the living forms surrounding us. His strong emphasis on "metamorphosis," on "the lure of becoming,"[65] where humans are part of the evolutionary process and subject to further transformation, also vividly brings home to us our embeddedness in nature.

It is probably in the new developments of ecotheology and ecospirituality that Teilhard de Chardin's ideas find most resonance. His understanding of the interrelatedness of humanity and nature provides us with strong elements for such an ecological spirituality. About a decade after completing his book *The Human Phenomenon,* Teilhard succinctly summarized this vision of the close interdependence of natural and human worlds in a study entitled *Man's Place in Nature: The Human Zoological Group.*[66] Based on lectures given in 1949, more than fifty years ago, this was certainly a pioneering vision among Catholic thinkers of his day. More recently the great contemporary Catholic ecologist, Thomas Berry, who himself has been much influenced by Teilhard de Chardin, has spoken of the "mutual enhancement of the human and natural" as a task which Christians must take on. For in Berry's view,

> the renewal of religion in the future will depend on our appreciation of the natural world as the locus for the meeting of the divine and the human. The universe itself is the primary divine revelation. The splendor and the beauty of the natural world in all its variety must be preserved if any worthy idea of the divine is to survive in the human community.[67]

To sustain life on our planet and renew the human community is an immense practical and spiritual task that Berry describes in *The Great Work: Our Way into the Future.*[68] He argues there for "reinventing the human," for, according to him, human survival on this planet is only possible if we radically restructure the basic establishments that determine the functioning of human life, and that includes the religious traditions. But he also mentions that there is fourfold wisdom available to us to guide us into the future: "the wisdom of indigenous people, the wisdom of women, the wisdom of the classical traditions, and the wisdom of science" which is only just in its beginning phase.[69] In other words, in order to renew the earth and humanity, we need to draw creatively on all our available spiritual disciplines and use all our educational, intellectual, and emotional resources. Teilhard de Chardin's thinking on spirituality and his example of Christian spiritual practice provide a very significant resource for this purpose. His integral vision can also be considered an example of the new wisdom of science joined to an ancient faith.

To some, the gaunt, austere figure of Teilhard de Chardin in his old age may still stand for a priestly asceticism too far removed from a truly embodied spirituality. Yet he wrestled with difficult questions about spirituality and sexuality, especially in his personal letters to his intimate friend and beloved, Lucile

Swan,[70] just as he raised many other challenging questions about how to live spirituality in practice—immersed in the modern world of work, of rapid social change, of an uncertain future—without necessarily finding satisfactory answers.

A strong aspect of Teilhard de Chardin's own spirituality was his profound loyalty, his fundamental faithfulness to his vows as a priest, his permanent, unshakable commitment to his Order and his Church, in spite of many personal difficulties, doubts, and temptations. One can see in him a contemporary example of a "faithful servant of God" who overcame all the vicissitudes of his life in faith, hope, and love. He certainly experienced a great deal of anxiety, questioning, and hesitation, even shortly before his death when he asked himself in his last essay, "The Christic,"[71] whether the wonderful diaphany of the divine at the heart of the universe, which transfigured everything for him, was perhaps no more than a mirage of his own mind. Was his glorious vision of the universal, cosmic Christ perhaps an illusion after all? Might Christianity perhaps become extinguished in the world? After weighing these large questions he eventually replied with a definite "no" and once again reaffirmed his belief in the overall coherence of the Christian faith and the contagious power of the love engendered by it. This strength of faith, this Christian fortitude to which Teilhard's life gives such eloquent witness, can also be a tremendous source of strength and inspiration for other people.

More than anything else, the fire of Teilhard's words and example may teach us a spiritual discipline that will ignite in each of us a spark allowing us to live in the divine milieu. The practice of what he calls "the divinization of our activities and passivities" is a particular way of seeing, of reflecting, and of responding to life events, that can transform every experience, whether perceived as good or bad, into a significant encounter, one that reveals to us the breath and touch of the spirit, the ever loving heart of God. Its potential for transforming ordinary human life into greater growth and wholeness, into a sense of plenitude and an experience of communion, is immense. Understood in this way, the heart of Teilhard de Chardin's spirituality is truly linked to the transfiguration of each life into an ardent adventure of the spirit.

Aimed at personal and social transformation, Teilhard de Chardin's mystical vision of the cosmic, human, and divine can nourish, strengthen, and sustain spiritual practice, meditation, and prayer.[72] It also makes a very significant contribution to contemporary Christian ecospirituality, by developing a responsive and responsible attitude towards the earth and nature and encouraging people to take on the task of caring for humanity and the earth community.

Notes

1. This chapter is a much revised version of my Brueggemann Lecture given at Xavier University, Cincinnati, Ohio, on November 15, 1999, and, in an earlier form, at St. James's, Piccadilly, London.

2. Professor Emerita of Theology and Religious Studies and Senior Research Fellow, Institute for Advanced Studies, University of Bristol; Professorial Research Associate, Centre for Gender and Religious Research, School of Oriental and African Studies, University of London.

3. Pierre Teilhard de Chardin, *The Heart of Matter*, trans. René Hague (London: William Collins Sons & Co, 1978), 15.

4. For more details about his life see my illustrated biography *Spirit of Fire: The Life and Vision of Teilhard de Chardin* (Maryknoll, NY: Orbis Books, 1996), which also lists other works on Teilhard's life.

5. Pierre Teilhard de Chardin, *Science and Christ*, trans. René Hague (London: William Collins Sons & Co, 1968), 37-85.

6. Pierre Teilhard de Chardin, *Christianity and Evolution*, trans. René Hague (London: William Collins Sons & Co, 1971), 96-132.

7. Pierre Teilhard de Chardin, *Toward the Future*, trans. René Hague (London: William Collins Sons & Co, 1974), 163-208.

8. See my 1996 Bampton Lectures delivered at Oxford University and published as *Christ in All Things: Exploring Spirituality with Teilhard de Chardin* (Maryknoll, NY: Orbis Books, 1997); *Towards a New Mysticism: Teilhard de Chardin and Eastern Religions* (London: William Collins Sons & Co and New York: Seabury Press, 1980); and *The Spirit of One Earth: Reflections on Teilhard de Chardin and Global Spirituality* (New York: Paragon House, 1989). Chapter 4 of the last book discusses other writers on Teilhard's spirituality and examines at length Teilhard's important essay, "The Phenomenon of Spirituality," written in 1937, published in his book *Human Energy*, trans. J. M. Cohen (London: William Collins Sons & Co, 1969), 93-112.

9. Teilhard de Chardin, *Heart of Matter*, 15-79.

10. Ibid., 16.

11. Ibid., 44.

12. Pierre Teilhard de Chardin, *Writings in Time of War*, trans. René Hague (London: William Collins Sons & Co, 1968).

13. Such as Blondel and Teilhard's friend Valensin; see Henri de Lubac, ed., *Blondel et Teilhard de Chardin: Correspondance Commentée* (Paris: Beauchesne, 1965). English translation New York, 1967.

14. See Teilhard de Chardin, *Toward the Future*, 128.

15. See especially his essay "Pantheism and Christianity" (1923) in Teilhard de Chardin, *Christianity and Evolution*, 56-75.

16. His first essay "Cosmic Life" (1916) is dedicated "To *Terra Mater*, and through her to Christ Jesus, above all things." See Teilhard de Chardin, *Writings in Time of War*, 13, 30.

17. Ibid., 14.

18. Ibid.

19. Ibid., 69-70.

20. First published in the collection of early texts, Pierre Teilhard de Chardin, *Hymn of the Universe*, trans. Simon Bartholomew (London: William Collins Sons & Co, 1970) but also found in Teilhard de Chardin, *Heart of Matter*, 67-77.

21. Teilhard de Chardin, *Hymn of the Universe*, 59-60.
22. Ibid., 64.
23. Ibid., 64-65.
24. Pierre Teilhard de Chardin, *The Human Phenomenon*, trans. Sarah Appleton-Weber (Brighton: Sussex Academic Press, 1999). This fresh translation of *Le phénomène humain* provides a much more accurate and poetic text. For the quotation from the Prologue, see Teilhard de Chardin, *Human Phenomenon*, 3. The earlier translation was published as *The Phenomenon of Man*, trans. Bernard Wall (London: William Collins Sons & Co, 1959).
25. Teilhard de Chardin, *Writings in Time of War*, 32.
26. Pierre Teilhard de Chardin, *Letters to Two Friends, 1926-1952*, ed. Ruth Nanda Anshen, trans. Helen Weaver (London: William Collins Sons & Co, 1972), 127.
27. See Donald Gray's detailed study of Teilhard's notion of creative union in *The One and the Many: Teilhard de Chardin's Vision of Unity* (London: Burns & Oates, 1969).
28. Teilhard de Chardin, *Writings in Time of War*, 70.
29. This is a more appropriate term for Teilhard's notion of "*survie*," wrongly translated as "survival" in the first translation of *Le phénomène humain*.
30. For some discussion of this, see Beatrice Bruteau, *The Grand Option: Personal Transformation and a New Creation*, Gethsemani Studies in Psychological and Religious Anthropology (Notre Dame and London: University of Notre Dame Press, 2001).
31. Many of these themes are discussed in the essays of his books, *Human Energy, The Future of Man*, trans. Norman Denny (London: William Collins Sons & Co, 1965); and *Activation of Energy*, trans. René Hague (London: William Collins Sons & Co, 1970).
32. Teilhard de Chardin, *Toward the Future*, 86-87.
33. David Tracy, "Recent Catholic Spirituality: Unity and Diversity," in Louis Dupré and Don E. Saliers, eds., *Christian Spirituality: Post-Reformation and Modern* (London: SCM, 1990, and New York: The Crossroad Publishing Company, 1989), 143-73, 155.
34. Teilhard de Chardin, *Human Energy*, 19-47.
35. Teilhard de Chardin, *Activation of Energy*, 229-43.
36. For a more detailed discussion of Teilhard's understanding of the spiritual contribution of world faiths, see my book *Christ in All Things* (see note 8 above), chap. 6 on "Interfaith Dialogue and Christian Spirituality."
37. Teilhard de Chardin, *Writings in Time of War*, 184.
38. See Ibid., 179-90.
39. I mention two excellent, earlier studies here: J. A. Lyons, *The Cosmic Christ in Origen and Teilhard de Chardin: A Comparative Study* (Oxford: Oxford University Press, 1982) and Christopher F. Mooney, *Teilhard de Chardin and the Mystery of Christ* (London: William Collins Sons & Co, 1966). *See also my* Christ in All Things, chap. 4.
40. Ursula King, "'Consumed by Fire from Within': Teilhard de Chardin's Pan-Christic Mysticism in Relation to the Catholic Tradition," *The Heythrop Journal* 40, no. 4 (1999): 456-77.
41. Pierre Teilhard de Chardin, *Le Milieu Divin: An Essay on the Interior Life*, trans. Bernard Wall (London: William Collins Sons & Co, 1963). Some editions use the title *The Divine Milieu* which I will use in my discussion. See this title in the Harper & Row Perennial Library edition, New York, 1960.
42. Ibid., 15.

43. Ibid., 11.

44. Teilhard de Chardin, *Heart of Matter*, 119-34.

45. Teilhard de Chardin, *Writings in Time of War*, 203-24.

46. This is the third of his published essays in the French edition of *Écrits du temps de la guerre* (Paris: Grasset, 1965), 85-107, but together with some other essays, it was not included in the English translation, *Writings in Time of War*. The English version is found in Teilhard de Chardin, *Hymn of the Universe*, 39-51.

47. Teilhard de Chardin, *Hymn of the Universe*, 40.

48. Ibid., 41.

49. Ibid., 45.

50. See Ibid., 49, 51.

51. Teilhard de Chardin, *Writings in Time of War*, 115-49.

52. Ibid., 177-90.

53. Ibid., 203-24.

54. Ibid., 249-69.

55. I have discussed the features of Teilhard's Christ in Chapter 4, "Christ in all Things: A Divine Center at the Heart of the Universe," of my book *Christ in All Things*.

56. Teilhard de Chardin, *Writings in Time of War*, 146.

57. Teilhard de Chardin, *Hymn of the Universe*, 32-33.

58. Ibid., 35.

59. As exemplified in Huston Smith's recent publication, *Why Religion Matter: The Fate of the Human Spirit in an Age of Disbelief* (San Francisco: HarperSanFrancisco, 2001).

60. This is how Jean Houston has described Teilhard's spiritual perspective as explained to her when she met him, unknown, as a teenager in Central Park in New York. Her encounter is movingly told in her book *A Mythic Life: Learning to Live Our Greater Story* (San Francisco: HarperSanFrancisco, 1996), 141-48.

61. Houston, *A Mythic Life*, 146.

62. See Brian Swimme, *The Hidden Heart of the Cosmos: Humanity and the New Story* (Maryknoll, NY: Orbis Books, 1996); Brian Swimme and Thomas Berry, *The Universe Story: From the Primordial Flaring Forth to the Ecozoic Era: A Celebration of the Unfolding of the Cosmos* (San Francisco: HarperSanFrancisco, 1992).

63. See Ian G. Barbour, *Religion and Science: Historical and Contemporary Issues* (San Francisco: HarperSanFrancisco, 1997).

64. See Ibid., 101-2, 247-49.

65. Houston, *A Mythic Life*, 145.

66. Pierre Teilhard de Chardin, *Man's Place in Nature: The Human Zoological Group*, trans. René Hague (London: William Collins Sons & Co, 1966). This book is based on a series of lectures given at the Sorbonne in Paris, February-March 1949.

67. See Thomas Berry, "Ecology and the Future of Catholicism: A Statement of the Problem," in Albert J. Lachance and John Carroll, eds., *Embracing Earth: Catholic Approaches to Ecology* (Maryknoll, NY: Orbis Books, 1994), xii. For a wide-ranging survey on ecotheology, see David Hallmann, ed., *Ecotheology: Voices from South and North* (Geneva: WCC Publications and Maryknoll, NY: Orbis Books, 1994).

68. Thomas Berry, *The Great Work: Our Way into the Future* (New York: Bell Tower, 1999).

69. Ibid., 176.

70. See the important correspondence, Thomas M. King, S.J., and Mary Wood Gilbert, eds.,

The Letters of Teilhard de Chardin and Lucile Swan (Washington, DC: Georgetown University Press, 1993); also Ursula King, "The Letters of Teilhard de Chardin and Lucile Swan: A Personal Interpretation," *Teilhard Studies 32* (1995).

71. Teilhard de Chardin, *Heart of Matter*, 80-102.
72. As an example, see the volume by Jesuit geologist James W. Skehan, *Praying with Teilhard de Chardin*, (Winona, MN: St Mary's Press, 2001).

TEILHARD'S ECOLOGICAL SPIRITUALITY[1]

MARY EVELYN TUCKER[2]

INTRODUCTION

Teilhard's sense of the spirit of the Earth and its evolution within the unfolding universe inspired his professional work as scientist and deepened his spirituality. His continual meditation on Earth's vast complexity and the nature and formation of the universe nurtured within him what might be called his ecological spirituality. Within the dynamic, unfolding universe and its expression in Earth's life systems, Teilhard encountered the divine in a vibrant and sustaining manner. These were a primary source of revelation for him.

Teilhard's pervasive sense of the natural world as a "divine milieu" is at the heart of his ecological spirituality. Timely and timeless, it provides a rich resource for our own period, one in which the deleterious effects of global climate change have become more evident. As we witness the extinction of species and the devastation of ecosystems, we would be wise to bring Teilhard's sense of geological time into our discussions. Only a large-scale evolutionary framework will help us to understand and interpret our loss. For we are now realizing that our destructive activities are causing the end of a geological era, the Cenozoic period, a period when millions of life forms have blossomed forth. Not since the dinosaurs went extinct 65 million years ago has Earth lost as many species as at present. We are thus in search of a deepening sense of the divine infusing the natural world in a manner that would prevent our continuing environmental destruction.

Teilhard's comprehensive vision of Earth and its interconnected life processes evolving over time is an important counterpoint to the modern instrumental view that nature is to be used exclusively for human ends. For many years there has been a belief that science and policy alone would be able to solve this ecological crisis. However, there is now a growing awareness that spiritual insight and ethical transformation along with a comprehensive evolutionary perspective will be indispensable. Teilhard's optimism about life's unfolding and the human participation in that process brings a wellspring of hope for the critical work needed to create a sustainable future. It is in this light that Teilhard's ecological spirituality may make a special contribution in our day, despite the fact that the scale of the global ecological crisis that we are facing was not evident during his lifetime.

A Journey into Teilhard's Thought

I first encountered Teilhard in high school and was immediately fascinated by his language, sense of poetry, and fervor. His writings seemed possessed of an inner fire, and while I could not absorb all of their complexities, their sheer intensity and scope captured my imagination. College intervened in the politically volatile times of the late sixties leaving Teilhard far behind. The turmoil of those years saw more of an existential angst among my peers than a groping toward spiritual answers. It was not until the decline of the political whirlwind in the mid-seventies that the deeper seeds of youthful discontent and frustration began to emerge. Many turned to forms of Hinduism and Buddhism to assuage the tides of a growing wave of alienation. There, in rituals and meditative disciplines, they sought paths of interiority, which were perceived as absent or as fossilized in our Western religious heritage. For some, a passage to traditions such as Buddhism or Hinduism resulted in a rigid adherence to that teaching, while for many more it became a vehicle for turning to secularism. Others came to appreciate the effectiveness of certain rituals or meditation previously rejected as archaic or ineffectual allowing them to reenter and repossess their Western tradition.

My own wanderings followed more of the latter pattern, although not always smoothly. After college I went to Japan to teach for a year and a half. I was fascinated with the different cultural and religious environment in which I found myself. This led to a particular interest in Zen Buddhism, in its meditative practices, and in the arts it had encouraged. My immersion in Zen came at a time when I was given some of Teilhard's works to read. The gardens and temples of Japan opened me to the larger process of nature's unfolding. By fortunate synchronicity, the experience of a cosmic sensibility that Zen provided was analogous to the expansive evolutionary framework Teilhard described so richly.

On reading Teilhard in Japan, I was captivated once again by his poetic intensity, but this time the words themselves took on a deeper meaning. It was, however, a very gradual process of understanding that began with Teilhard himself and, then only after learning more about him, with his thought. As I read through his letters written during World War I, it was Teilhard the person who was initially so appealing.[3] An extraordinary personality emerges in these letters that record a touching friendship and correspondence between Teilhard and his cousin Marguerite who later wrote of his experience during those war years: "Of the outside events in Pierre Teilhard's life the war was probably the most decisive of all. It had a profound effect on his whole being."[4] During those four and a half years on the front lines of the French army, Teilhard was baptized in the crucible of war.

Reading these letters I was struck with Teilhard's extraordinary humanness and breadth of mind. His concern for those around him, while undergoing the shattering effects of war, was remarkable. Even more compelling, however, was his conviction that, despite its destructive effects, the war could have some mysterious purpose in the larger evolution of things.

Teilhard's optimistic sense in the midst of destruction was singularly appealing. Of what did this faith consist that was at once so poetical and so practical? Seeking an answer I turned to examine this question in Teilhard's short essay, *How I Believe*. Here his intense love for the world and his unwavering love for God stand as the dual poles of his faith. An attraction both to matter and to spirit constituted the heart of his belief. At an early age he was drawn to rocks as enduring, solid substances, an interest that found expression in his work as a paleontologist. His early religious zeal likewise found fulfillment in his vocation as a priest. A dual commitment to the divine and to the world seeded Teilhard's great spiritual vision.

As I continued my reading, I became fascinated by the spiritual drive that animated his life and work. His book, *The Divine Milieu*, revealed this dynamic impulse most explicitly with its concern for, as Teilhard puts it, "the sanctification of human endeavour"[5] and "the humanization of Christian endeavour."[6] In this book, Teilhard details the process of divinizing one's activities, actions that contribute to the world, and one's passivities, sufferings that humans undergo. He confronts boldly the great problem of a two-fold spirituality, namely, love of God and love of the world. He observes how many people become schizophrenic in their religious practices, seeing their activity in the world as something only to be endured until the next life. For Teilhard, the problem of human action is central to the spiritual venture. Few people withdraw from the world to spend their lives solely in contemplation and prayer. Rather, most labor in the midst of the world, the results of their activity contributing to Earth's unfolding processes.

Teilhard urges us to become conscious of the larger dimension of our efforts. He says in *The Divine Milieu* that the human must construct "a work, an *opus*, into which something enters from all the elements of the Earth." Each person "makes his own soul throughout all his earthly days; and at the same time he collaborates in another work, in another opus, which infinitely transcends ... the perspectives of his individual achievement: the completing of the world."[7] It is this concept that Thomas Berry develops in his book, *The Great Work*.[8]

For Teilhard, then, the human and the world are intimately linked, for it is in the Earthly milieu of the divine that human beings find their purpose and direction. It was Teilhard's ability to express this groping toward meaning that so impressed me. In *The Making of a Mind*, it was his vision of a mysterious purpose in life's unfolding despite the awesome tragedy of the war around him; in *How I Believe*, it was his powerful attraction to both matter and spirit as a perspective for faith; and, finally, in *The Divine Milieu*, it was his concern with the practical and the personal with the importance of human action in relation to the world at large. These key elements of Teilhard's thought, perspective, purpose, practicality, and personalization, could well inform our search for an ecological spirituality, our response to the ecological crisis that has beset us. It is in this area that Teilhard's thought acquires special meaning for our time.

The Roots of an Ecological Spirituality

An ecological spirituality is emerging as we penetrate Earth scientifically and technically and as we examine other cultures spiritually and historically. The search for origins, for the nature of the primeval fireball, and for the residual energies of the "big bang" comes at a time in human history when we are exploring ever more vigorously the origins of our spiritual traditions for sources of wisdom in the contemporary world. As we press further into the past for guides to the future, we are translating each other's great religious texts and experimenting with one another's ancient spiritual disciplines. Since the end of World War II, when we encountered Asian traditions and began to establish departments of Asian studies in North American universities, we have been experiencing a new phase, the dialogue of civilizations. This encounter has resulted in one of the most comprehensive processes of inter-religious dialogue the world has ever seen. The potential of this encounter has still to be fully realized, perhaps in a common concern for the ecological crisis of our planet. At the moment there are still competing claims by the religious traditions to reassert their uniqueness in the values of justice in Judaism, of salvation in Christianity, of submission in Islam, of insight in Buddhism, of liberation in Hinduism, and of integration in Confucianism.

These values were not the primary concerns of early religious beliefs among indigenous peoples. In modern times, many of the world religions have confined themselves to personal salvation and interpersonal ethics which have become the norm for defining the religious life. Indigenous peoples, broadly speaking, do not isolate the human from the divine but rather relate the human to the numinous creative world of nature. This is a perspective that we need to reevaluate in our discussion of religion and its role in the future. If religious concerns are limited to human salvation and interpersonal ethics, where will we find the models for interacting with the natural world in a mutually sustainable and non-destructive manner? Our obsession with the divine-human relationship causes us to lose sight of the very sphere in which the divine has traditionally been encountered, namely, in and through the natural world itself.

Would we understand death and rebirth symbolism as well without its constant reflection to us in the natural world? Would our sacramental symbols, such as water for baptism, have the same rich implications if we were not first to witness its natural cleansing and purifying powers? Our divorce of the natural from the supernatural resulted in the burden of secularization, the loss of transcendence. We now lament the death of God, the impact of atheism, and most especially, the absence of the sacred in the modern world.

One may wonder whether this yearning for transcendence and this mourning the impact of secularization do not represent on another level the subconscious search for an ecological cosmology that would reintegrate the supernatural and the natural. How to do this, at what cost, and for what ends are questions that may be justly raised. Yet the issue of an ecological spirituality presents itself in many forms today with a resurgent interest in mythology, in ritual, in symbol systems, in native religions, in esoteric traditions, and in feminist spirituality. These may very well be elements of a more widespread groping toward a convergence of the natural and the supernatural spheres. How this can be done is an issue that deserves to be at the forefront of our thinking, theological and otherwise.

We cannot simply turn to native traditions in a romantic back-to-nature quest that tries to incorporate ancient mythologies or symbol systems into a contemporary setting. Yet we must not merely dismiss as so much superstition or pantheism the religious beliefs of much of the human community that searches for an intimate spiritual experience of the natural world. Indeed, we may be well advised to take seriously their experience of the numinous in nature and thus realize a spirituality that embraces the very life processes that sustain us.[9]

In addition, there are numerous grassroots environmental projects inspired by religious values and ethics that have flourished around the world. These distinctive expressions of ecological spirituality are overcoming the split between the natural and supernatural spheres. Like Teilhard, those who practice these ecological spiritualities view the natural world as part of the divine milieu.

THE BIFURCATION OF SCIENCE AND RELIGION

The reintegration of the natural and supernatural spheres occurs at a time when we are plumbing the Earth in a scientific quest to understand the macrophase: the origins of the universe and the dynamics of the evolutionary process. At the same time, we are exploring the microphase: the basic life of the cell, the constituent building blocks of molecules, and the inner structure of the atom itself. These studies are uncovering structures and patterns in the natural world which co-exist with random change and mutations. Here we find the great paradox of apparent purpose and purposelessness mutually present in nature, and are faced with the reality of order and disorder, of necessity and chance, at the heart of our evolution.

This great paradox becomes even more striking when we see its bifurcation in the scientific and the religious communities. Scientists, for the most part, reject purpose or meaning in the natural world and in evolutionary processes. Similarly, theologians are unwilling to relinquish their scriptural context for interpreting the purpose and direction of the universe. The scientist reads the book of nature and often finds it filled with random, chaotic, disconnected events. At the same time, the theologian reads the book of scripture, and finds nature to be a purposeful expression of a divine creator. For the scientist, nature is a primary source of scientific truth; for the theologian, God is the primary source of revealed truth. Teilhard recognized this problem clearly. In *The Human Phenomenon* he writes,

> As I said, all scientists are now in agreement about the general fact that there is *an* evolution. But whether or not this evolution is *directed* is quite another matter. Ask a biologist today if he accepts that life is going *somewhere* in the process of its transformations, and nine times out of ten he will answer no— even vehemently.[10]

This clash between claims of truth remains unresolved in contemporary society. As a result, we continue to conceptualize and pass down in our educational system two ways of knowing that seem to be mutually exclusive—the scientific story of the universe as objective fact devoid of meaning, and the religious story of salvation encompassing all questions of meaning and calling forth a response of unswerving faith and belief. The clash of objective fact and interpretive meaning, of randomness and purpose, of chance and necessity, perpetuated by the scientific and religious communities, is one of the unconscious sources of the secularization of the modern world. There is an acute need for an ecological spirituality that will reunite the religious drive of the human with Earth processes themselves. The starting point for such a spirituality can be located in the thought of Teilhard, and so it is to him I turn to suggest the ground from which a new ecological spirituality can and will emerge.

TEILHARD'S COSMIC PERSPECTIVE

The themes of perspective, purpose, practicality, and personalization capture the seminal ideas of Teilhard's spiritual vision. In the spiritual and material poles of his faith, Teilhard was able to view the dynamic undercurrent of the whole evolutionary process. One of Teilhard's greatest contributions to modern religious thought is his conception that all of reality is composed of both spirit and matter, of psychic and physical components, a within and a without. It was his aim in the early chapters of *The Human Phenomenon* to demonstrate that the numinous dimension of life was present from the beginning. This radically alters our perspective of matter itself. No longer is matter seen as dead and inert, and as a consequence, the divine is no longer to be sought only in a transcendent union with a merciful God. This suggests a remarkable change in our religious quest, which had previously been directed toward other–worldly goals realized only after death. In *The Human Phenomenon* Teilhard appeals to ordinary experience to assert the within of all things:

> Indisputably, deep within ourselves, through a rent or tear, an "interior" appears at the heart of things. This is enough to establish the existence of this interior in some degree or other everywhere forever in nature. Since the stuff of the universe has an internal face at one point in itself, its structure is necessarily *bifacial*; that is, in every region of time and space, as well, for example, as being granular, *coexistensive with its outside, everything has an inside.*[11]

Teilhard's sense of the *within* is critical to going beyond a mechanistic or reductionist view of the world as nothing more than inanimate matter. He suggests that life could not arise without a sense of pre-life or some kind of interiority:

> Although disconcerting for our imagination, the picture of the world that logically follows from this is in fact the only one our reason can absorb. Taken at its lowest point, exactly where we placed ourselves at the beginning of these pages, matter at its origins is something more than the particulate swarming so marvelously analyzed by modern physics. Beneath this initial mechanical sheet we must conceive the existence of a "biological" sheet, thin in the extreme, but absolutely necessary to explain the state of the cosmos in the times that follow. Inside, consciousness, and spontaneity are three expressions of one and the same thing, and we can no more legitimately set an experimental absolute beginning for them than for any other of the lines of the universe.
>
> *In a coherent perspective of the world, life inevitably presupposes a prelife before it, as far back as the eye can see.*[12]

Teilhard redirects our vision to what is close at hand and yet co-extensive with the birth of creation itself. He points out that the interiority of the universe is a key component to all future forms of spirituality. He notes repeatedly that unless there were an interior aspect to matter, consciousness and spontaneity could not emerge in the human. The human should not be seen as something extrinsic or added on to the evolutionary process, but as a culmination and outgrowth of what went before. To understand that reality, from the tiniest atom to the most intelligent human, is composed of a within and a without, gives us a very different perspective on our universe.

The effect of this insight for spirituality is to achieve a reciprocity with both the particular and the whole of the natural world in a way scarcely imagined until now. Before, our hope was transcendent union; now, that is balanced by a new understanding of an immanence in the depths of matter. That is not, of course, to disallow the considerable differences in the intelligence and intentionality of a human, an animal or a plant. Yet not to see the essential link between all phases of life is to deny the very capacity of life to structure and reproduce itself. The mystery behind the process lies precisely in the interiority of matter that in its self-organizing dynamics finds one of its greatest expressions in human beings, especially in their spiritual life.

Teilhard believes this new perspective will permit the human to appreciate again the fundamental unity of life. Knowledge of such unity is beginning to dawn on human consciousness through the discoveries of science. A sense of the cosmos is becoming a part of the popular imagination. A cosmic sensibility is actually quite old in the human community, but has been lost in the modern period beneath data, verification, and empiricism. We scarcely see the forest for our focus on the tree. Yet Teilhard recognizes how ancient this sensibility of the whole really is. In his book *Human Energy* he writes:

> The cosmic sense must have been born as soon as man found himself facing the forest, the sea and the stars. And since then we find evidence of it in all our experience of the great and unbounded: in art, in poetry, in religion. Through it we react to the world as a whole as with our eyes to the light.[13]

He describes the effects of this new perspective on the unity of life as follows:

> Whereas for the last two centuries our study of science, history and philosophy has appeared to be a matter of speculation, imagination and hypothesis, we can now see that in fact, in countless subtle ways, the concept of Evolution has been weaving its web around us. We believed that we did not change; but now, like newborn infants whose eyes are opening to the light, we are becoming aware of a world in which neo-Time [evolution] is endowing the totality of our knowledge and beliefs with a new structure and a new dimension.[14]

The impact of the discovery of evolution on human consciousness is immense and still unfolding. It is as if we are becoming alive to a whole new perspective and dimension which we are still absorbing.

> For our age, to have become conscious of evolution means something very different from and much more than having discovered one further fact, however massive and important that fact may be. It means (as happens with a child when he acquires the sense of perspective) that we have come alive to a new *dimension*. The idea of evolution is not, as sometimes said, a mere hypothesis, but a condition of all experience.[15]

The monumental psychological change that this new perspective is requiring of humans is evident in our contemporary period, and will require several more centuries to absorb more fully. After all, Darwin's *Origin of Species* was only published in 1859: "This is something we must understand once and for all: for us and for our descendents, there is henceforth a final and permanent change in psychological time-relationships and dimensions."[16]

Such a change in the understanding of evolution might be defined as one of perspective and purpose. It is undoubtedly this new evolving context of human life that remains one of the richest sources for dynamizing human energies. We are awakening to the fact that the Earth and its inhabitants are much older than we thought. Although the theory of evolution was discovered a little more than a century ago, its implications are still being absorbed by the human mind. As we gradually begin to connect ourselves both scientifically and poetically to this vast evolutionary process, we are tapping unexplored resources in the human psyche and spirit for redirecting our sense of perspective and purpose. It is Teilhard who has given us some of the first metaphors to describe our role as the consciousness of the Earth itself.

In terms of perspective, then, Teilhard offers a vision of the unity of life that resituates the human in the whole cosmic order. It provides a means of reciprocity and reverence with the natural world, which our previous scientific view of matter did not take into consideration. Matter was dead, inert and radically different from the human. Our capacity for communication with nature is greatly enlarged and revitalized when we recognize its essential connectedness with ourselves. Surely this has important implications for our understandings of spiritual purpose.

THE ISSUE OF HUMAN PURPOSE

Purpose may be the greatest problem facing the contemporary human community. We have already witnessed considerable inroads into the teleological thrust of religion by the existentialist and postmodern critics who wish to bracket out all concepts of shared purpose or values of evolutionary processes. Such critics speak of a sense of purposelessness in the universe mirrored by the apparent lack of direction so deeply imbedded in individuals and in our society at large. At the crux of the problem of purpose is the meaning of human life in an evolving universe. To ask the question "Does evolution have a goal?" becomes a vital question for spirituality, not simply an academic endeavor. In our spiritual quest we are now learning to seek the largest possible frame in which human energies become activated and dynamized.

For Teilhard this rests precisely on the evolution of spirit and matter over time. Teilhard's ability to see the relationship between spirit and matter or mind and nature is the starting point for understanding the larger design of things. As theologian John Haught notes in *Nature and Purpose*, it is precisely the capacity to understand the relationship between mind and nature that may have such an effect on the sense of human purpose and commitment. He stresses the significance of this unity for the crisis of meaning in the modern world.

The starting point of a link between mind and nature described by Haught is at the heart of the question of spiritual purpose. If matter did not have an inner intentionality or entelechy, the larger scheme of things would also lack such direction. Here arises the complex issue of the evolutionary process in terms of random change or underlying purpose, often noted as the problem of chance and necessity. In other words, is evolution simply a series of arbitrary mutations over some four and a half billion years with no explanation or long range goal? Or does the very fact that life has evolved into increasingly complex forms suggest an inherent design and purpose?

> It is possible in theory to anticipate, therefore, the enormous implications that a new alliance of nature and mind might have for the contemporary crisis of meaning. Nothing less imposing than the significance of our lives is bound up with the quest for a union of mind and nature established on solid grounds compatible with reason, common sense and science. If we could grasp somehow that our subjectivity is a blossoming forth of nature itself, and not some enigmatic nothingness or separate substance over against nature, we would have at least the context in which to discuss once again the question of nature and purpose.[17]

This debate is currently being carried on in the halls of science with many subtle variations on the broad positions outlined above. Part of the problem for the Western monotheistic traditions lies in their inability to embrace both sides of the discussion, as they try to maintain the traditional perspective that purpose arises because God created the world and set it in motion. This most crucial point of creation versus evolution has appeared across the country in classrooms, in churches, and in courtrooms.

Many religions have been unable so far to include both chance and necessity in the newly emerging perspective on evolution. To accept change and mutation at many points in the microphase by no means negates the sense that evolution has a direction in its macrophase. Just as in human life we cannot deny the existence of malformations, disease, or death, so in evolution the survival of the fittest has resulted in the adaptation or extinction of many species and forms of life. Nonetheless, when we step back from the particular to the general sweep of evolution we cannot but be impressed with the sense of patterning and design.

One may well ask what effect this has on contemporary spirituality. The answer is a very significant one. If spirit and matter are the dynamics of evolution, we have a radically new perspective for situating the whole idea of purpose. No longer can the human be viewed as the existentialists have proposed, as a random event in an empty, purposeless universe. Rather, we are intrinsically linked to the evolution of spirit and matter in the universe as a whole. In fact, we are at a moment in history when we must take responsibility for guiding this evolutionary process in a sympathetic awareness of its profound connection to ourselves.

For the first time, and on a global scale, we have the capacity to say which species may live, what air or water will remain pure, what land or sea areas may be exploited, and even when human life might be conceived or terminated. The numerous issues confronting us in genetic and medical ethics are only phases of an important process in the increasing responsibility of humans to work for the continuance and survival of life in all its forms. All of these are profoundly intricate questions that bring new challenges to scientists and theologians alike. They especially challenge us to expand our idea of spirituality, to see it as more than an other–worldly goal or as a series of ritual acts which put us in communion with the divine for the sake of personal salvation. Rather, it is something that requires our energies on a scale never imagined before. As Teilhard advises, we can live with the explicit consciousness of being an atom adrift or a citizen of the universe. This sense of perspective and purpose is now so widely drawn as to be a dramatic challenge to all traditional spiritualities.

We are now confronted with the challenge of resituating world's religions that claim some four thousand years of history into a perspective which reveals Earth to be four and a half billion years old. The imperative is to shift our viewpoint from human historical time to cosmic and geological time. The epochal change of paradigm is from the divine as simply transcendent to the world, to a sense of the divine within the world, from a perspective which saw spirit and matter as always separate, to one that sees their destinies intertwined in evolution, from a perspective that saw the Logos as given from without, to one which begins to discover an inner–ordering Logos at the heart of all matter.

The transition in terms of purpose is from a wish to embrace design and directionality while rejecting change and mutation. In other words, it is a movement from a radical separation of good and evil in nature and in the human to that which sees these two forces as the dynamizing drive of evolution itself. These two forces should not be seen as mutually exclusive, but rather in a creative tension within the human psyche and spirit. (There is much in modern depth psychology that has contributed to our awareness here.) Our spiritual goals are thus reoriented from a quest toward other–worldly perfection and goodness to a quest toward the dynamic evolutionary process close at hand. Our spiritual purpose and perspective, then, is expanded and refocused to embrace both four and a half billion years of Earth history and the immediate contemporary challenges to the planet and the evolution of human life.

PRACTICALITY AND PERSONALIZATION

I come, then, to my last two points with regard to Teilhard's spiritual vision, namely practicality and personalization. If our sense of spiritual perspective and purpose has been expanded by Teilhard, what are the consequences for human action and spiritual practice? Teilhard's vision is eminently practical, not simply a misplaced abstraction for spiritual growth. Rather, it has consequences for spiritual practice in at least three ways, specifically for prayer, sacrifice, and action.

With regard to prayer, Teilhard gives us numerous examples of his devotionalism, the spirit of which may be instructive for our own prayer life. Teilhard's cosmic purview gives us a context in which to pray with and through all the elements in the universe. We can pray with a new organic and ecological sense of reverence. The winds, the stars, the waves, and fire become a symphony of praise to the divine—something the Psalmists and St. Francis understood intimately. This grand dimension of life in Christocentric prayer found early expression in the epistles of Paul. In the early modern period of Christianity, this cosmological sense of Christ waned, and an emphasis on redemption predominated, based on a devotional imitation of Christ. We may now reintegrate a focus on the historical Christ of social justice with the Cosmic Christ, the Logos at the heart of the universe.

A sympathetic resonance with nature and an understanding of the Cosmic Christ become sources of enormous richness for prayer, worship, and meditation. To pray with all the elements and with matter itself becomes a way of drawing strength from the enduring powers of nature in the evolutionary process. Finally, to pray in this enlarged context becomes a means of overcoming the awesome forces of alienation and impersonalism that pervade modern culture. We are indeed citizens of the universe and our prayer is the voice of all the elements in this extraordinary creation. Teilhard gives us many examples of such an expanded mode of prayer, some of the most striking of which are found in *Hymn of the Universe*. Teilhard's "Mass on the World," offered when he was without bread or wine during a scientific expedition in the Ordos desert of China, and his powerful "Hymn to Matter" both demonstrate a new ecological mode of prayer:

> "I bless you matter and you I acclaim; not as the pontiffs of science or the moralizing preachers depict you, debased, disfigured—a mass of brute forces and base appetites—but as you reveal yourself to me today, in your totality and your true nature.

> "You I acclaim as the inexhaustible potentiality for existence and transformation wherein the predestined substance germinates and grows.

> "I acclaim you as the universal power which brings together and unites, through which the multitudinous monads are bound together and, in which they all converge on the way of the spirit.

> "I acclaim you as the melodious fountain of water whence spring the souls of men and as the limpid crystal whereof is fashioned the New Jerusalem.

> "I acclaim you as the divine milieu, charged with creative power, as the ocean stirred by the Spirit, as the clay molded and infused with life by the incarnate Word."[18]

In terms of sacrifice, which is one of the central ideas for spirituality, Teilhard again provides us with a frame that enlarges our understanding of traditional ideas. From the supreme sacrifice of Christ on the cross, Teilhard points to the sacrificial nature of the whole evolutionary process in which the human has a central role. In other words he sees the backward movement of evolution as its entropy phase and the forward movement as its energy phase. These are the catalysts in the larger dynamic of spirit and matter evolving. Teilhard situates evil and entropy in the cosmic order not simply in the human because of original sin. He sees natural disasters, mutation, sickness, and tragedies as part of the groping of both nature and the human to fulfill their deepest purposes. Without the struggle of life there would not be the heroic potential of the human to overcome his or her particularity. This drive for communion with the Divine through Earth lies at the heart of an ecological spirituality.

Such a spirituality should offer us the largest context possible to situate our own yearnings toward meaning. In this way, for Teilhard and for us, sacrifice takes on a powerful cosmic dimension. Through the sacrifice of the human in suffering and of the Earth itself in physical changes, evolution unfolds. Teilhard describes its unfolding in terms of the power of human suffering to transform energy into activity:

> Human suffering, the sum total of suffering poured out at each moment over the whole Earth, is like an immeasurable ocean. But what makes up this immensity? Is it blackness, emptiness, barren wastes? No indeed; it is potential energy. Suffering holds hidden within it, in extreme intensity, the ascensional force of the world. The whole point is to set this force free by making it conscious of what it is capable. . . . If all those who suffer in the world were to unite their sufferings so that the pain of the world should become one single grand act of consciousness, of sublimation, of unification, would not this be one of the most exalted forms in which the mysterious work of creation could be manifested to our eyes?[19]

Finally, in terms of human action, Teilhard's spiritual vision again has eminently practical implications. By now it is clear that Teilhard's expansion of our perspective and purpose has enormous potential for dynamizing human energies. His concern to activate a zest for life and a will to participate in evolution was one of the major recurring themes in his writings. Human action assists the evolutionary advance and applies to every field of enterprise—business, science, education, law, agriculture, social services, cultural and artistic pursuits—all of which are involved in a transforming process much greater than themselves. How to activate human energy and consciousness in this direction was one of Teilhard's greatest concerns for spirituality.

I come now to my final point, that of personalization. Teilhard was intensely concerned that his spiritual vision might be misunderstood as a pantheistic union with the cosmos. He also recognized the growing tendency of the modern world to depersonalize or impersonalize reality. In *The Human Phenomenon*, Teilhard cites two reasons for this depersonalizing tendency.[20] The first is the technique of analysis and objectification that we have inherited from the scientific method. The second is the discovery and exploration of outer space that seems to dwarf the human in relation to the cosmos. Having identified these two factors, Teilhard goes on to acknowledge that it may seem incongruous or inappropriate to associate an Ego with the All of the universe. In other words, we cannot simply anthropomorphize the cosmos, nor can we easily embrace an impersonal cosmos. We are left straddling a heritage of personal deity, while groping toward a larger intuition of a numinous presence in the cosmos.

Here is one of the most critical transitions that our period is facing in terms of spirituality. For centuries many of the world's religions have concentrated on a divine-human relationship expressed in personal devotionalism. While this dynamic has been and will continue to be an energizing force in the human community, the scope in which we acknowledge such a relationship must be greatly enlarged. This is precisely what Teilhard has begun to do for us.

We are now at a point of contemplating the role of the human in the vast evolutionary process. Just as the immensity of geological time is revealed to us, so do doubts about the human and our past begin to plague us and we draw back from anthropomorphizing the cosmos. A complacent anthropomorphism no longer seems a satisfactory stance. In reexamining history we are less inclined to exalt the human in light of a continuing inhumanity to persons and of an assault on the Earth. More than ever before, we question our purpose, our function, and indeed our very being. Perhaps terrorism and the nuclear threat are only a shadowy manifestation of the deep doubts that lies buried in human consciousness about our own existence. Doubts about ourselves lead to doubts about the whole cosmos.

In earlier periods the universe was seen as the Great or Cosmic Person. To reassert meaning for the human venture, we must first rediscover the personal in the cosmos. Teilhard points toward this when he identifies personalization with centration whence there are, in the heart of matter, various centering elements and attracting forces. Physicists continue to study the attraction of particles for one another down to the quantum level as they form patterns that still retain elements of indeterminacy and mystery.

The act of reawakening both our primordial sense of the cosmos as a whole, along with our scientific insight into nature, may point us toward a new vision of the numinous dimension or patterning within material reality. In this spirit Teilhard articulated the personal quality of the universe as a center which draws all elements to itself. This is what he described as the divine milieu. The following passage illustrates the power of the center as the sustaining force of all reality:

> However vast the divine milieu may be, it is in reality a *centre*. It therefore has the properties of a centre, and above all the absolute and final power to unite (and consequently to complete) all beings within its breast. In the divine milieu all the elements of the universe *touch each other* by that which is most inward and ultimate in them. . . .
>
> There we shall one day rediscover the essence and brilliance of all the flowers and lights which we were forced to abandon so as to be faithful to life. The things we despaired of reaching and influencing are all there, all reunited by the most vulnerable, receptive and enriching point in their substance. In this place the least of our desires and efforts is harvested and tended and can at any moment cause the marrow of the universe to vibrate.
>
> Let us establish ourselves in the divine milieu. There we shall find ourselves where the soul is most deep and where the matter is most dense. There we shall discover, with the confluence of all its beauties, the ultra-vital, the ultra-sensitive, the ultra-active point of the universe. And, at the same time, we shall feel the plenitude of our powers of action and adoration effortlessly ordered within our deepest selves.[21]

One aspect of the centering power of nature to draw all elements together is known in the physical order as gravity; its counterpart in the human is love. Both of these become expressions for the attractive forces of centering, individualization, and personalization. Again Teilhard speaks most eloquently in this regard:

> Love dies in contact with the impersonal and the anonymous.[22]
>
> Love is by definition the word we use for attractions of a personal nature. Since once the Universe has become a thinking one everything in the last resort moves in and towards personality, it is necessarily love, a kind of love, which

forms and will increasingly form, in its pure state, the material of human energy. . . . Love is the most universal, the most tremendous and the most mysterious of the cosmic forces.[23]

Teilhard's spiritual vision is one that brings us an expanded sense of perspective and a new sense of purpose. Its effect, however, is eminently practical and personalized for it implies nothing less than the dynamizing of human energies with a new hope in the thrust of evolution. At the same time, when we are experiencing a crisis of physical energy sources and diminished ecosystems we are also passing through a great change in the activation of human energies. Just as our physical capacity to live on the Earth is undergoing a radical transformation due to the ecological crisis, so is our groping for new sources of spiritual energy.

I conclude with a passage where Teilhard offers possibilities of a new ecological spirituality for our times:

> . . . if each of us can believe that he is working so that the Universe may be raised, in him and through him, to a higher level—then a new spring of energy will well forth in the heart of Earth's workers. . . .

> Indeed, the idea, the hope of the planetization of life is very much more than a mere matter of biological speculation. It is more of a necessity for our age than the discovery, which we so ardently pursue, of new sources of [physical] energy. It is this idea which can and must bring us the spiritual fire without which all material fires, so laboriously lighted, will presently die down on the surface of the thinking Earth: the fire inspiriting us with the joy of action and the love of life.[24]

Here is Teilhard's spiritual testimony, one that challenges us with its optimism, inspires us with its perspective, and renews us with its powerful sense of purpose. His vision may well be a source of inspiration amidst the formidable challenges facing us at present. As the twenty-first century unfolds, we must seek such grounding to help shape the transformations that will be needed to create a sustainable future for our Earth.

Notes

1. Published in similar form as Mary Evelyn Tucker, "The Ecological Spirituality of Teilhard," *Teilhard Studies 51* (Fall 2005).

2. Senior Lecturer and Research Scholar, Yale School of Forestry and Environmental Studies and Yale Divinity School; Environmental Ethicist-in-Residence, Interdisciplinary Center for Bioethics, Yale University, Hartford, CN 06520; Vice President, American Teilhard Association.

3. These letters are collected in Pierre Teilhard de Chardin, *The Making of a Mind: Letters from a Soldier-Priest, 1914-1919*, trans. René Hague (New York: Harper & Row, 1965).

4. Ibid., 23.

5. Pierre Teilhard de Chardin, *The Divine Milieu*, trans. Bernard Wall (New York: Harper & Row, 1960), 65.

6. Ibid., 68.

7. Ibid., 60-61.

8. Thomas Berry, *The Great Work* (New York: Bell Tower, 1999).

9. This process of trying to understand the varied spiritual experiences of the natural world as expressed in the world's religions is what inspired the Harvard project on world religions and ecology. From 1996-98 a series of ten conferences were held at the Center for the Study of World Religions at Harvard Divinity School. Over 800 scholars and environmentalists participated and a ten-volume book series was published from Harvard. There has subsequently emerged within academia a field of study in religion and ecology. See www.environment.harvard.edu/religion

10. Pierre Teilhard de Chardin, *The Human Phenomenon*, trans. Sarah Appleton-Weber (Brighton: Sussex Academic Press, 1999), 91.

11. Ibid., 24.

12. Ibid., 24-25.

13. Pierre Teilhard de Chardin, *Human Energy*, trans. J. M. Cohen (New York: Harcourt Brace, 1971), 82.

14. Pierre Teilhard de Chardin, *The Future of Man*, trans. Norman Denny (New York: Harper & Row, 1969), 88.

15. Pierre Teilhard de Chardin, *Science and Christ*, trans. René Hague (New York: Harper & Row, 1969), 193.

16. Pierre Teilhard de Chardin, *Activation of Energy*, trans. René Hague (New York: Harcourt Brace, 1970), 256.

17. John Haught, *Nature and Purpose* (Lanham, MD: Rowan & Littlefield, 1980), 14.

18. Pierre Teilhard de Chardin, *Hymn of the Universe*, trans. Simon Bartholomew (New York, Harper & Row, 1961), 69-70.

19. Ibid., 93-94.

20. Teilhard de Chardin, *Human Phenomenon*, 257.

21. Teilhard de Chardin, *Divine Milieu*, 92-93.

22. Teilhard de Chardin, *Human Phenomenon*, 192.

23. Teilhard de Chardin, *Human Energy*, 145-46, 32.

24. Teilhard de Chardin, *The Future of Man*, 118.

TEILHARD AND THE QUESTION OF LIFE'S SUFFERING

JOHN F. HAUGHT[1]

Many evolutionists today subscribe to a version of scientific naturalism that claims to be able to explain all aspects of life, including suffering, in purely biological terms and without having to resort to theological understanding at all. From the perspective of Darwinian biology, suffering (which I shall take to be inclusive of the sensation of pain by all sentient life[2]) is nothing more than an adaptation that enhances the probability of survival and reproductive success in complex organisms.

The question I want to address in this essay, therefore, is whether it is true that theology can add nothing of substance to the Darwinian naturalist's account of suffering.[3] Darwin himself came to doubt that the idea of God could illuminate the suffering of living beings. He observed that suffering is "well adapted to make a creature guard against any great or sudden evil."[4] Suffering, he speculated, is life's warning system, and, if at times the torment it brings seems exorbitant, this tragic excess is still consistent with a purely naturalistic understanding of life.[5] Today, according to many Darwinians, religious and theological responses to suffering have no comparably lucid explanatory value. Some neo-Darwinians account for the suffering of sentient life in terms of the "attempt" by genes to make their way into subsequent generations. Genes somehow sense that they cannot expect to survive unless they fashion organic "vehicles" endowed with sensory feedback equipment that can send messages instructing them when their survival is in jeopardy. From a contemporary biological point of view, genes cunningly manufacture delicate nervous systems in order to assure their immortality. Such machination may seem intelligent and even ingenious, but to countless biologists today the whole show is at bottom blind and impersonal.[6]

In the process of writing The *Origin of Species* and thinking about its implications, Darwin himself gradually gave up his earlier belief in divine providential governance of the universe. He was tormented, for example, at how ichneumon wasps lay their eggs inside living caterpillars so that the newly hatched larvae would have fresh meat on which to nourish themselves. Resourceful as this snapshot from the life-story may appear when viewed from the wasp's perspective, it is difficult, Darwin concluded, to attribute the caterpillar's fate to a beneficent divine agency. Going beyond Darwin, the renowned ethologist Richard Dawkins claims that such inconsiderate genetic engineering is reason enough for atheism. "So long as DNA is passed on," he says, "it does not matter who or what gets hurt in the process. It is better for the genes of Darwin's ichneumon wasp that the caterpillar should be alive, and therefore fresh, when it is eaten, no matter what the cost in suffering. Genes don't care about suffering, because they don't care about anything."[7] And any universe that puts up with such unseemly behavior, he goes on, is purposeless, blind, and indifferent.[8]

After Darwin, any coherent theological response to the brute fact of suffering cannot fail to notice ichneumon wasps and similar instances of nature's indifference to suffering. Clearly earth was no paradise even prior to the appearance of human beings capable of perpetrating their own kind of evil. Pain, struggle, death, and periodic extinctions have been essential, not just incidental, to the ongoing creation and diversifying of life. Religious hope encourages us to anticipate that in God's good time all tears will be wiped away and death will be vanquished. And for those touched by the biblical sense of promise, it should not be too much to expect that God's redemption will cover *all* of life's suffering. But religions and theologies still generally avoid the issue of why evolution involves so much struggle, travail, and death in the nonhuman chapters of the life-story. Theology still needs to consider in depth what evolution entails regarding the meaning of God, sin, evil, hope, redemption, and especially suffering in the wider world of life.[9] I hope to show how theology's encounter with the thought of Teilhard de Chardin can be a proper stimulus to such reflection.

EVOLUTIONARY NATURALISM
AND THE SUFFERING OF SENTIENT LIFE

Scientific naturalists now insist that theology is of no help at all in the understanding of life. Darwin, they claim, has given a fully satisfying "naturalistic" answer to the question of why sentient organisms are subject to suffering. To those who believe that nature is all there is and the universe devoid of purpose, all suffering must be accounted for scientifically. In the intellectual world today, this has increasingly come to mean that suffering is an evolutionary adaptation whose sole function is that of promoting the survival of human genes.[10] Evolutionary naturalists see no need to complicate accounts of suffering by bringing in religious interpretations. Religious myths about suffering, along with the theologies they inspire, are hopelessly complicated in comparison with the elegant simplicity of evolutionary accounts.

This negative judgment applies to theodicy no less than to mythology. In its narrowest meaning, "theodicy" is any theological or philosophical attempt to "justify" the Creator's existence in the face of evil and suffering. The so-called "theodicy problem" asks whether it is reasonable to believe in an all-good and all-powerful God, given the fact that the creation has room for so much suffering and moral evil. A theodicy is any attempt to respond to this "problem" in such a way as to defend the idea of God. Typically theodicies are philosophically abstruse, and they are notorious for their failure to comfort people who are actually suffering. Nevertheless, even the most abstract theodicies are expressions of an irrepressible need by people of all times and places to make some sense of suffering. Indeed, *any* attempt to understand suffering, including those of the most entrenched evolutionary naturalists, can be called a kind of "theodicy."[11] For many thoughtful people today, Darwinism itself has come to function as a theodicy, inasmuch as it gives a meaning to suffering, accounting for it along with all other traits of living beings in terms of the easily understandable idea of evolutionary adaptation. Such a theodicy is all the more appealing because it professes to have a simplicity absent in the convolutions of mythic and theological attempts to come to grips with pain and other kinds of evil. On the question of theodicy, Darwinism apparently satisfies the requirement known as Occam's razor according to which there is no need to appeal to complicated explanations if a simpler one is available. Surrendering the consolations provided by religious hope is a small price to pay for the intellectual lucidity of the Darwinian justification of pain.

Nevertheless, scientific and evolutionary naturalists will have a hard time convincing the masses that they now need to give up their venerable religious and theological sources of comfort. Even in the age of science and amidst the growing popularity of Darwinism in the academic world, most people, including educated believers, remain unconvinced. Religions and theodicies still persist in the face of naturalistic debunking.[12] Is this simply because we are irrational beings crippled by inferior science education? Why do so many intelligent people still believe in God even after they have been exposed to evolutionary science?

The standard contemporary Darwinian response is that religious myths of suffering continue, even after Darwin, to have an adaptive function, and that is why they persist. Even illusions, according to evolutionist debunkers of religion, can trick people into believing that life is worth living, and that it is good to have offspring who can enjoy the same illusions. The Darwinian naturalist, of course, professes to see through our fantasies of meaning: what is *really going on* in religion is that our genes are trying to get passed off to the next generation, and an inherited tendency to be religious facilitates the flow. This is the *true* reason why religions and theodicies do not just disappear overnight. Loyal Rue, a philosopher who exemplifies very well what I mean by an evolutionary naturalist, even seems to suggest that scientists should be careful about letting the rest of us in on the discovery that our religions are adaptive illusions. If we all find out tomorrow what is *really going on*, we might too precipitously dispose of our religious beliefs and sacred theodicies. In that case we would be deprived of one of the human traits that have allowed our genes to survive for so many thousands of years. If we expose our religions as the lies they really are, humanity might go extinct.[14]

Recently a less simplistic version of Darwinian naturalism has begun to concede that religions and theodicies are quite possibly not adaptive *per se*. Rather, they are "parasitic" complexes that attach themselves to certain brain functions or cerebral modules that originally proved adaptive for reasons not having anything to do with religion. These physiological adaptations occurred one to two million years ago, but they have now become colonized by religious ideas and activities quite foreign to what evolution and our genes originally had in mind. Pascal Boyer, Scott Atran, and more recently Daniel Dennett, for example, claim that religion implants itself in human brains so easily because hominid and early human brains, for the sake of survival, had to become good at "agent detection."[15] Present-day religious illusions of invisible supernatural entities, Atran writes, are "the by-products of a naturally selected cognitive mechanism for detecting agents—such as predators, protectors, and prey—and for dealing rapidly and economically with stimulus situations involving people and animals."[16]

In response to both versions of the evolutionist debunking of religion and theodicy, I believe the thought of Teilhard de Chardin still has considerable relevance. Teilhard fully embraced evolution while at the same time finding a legitimate place for a theological understanding of life's suffering. I shall summarize his proposal below, but first it is important to examine further the naturalist claim that the suffering of sentient life can be understood exhaustively in Darwinian terms.

IS DARWINISM SUFFICIENT?

Darwinian biology provides a relatively simple explanation of life's diversity, and the notion of natural selection can also say why many organisms eventually acquired a high degree of sentience and a capacity to experience pain. From an evolutionary point of view, such attributes give organisms an adaptive advantage over those less generously endowed with feelings. The capacity for suffering can serve the cause of survival and reproduction by allowing an organism to be informed when it is in danger. Were it not able to feel pain, an organism could easily acquiesce in its own extinction. Today some scientific naturalists, in particular those impressed by Darwinian explanation, claim that the survival of genes is the *ultimate* reason why suffering occurs in the life-world. The intensity of suffering is often excessive, but to the evolutionary naturalist, such overkill is not surprising in a purposeless universe.

But can Darwinian naturalism account *fully* for the emergence of either sentience or suffering, especially since these can be actualized only if there first exist *subjects* that can feel? Subjectivity, if it is indeed an aspect of nature, also needs explaining. And, given the abstract, public, and objectifying method of acquiring scientific understanding, one must ask whether modern science, including Darwinian biology, can tell us anything about the *inner* worlds of actual subjects. Science has no formal access to the mysteriously hidden world of subjectivity (animal as well as human), even though evolutionary biology makes no sense unless sentient, struggling subjects are assumed to exist. Scientific method limits its attention to what is objectively or publicly accessible, and so it always leaves out any focus on the *insideness* of suffering organisms. It is only by a nonscientific, "personal" empathy rather than by an objectifying method of study that scientists can attribute sentience and suffering to organisms at all.

As Teilhard rightly asserts, however, the subjectivity or insideness of sentient life is as much a part of nature as rocks and rivers. Science cannot see subjects as such, but this does not mean that subjects are not part of the cosmos. Natural selection can help explain why nervous systems become more complex and hence why sentience and suffering can become more intense in the course of natural history. But no science as such can get inside of subjects or explain why subjectivity has found its way into nature in the first place.[17]

Moreover, according to Darwin, sentient subjects have to *struggle* for existence. Struggling, of course, is an instance of *striving*, but it is only subjects that can strive or aim intentionally at achieving a goal. According to philosopher Michael Polanyi, living beings can be identified as alive only because they are centered and striving, able either to succeed or fail in the attainment of their goals. That is, living beings act according to the "logic of achievement."[18] Living beings, unlike nonliving, exert effort, and it is only because of our own personal experience of striving, succeeding, and failing that we can recognize, by way of personal rather than scientific knowing, that other sentient beings are also subjects able to strive, struggle, and suffer.[19] Since conventional science has no room for subjects in its maps of the world, it has no way of accounting in a foundational way for suffering either. Darwinism, insofar as it is scientific, *presupposes* but does not account for subjectivity, sentience, and striving.[20]

One of the important contributions of Teilhard to the discussion of suffering in evolution is that he held on stubbornly to the obvious fact of subjectivity, or insideness, and made it an integral aspect of his vision of nature. He even wanted to expand the scientific method beyond its usual meaning so that it would embrace both the inside and outside of nature. I believe this was a strategic mistake, but it is only fair to point out that his reason for doing so was to ensure that empirically minded thinkers would not leave out any aspect of nature, including what cannot be fully objectified. Teilhard cannot be blamed for seeking a wider empiricism than modern science practices.

In any case, the scientist requirement that subjectivity be banished from a truly enlightened picture of nature is impossible to obey consistently. Even contemporary gene-centered Darwinism, for example, cannot cleanse from its own discourse oblique references to subjectivity. Instead, it simply displaces the implicitly acknowledged subjectivity of living beings onto clusters of genes intent upon accomplishing their own aims. In neo-Darwinian writings, the logic of achievement remains obvious in spite of almost desperate evolutionist attempts to exorcize it from an enlightened view of nature. Matt Ridley, for example, employs the category of subjectivity when he says we must "think of genes as analogous to *active and cunning individuals*"[21] (emphasis added). Ridley knows that biologists should ideally avoid all reference to subjects, but in biology's contemporary discourse, genes are endowed with intentionality and even personality. "A gene has only one criterion by which posterity judges it: whether it becomes an ancestor of other genes. To a large extent it must *achieve* that at the expense of other genes"[22] (emphasis added). Genes, Ridley goes on, form *strategies* to ensure their survival.[23] Here the logic of achievement shows up in what is supposed to be purely scientific understanding.

The lesson is that science cannot completely disregard subjectivity, try as it might. Evolutionary biology is right in saying that suffering is adaptive, but it cannot by itself account for the mystery of interiority. It cannot tell us why *subjects* able to sense, struggle, and suffer came into the universe at all. This breakdown in consistency carries over into Darwinian attempts to explain fully why human subjects engage in religious striving, why they cannot help looking for appropriate theodicies, and why religions are so persistent. Religious persons are themselves instances of striving that can be located in an unbroken evolutionary succession of struggling subjects—going all the way back to the most primitive instances of life. Religious subjects strive to find pathways beyond evil, suffering, and death.[24] Thus religion is a most concentrated instance of life's perpetual striving. And, since all striving arises from within the hidden world of subjects, one may conclude that Darwinian biology cannot carry us inside the world of religion any more than it can take us inside any kind of subjectivity. Evolutionary accounts rightly note that suffering and religion can be adaptive, but the actual subjective experiential content of suffering and religion is no more reducible to adaptation than the words on this page are reducible to ink and paper. Darwinian processes may still be operative at some level in the worlds of feeling, thought, and faith, but evolutionary science can tell us very little about what is really going on in these worlds.

TEILHARD AND THEODICY AFTER DARWIN

However, if a Darwinian account of suffering is inadequate, what shape must a religious theodicy assume in an age of evolution? It seems to me that theodicy cannot remain exactly the same after Darwin as it was before. Science has now demonstrated that there have been millions of years of struggle and suffering in life prior to our own emergence as a distinct species. This fact, it seems to me, raises significant questions about the one-sidedly anthropocentric focus of classical theology's treatment of suffering. Suffering is a characteristic of *all* of life, as Buddhism makes clear, and so any convincing theodicy must take into account the larger biological domain, not just that of humans and their struggles. Any theodicy that remains oblivious to the pre-human evolutionary trail of striving, pain, disease, predation, and extinction is leaving out something essential to a theologically rich understanding of God, creation, and redemption. What happens in the wider cosmic drama and life-story must now be made integral to any careful theological treatment of life's suffering.

Above all, this will mean that the theme of expiation, where guilt must be paid for by suffering, cannot plausibly function any longer as the foundation of theodicy. As the Book of Job had long ago complained, the idea that suffering exists in order to expiate guilt has no applicability wherever suffering is innocent. And Christian interpretations of Jesus' suffering as substitutionary satisfaction for human sin provide no answer to why animals or infants suffer and what the meaning of this suffering might be.[25] The expiatory understanding of suffering, nevertheless, still influences much religious thought and popular spirituality. When Christians look for meaning in suffering, they are still under the spell of ancient mythic theodicies that interpreted suffering as the outcome of free human acts of rebellion, beginning with the spoiling of an original cosmic perfection. Such an emphasis will be exposed as inadequate, however, as soon as theology and theodicy connect religious belief with the *whole* story of suffering in evolution.

Teilhard's thought is especially relevant to this project because it views suffering in the context of an *unfinished creation* rather than exclusively in terms of expiation. In the wake of Darwin and contemporary cosmology, it is difficult, Teilhard often points out, to conceive of any time in the past when the cosmos had attained perfection.[26] Logically speaking, then, the cosmos would have been imperfect from the beginning. There would always have been a dark side to the cosmos.[27] Consequently, no *loss* of primordial perfection could ever have occurred, and thus any reason to expiate an imagined initial transgression would be ruled out. The cosmological assumptions that undergird the need for expiation, self-punishment, resentment, and victimization have now been overturned.

Theodicies centered on the idea of expiation have, of course, been influenced especially by the biblical story of Adam and Eve and their expulsion from paradise. This narrative is an expression of what philosopher Paul Ricoeur calls the "ethical vision of existence" which attributes the cause of suffering to human guilt.[28] The ethical vision assumes that wherever suffering exists, it must have been caused by human acts of disobedience. Guilt must be paid for in the sterling of suffering in order to balance the books. Consequently, as Teilhard observes, a tendency toward scapegoating has come into human history—and still exists—as the tragic underside of the expiatory strain of Christian theodicy.[29] One of the sad consequences of this kind of theodicy is that it inevitably leads people to expect punishment and/or look for culprits wherever suffering shows up, no matter how innocent the suffering really is.[30] What is intended to provide an answer to the theodicy problem ends up contributing even more misery to the cumulative history of suffering. Teilhard is deeply disturbed by the narrowness of such a perspective:

> In spite of the subtle distinctions of the theologians, it is a matter *of fact* that Christianity has developed under the over-riding impression that all the evil round us was born from an initial transgression. So far as dogma is concerned we are still living in the atmosphere of a universe in which what matters most is reparation and expiation. The vital problem, both for Christ and us, is to get rid of a stain. This accounts for the importance, at least in theory, of the idea of sacrifice, and for the interpretation almost exclusively in terms of purification. It explains, too, the pre-eminence in Christology of the idea of redemption and the shedding of blood.[31]

Teilhard is not denying that life is sacrificial. What he is questioning is the entrenched religious habit of associating pain primarily with expiation. For Teilhard, the fact of suffering, along with all other kinds of evil, gains a foothold in a more fundamental cosmic "fault," namely, that God's creation is still unfinished. Therefore, what needs explaining, even more than the fact of suffering, is why God would create an unfinished universe to begin with. Teilhard's answer is that any other kind of initial creation would be theologically inconceivable. An initially finished creation would be frozen everlastingly in a finalized state, with no room left for more being. Such a product would be dead on arrival, for in its fixed completeness it would have no room for a future, freedom, or even life. Above all, it would not be truly other than God. It would not be a world at all.[32]

The idea of an initially finished or perfected creation, it needs to be emphasized, is not incidental to the expiatory version of theodicy. Cosmology, contrary to those theologians who dismiss its importance, does indeed make a great difference theologically. The idea of a static universe, for example, allowed theology for centuries to assume that God's original creation was perfect and complete, and that this primordial perfection was then violated by an "initial transgression." If a perfect creation existed in the beginning and then became defiled by human guilt, it is tempting to look for someone or something to blame for such a breach. And then it is also easy to picture redemption as a *return* to paradise, and to understand all suffering as penalty for an original fault. For if one assumes an originally perfect creation, then the initial transgression that messed everything up will seem so momentous as to require a proportionate penalty. Before geology, evolutionary biology, and Big Bang cosmology came along, it was much easier for theology and spirituality to suspect that suffering is essentially punishment than it is afterwards.

Yet no matter how tidy and appealing this Adamic vision may initially appear to be as an answer to the question of suffering, it has all too readily accommodated the history of self-righteous acts of blame, witch-hunting, and other kinds of revenge. The inner logic of an expiatory understanding, after all, is to demand that things be made right once again, and suffering can easily be understood as an essential part of restitution. In a pre-evolutionary universe, setting things right is likely to imply the *restoration* of a perfection that once was and is now no more. It is by going *back* to the perfection of the cosmic past, rather than *forward* toward a radically new creation, that the expiatory religious imagination is inclined to envisage redemption.

However, as Teilhard's many writings imply, the fact of an evolving, and hence unfinished, universe, alters dramatically the cosmic context in which theology and theodicy must now function if they are to be believable. If the universe, as Teilhard emphasizes, is *still* coming into being, if it is even now being drawn toward a new future from its original condition of fragmentation and simplicity, it could never have existed in any initial state of perfection. The universe, in a sense, does not fully exist even yet, so how could it have been fully actualized in the past? Teilhard's synthesis of faith and evolution, makes it clear that in the absence of any past state of completed creation, the idea of restoration is no longer applicable. What reason, therefore, would there be for theodicies of expiation, or for the sad human history of scapegoating violence, if there has never existed a perfect universe *in principio*?

Teilhard proposes an alternative cosmological framework, one that is fully supported by science, to serve as the context for theology's reflections on the meaning of suffering—and here I am talking about all of life's suffering and not just our own. In a universe that is still unfinished—one that is even today emerging from the "nothingness" of primal multiplicity—the attribute of perfection can be applied only to a future cosmic unity that will occur in the everlasting care of a God who calls the universe into being from up ahead in the future. The logic of evolution has now permanently closed off the path of restoration and expiation. Evolution places in question all theodicies that have nourished themselves on nostalgia for a lost paradise. It leaves no legitimate room for resentment that paradise has been lost since creation has never (yet) been a paradise. Both the biblical logic of promise and the pattern of evolution have together barred the door to our ever returning to Eden. Henceforth our attempts at theodicy must purge themselves of all motifs of expiation, and place life's suffering and sacrifice in the context of hope for future fulfillment.

SUMMARY AND CONCLUSION

Teilhard's great synthesis invites theologians to think out more consistently what it means for theodicy if the universe is unfinished and the world is still being created. Because science rules out any past moment of created perfection, Teilhard is proposing that sadness over the imagined loss of paradise be supplanted by a common hope for new creation that can energize human action. The cosmos and life are still coming into being, so our religious aspirations can now veer away from a pining for the past and extend themselves irreversibly toward an eschatological fulfillment in God's future. It is only up ahead that our native longing for perfection can conceivably be satisfied. The biblical theologies of promise and hope can now live quite comfortably alongside a scientific understanding of nature. In a universe that is still being created, we can only look, along with Abraham, the prophets, Jesus, and Paul toward the horizon of the future. It is from there that we expect the coming of God and new creation.

Unfortunately, however, the temptation is strong to enshrine as eternally normative some imagined past epoch of perfection, whether in cosmic or human history, rather than open ourselves to the refreshing novelty of God's future. Nostalgia can easily become a substitute for hope. Any past victory in life's ascent or in human history is only an intimation or analogy of what is to come, but nostalgia can turn such fragmentary glimpses of the future into absolutes that we must at all costs restore. Thus the spirit of Abrahamic adventure into the wide openness of the future can give way to a religiosity whose entire energy is bent on recovering some idyllic past moment, whether in religious, natural, or secular history, as though it were the goal of all becoming.

An earnest encounter by theology with Teilhard's interpretation of evolution forbids such idolatry. At the same time, Teilhard's thought can lead theodicy to decentralize the expiatory interpretation of suffering that adheres most readily to a pre-evolutionary understanding of the universe. A vivid awareness of evolution no longer permits our theodicies to overlook the possibility that a great portion of life's suffering has been tragic and innocent, having nothing at all to do with guilt. Sentient striving and failure have existed for many millions of years prior to human emergence. A sense of our human solidarity with the suffering of all sentient life, therefore, can no longer permit an understanding of suffering, including human suffering, as primarily punishment.

Therefore, going far deeper than the Darwinian understanding of suffering exclusively in terms of adaptation, Teilhard's approach shows that the meaning of suffering—at the very least—is that of turning the story of life, especially in its recent mode of human sensitivity and striving, irreversibly toward a new future, one in which there is room for hope that all suffering will be healed and all tears wiped away. Instead of looking for culprits and scapegoats, or indulging in interminable acts of expiation, hope seeks companionship and community on the cosmic journey into an uncertain future that will ultimately be taken up into the eternal love of God. By participating in a "great hope held in common"[33] we numb the roots of violence and gather our energy cooperatively toward the ushering in of new being. In an evolutionary setting, we can believe more readily than ever before that the age of expiation, as the Letter to the Hebrews also implies, is altogether a thing of the past.[34]

Consequently, theodicy from now on should not try to force the fact of suffering to fit a cosmography that allows pain to be taken as punishment. Instead, it should inquire, along with Teilhard, why an all-good and all-powerful

God would create an *unfinished, imperfect* universe to begin with. Could it be, as Teilhard seems to hold, that a truly loving God has no alternative? Could an initially finished cosmos really be distinct enough from God to be called a creation at all? In any case, an unfinished universe is the one we have, and it is one that still has a future. It is a universe in which there is room for "more being" and hence for hope. A still evolving universe turns theodicy away from nostalgia for an imagined state of cosmic perfection allegedly existing in the remotest past.[35] Theodicy after Darwin and Big Bang cosmology may now take advantage of an entirely new setting in which, following Teilhard's account, the universe is pictured as still emerging into being, rather than having been completed in the beginning. There is no need any longer to think of the universal perfection to which human hearts always rightly aspire as though it were something that has ever existed on the plane of natural or human history. Instead, we may now hope that the universe that is still coming into being may attain a fully actualized state of perfection in the future, and that our own strivings, strugglings, and sufferings—along with our joys and creations—will in some way be taken into the everlasting bosom of the God who awakens the world to becoming more.

Notes

1. Distinguished Research Professor, Department of Theology, Senior Fellow, Science and Religion, Woodstock Theological Center, Georgetown University, Washington, DC, 20057.

2. Some writers do not attribute "suffering" to nonhuman animals, but instead attribute to the latter only "pain." However, I consider the distinction somewhat arbitrary and unnecessarily anthropocentric.

3. This essay considerably revises, adapts, and expands ideas first presented in my Sophia Lecture given at the Washington Theological Union in 2004. An abbreviated version of that lecture appears in "What If Theologians Took Evolution Seriously?" *New Theology Review* 18 (November 2005): 10-20. A more recent development of the theme of suffering and evolution appears in my book, *Is Nature Enough? Meaning and Truth in the Age of Science* (Cambridge: Cambridge University Press, 2006).

4. Nora Barlow, ed., *The Autobiography of Charles Darwin* (New York: Harcourt, 1958), 88-89.

5. However, as we now realize, viruses and other kinds of disease, such as hypertension, can invade organisms painlessly, so life's warning systems, like other evolutionary adaptations, are not perfect. See John Hick, *Evil and the God of Love* (Norfolk, England: The Fontana Library, 1968), 333-38.

6. See Charles Sherrington, *Man on His Nature* (Cambridge: Cambridge University Press, 1951), 266.

7. Richard Dawkins, *River Out of Eden* (New York: Basic Books, 1995), 131.

8. Ibid., 133.

9.   Among recent attempts to understand theologically the suffering of sentient life, John Hick's *Evil and the God of Love* is impressive, but even his theodicy is not deeply informed by evolutionary biology.

10. Biologists often employ teleological language in their characterization of evolutionary adaptations, but for them this is not indicative of any wider purpose in nature. However, the question of teleology in life is still being debated: see Michael Ruse, *Darwin and Design: Does Evolution Have a Purpose?* (Cambridge: Harvard University Press, 2003).

11. Here I am following the broad usage of the term by sociologist Peter Berger in *The Sacred Canopy* (Garden City: Anchor Books, 1990), 53ff.

12. See Robert Hinde, *Why Gods Persist: A Scientific Approach to Religions* (New York: Routledge, 1999); Walter Burkert, *Creation of the Sacred: Tracks of Biology in Early Religions* (Cambridge, MA: Harvard University Press, 1996); Pascal Boyer, *Religion Explained: The Evolutionary Origins of Religious Thought* (New York: Basic Books, 2001).

13. See, for example, E. O. Wilson, *Consilience: The Unity of Knowledge* (New York: Knopf, 1998).

14. Loyal Rue, *By the Grace of Guile: The Role of Deception in Natural History and Human Affairs* (New York: Oxford University Press, 1994), 82-107.

15. Boyer, *Religion Explained*; Scott Atran, *In Gods We Trust: The Evolutionary Landscape of Religion* (New York: Oxford University Press, 2002); Daniel Dennett, *Breaking the Spell: Religion as a Natural Phenomenon* (New York: Viking, 2006).

16. Atran, *In Gods We Trust*, 15.

17. One could also ask whether the neo-Darwinian notion of adaptation has *fully* explained why life has had a tendency to *complexify* at all, especially since simple forms of life, like bacteria, have proven to be quite adaptive and persistent in time without ever becoming complex enough to suffer sentiently.

18. See Michael Polanyi, *Personal Knowledge* (New York: Harper Torchbooks, 1962), 327ff.

19. Ibid.

20. So resistant is subjectivity to objectification that some philosophers of mind even deny that it has real existence. See, for example, Paul Churchland, *The Engine of Reason, The Seat of the Soul* (Cambridge, MA: Bradford Books, 1995), and Daniel Dennett, *Consciousness Explained* (New York: Little, Brown, 1991). For a critical discussion I recommend especially Alan Wallace, *The Taboo of Subjectivity: Toward a New Science of Consciousness* (New York: Oxford University Press, 2000).

21. Matt Ridley, *The Red Queen: Sex and the Evolution of Human Nature* (New York: Penguin Books, 1993), 92-93.

22. Ibid., 94.

23. Ibid., passim.

24. See John Bowker, *Is Anybody Out There?* (Westminster, MD.: Christian Classics, Inc., 1988); 9-18, 112-43.

25. For a rich discussion of traditional themes of expiation and satisfaction, see Gerard Sloyan, *The Crucifixion of Jesus, History, Myth, Faith* (Minneapolis: Augsburg Fortress Publishers, 1995), 98-122.

26. This point is insinuated in many of Teilhard's writings, but I find it most explicit in Pierre Teilhard de Chardin, *Christianity and Evolution*, trans. René Hague (New York: Harcourt Brace & Co., 1969).

27. Ibid., 40.

28. Even in the Adamic myth, however, the figure of the serpent represents the intuition that evil is more than a human product. Paul Ricoeur, *The Conflict of Interpretations: Essays in Hermeneutics*, ed. Don Ihde (Evanston, IL.: Northwestern University Press, 2004), 294-95.

29. Ibid.

30. See Teilhard de Chardin, *Christianity and Evolution*, 81.

31. Ibid.

32. Here I am summarizing a theme that recurs especially in the essays in *Christianity and Evolution*.

33. Pierre Teilhard de Chardin, *The Future of Man*, trans. Norman Denny (New York: Harper Torchbooks, 1964), 75.

34. Gerd Theissen, *The Open Door* (Minneapolis: Fortress Press, 1991), 161-67.

35. John Hick, in a manner similar to Friedrich Schleiermacher, tries to salvage the notion of an original human perfection by redefining perfection to mean having the possibilities for development. *Evil and the God of Love* (New York: Harper & Row, 1966), 225-41. But the very definition of perfection is the "full actualizing of possibilities." And from all the evolutionist can see, humans have always been part of a universe in which life feeds on life, and in which suffering and death are pervasive, one in which the world's possibilities are still far from fully actualized.

TEILHARD: *LE PHILOSOPHE MALGRÉ L'ÉGLISE*

Donald Wayne Viney[1]

Two facts about Pierre Teilhard de Chardin are beyond dispute: his unfailing loyalty to the Church and his unflagging commitment to evolution. This dual aspect of Teilhard is nowhere more evident than in the "crisis of obedience" that reached its peak in July 1925, coincidently the same time as the Scopes Trial in Tennessee.[2] As a condition of fidelity to Rome, Teilhard was directed to sign a document listing six teachings of the Church on matters that brought it into apparent conflict with evolution. It is unknown in precise terms what these six propositions were.[3] What is known is Teilhard's anguish as he weighed his vows as a Jesuit against his integrity as a scientist. He signed the paper. Thereafter, his religious superiors instructed him to avoid philosophy and theology and focus on strictly scientific research. This first confrontation with Rome ended Teilhard's naiveté concerning the power of the Church, and its willingness to use that power, to prevent the dissemination of his ideas, including ideas that he considered the Church most in need of assimilating.

In my view, commentators are often not careful to take into account the effect that the crisis of obedience had on the ways in which Teilhard expressed his thought. After 1925, he was more cautious about how he presented his ideas for publication. His correspondence with his most intimate friends reveals a man impatient with the theologians of his day and the metaphysical views they propounded—the Thomists and Thomism. It was not simply their nervousness about the scientific theory of evolution that bothered him, but their refusal to come to terms with the philosophical and theological implications of evolution. Paul Grenet called Teilhard a philosopher in spite of himself—*un philosophe malgré lui*.[4] With apologies to L'Abbé Grenet (and to Molière), I modify this description somewhat by calling Teilhard a philosopher in spite of the Church—*un philosophe malgré l'Église*. In his last years, when it was painfully evident that Rome would remain intransigent to the end, never allowing him to publish his most cherished writings, he willed his works to Jeanne Mortier—the woman who volunteered her services as his secretary—so that future generations could decide for themselves as to the value of his thought.[5]

A Brief Account of Teilhard's Relations with Rome[6]

Teilhard was, from an early age, a loyal son of the Church. Our account, however, of his relations with Rome that resulted in discipline and exile should begin with mention of his wartime essays that he sent to his cousin Marguerite Teilhard-Chambon and that are now collected in the volume *Écrits du Temps de la Guerre (1916-1919)*.[7] These caught the notice of his religious superiors because of their unorthodox theology, for they cast doubt on the existence of Adam and Eve, the doctrine of original sin, and the concept of creation *ex nihilo*. The essays did not, however, raise great enough alarm to prevent Teilhard from taking his vows after the war. The seeds of Teilhard's official troubles with the Church were sewn in 1922 when he wrote, "Note on Some Possible Historical Representations of Original Sin."[8] The essay was written at the request of a colleague in dogmatic theology and was never meant for publication. Mysteriously, the essay found its way to Rome and was the major contributing factor in the crisis of obedience. But Teilhard was oblivious to the looming crisis for he was preoccupied with his first trip to China, between April 1923 and September 1924.

Late in 1924, Teilhard was back in Paris teaching at the Institut Catholique. His extreme popularity with students did not help his cause. Students at Hastings—among them the young Henri de Lubac—had referred to him and other advanced Jesuit thinkers of the time simply as *La Pensée* (The Thought).[9] A conservative group of French Bishops lobbied the Holy Office to pressure the Jesuits into curbing Teilhard's activities.[10] As noted above, the crisis broke in July 1925, and Teilhard was obliged to sign a statement repudiating his ideas on original sin in deference to the authority of the Church. His inner struggle was excruciating. Some of his friends advised him to leave the Jesuits; L'Abbé Breuil said, "Vous êtes mal marié. Divorcez-la!" (You are in a bad marriage. Get a divorce).[11] Auguste Valensin, on the other hand, advised Teilhard to sign the confession, not as a statement of the condition of his soul—which Valensin argued, God alone could judge—but in order to signal his obedience to the Jesuits. The immediate result of the "crisis" was that Teilhard could no longer teach at the Institut Catholique and that he was sent back to China, this time against his wishes.

While officially obedient to Rome, Teilhard confided to Valensin that his attitude toward the Church had changed. From Paris on January 10, 1926, he wrote:

> In some way, *I no longer have confidence* in the outward manifestations of the Church. I believe it is by it that the divine influence will continue to reach me. But I no longer believe very much in the immediate, tangible, critical value of official decisions and directions. There are some who feel happy in the visible Church; as for me, it seems I will be happy to die to be rid of it, that is to say, to find Our Savior outside of it. I speak to you thus naively—without bitterness it seems to me—because it is true, and because I *cannot* see things otherwise.[12]

Teilhard continued to question the "critical value of official decisions and directions" to the very end of his life. It is a testimony to his character that he never allowed bitterness to consume him, despite repeated frustrations in his attempts to publish. In 1927, he expressed the hope that his devotional masterpiece, *The Divine Milieu*, would be considered orthodox. In July 1929, he received word that the book was going to be published, but a censor held it up. By August 1930, it was clear that the book would not be published.[13]

Similar frustrations dogged Teilhard's efforts to see *The Human Phenomenon* in print. In October 1948, Teilhard went to Rome seeking ecclesiastical approval for publication, as well as permission to accept an invitation to a Chair at the Collège de France. Teilhard prepared himself "to stroke the tiger's whiskers."[14] In Rome, Teilhard met the Dominican theologian Réginald Garrigou-Lagrange (1877-1964) who had been one of Teilhard's harshest critics. Nevertheless, Teilhard told Pierre Leroy that the meeting was cordial. "We smiled and talked about Auvergne."[15] Teilhard's requests for permission to publish and to accept the invitation to the Chair were denied. In February 1949 at the Sorbonne, Teilhard gave one of six talks, but an attack of pleurisy cut short the lecture series. It was less Teilhard's health, however, than it was the Church that limited his freedom. He wrote what would have been the Sorbonne lectures into a book, *The Human Zoological Group*, but Rome refused to see it published.

Teilhard was aware of the obstacles he faced. As early as 1934, he wrote to Léontine Zanta: "I've obviously a loaded dossier against me, and there are plenty of mines lurking in the waters where I sail."[16] His reputation as a priest involved in some of the most well-known digs in paleontology—like so-called Piltdown man in 1912 and *Sinanthropus* in 1929-30—made him an object of curiosity in the public eye.[17] When he appeared at Philadelphia's Academy of Natural Science in 1937, *Newsweek* reported on the event, complete with a photograph of Teilhard. The reporter wanted to know how a Jesuit reconciled his religious and scientific beliefs.[18] Teilhard's reply, as reported, is disappointing: "The lack of understanding that exists in some quarters on the evolution of man can be classified solely as a lack of understanding." Perhaps Teilhard was misquoted. He wrote to Lucile Swan that he was, on the whole, "rather disgusted by the press...."[19]

In fairness, one must say that Teilhard was not innocent of stoking the fires of controversy. Despite the fact that the Church denied him permission to publish his religious-philosophical works, many of them were widely known because he authorized stenciled copies to be distributed—he referred to them as *clandestins*. These booklets contributed to his being something of a *cause célèbre*. I know of no assessment of the number of *clandestins* that were in circulation, but it must have been considerable. In a 1937 letter to Swan, he speaks of "a real clandestine shop" at the residence of Simone Bégouën in Paris.[20] Later, Jeanne Mortier became Teilhard's *de facto* secretary. His letters to her are filled with requests for more *clandestins* and requests that she send them out to this or that colleague or friend. Whatever the number, it was great enough to cause controversy. It is in this context that we should interpret Teilhard's words to Leroy in 1950, "I'm quite aware I'm not as innocent as all that."[21]

A favorable article written by André Billy of the Academy Goncourt appeared in *Figaro Littéraire* in August 1950. Billy referred to Teilhard as "a great semi-underground poet." That Teilhard did not work entirely underground (*à demi clandestin*) means, in the first place, that he willingly submitted himself to the censure of his religious superiors, and in the second place, that the Church authorities did not prohibit the distribution of his *clandestins*. Billy had access to three *clandestins* lent to him for fifteen days by one of Teilhard's followers.

He had tried to acquire a fourth, *Human Energy*, but without success. Billy ended with these words: "He is our greatest prose poet. What a shame that it is so difficult to put one's hands on his works."[22] Billy's praise of Teilhard as a "staggering visionary" heralding a new religion might have been more hindrance than help except that he confessed difficulty acquiring the *clandestins*. Teilhard thought that this would mute criticism from Rome. Afterwards, Teilhard sent Billy a copy of *Human Energy*.[23]

Teilhard's critics were also busy. Two books were published prior to his death which used his *clandestins* to launch criticisms. The first, by an unnamed author—perhaps L'Abbé Luc Lefèvre, founder of *Pensée Catholique*—is titled *L'Evolution Rédemptrice du P. Teilhard de Chardin* (The Redemptive Evolution of Father Teilhard de Chardin).[24] While the author does not directly impugn Teilhard's character, Teilhard's thought is said to express an "almost luciferian pride."[25] The reader is reassured that Christianity has no need of evolution considered either as an objective reality or as a type of explanation. Like it or not, introducing evolution into Christianity runs a strong risk of altering certain fundamental dogmatic truths.[26] The author is alarmed by the effect that Teilhard's "barely Christianized Hegelianism"[27] might have on the theologically untrained. In a notice published in the Jesuit journal *Études*, Teilhard referred to the book as a "lampoon" in which there was nothing to say unless that, "I absolutely do not recognize in it the expression of my thought."[28] The title of the book itself betrays misunderstanding since it attributes to Teilhard a belief in the redemptive value of cosmic becoming.

In 1952, Louis Cognet's *Le Père Teilhard de Chardin et la Pensée Contemporaine* (Father Teilhard de Chardin and Contemporary Thought) appeared, the second book critical of Teilhard's thought. Cognet wryly expressed the wish to avoid the systematic hostility of the "courageous anonymous author" of *L'Evolution Rédemptrice* who in every chapter seemed intent on collecting firewood in preparation for a heresy tribunal.[29] In this, Cognet succeeds, although his book—title notwithstanding—is not a discussion of Teilhard and contemporary thought. It is, rather, an extended argument that Teilhard seriously compromises traditional Catholic teaching concerning especially the transcendence of God, the essential difference between the human and the non-human, the fallen nature of creation due to human sin, the role of the devil in the economy of evil, and the gift of redemption accomplished through God's incarnation in Christ. The message iterated throughout Cognet's book is neatly captured in what he says about the problem of evil: "Reassuring perhaps for certain contemporary consciences, the affirmations of Father Teilhard de Chardin would ill suffice to satisfy a Saint Augustine or a Saint Thomas."[30]

Cognet never seriously confronts the problems that most concern Teilhard, which is to say, how to make sense of Christianity in relation to an evolutionary worldview, and how to understand evolution from a Christian point of view. Cognet simply says that the work of a Christian who is a scientist should be carried out in such a way that it "not be contrary to the traditional Christian view of the world."[31] Teilhard wrote to Leroy concerning the book:

> But what an *enfant terrible* [Cognet] is in the frankness with which he pushes the logic of original sin and Christian catastrophism as far as it can go! This categorical affirmation that humanity (historically) reached a high point in some terrestrial paradise and that, since then, Christianity is by nature back-ward-looking. . . . But at least he is frank and logical to the end—at which point one recoils, as before a bad joke.[32]

Teilhard also remarked, "It's a shame I can neither explain nor answer him."[33] Teilhard wrote to Mortier that perhaps Cognet had done him a service by opening Pandora's Box.[34] He realized, however, that the controversy was fueled by his *clandestins*.

The suspicion of Teilhard's work was indicative of the Church's stiffening attitude toward evolution. Leroy tells how, in 1950, Msgr. Feltin, the archbishop of Paris, returned from Rome with the directions that during Lent there were to be "three burning subjects": Communism, evolutionism and Thomism. "When one spoke of the first two, one must be against them; when one spoke of the third, one must be for it."[35] Leroy speaks of evolutionism rather than evolution. This is important, for the Church did not categorically deny the scientific theory of evolution, even if, as Teilhard believed, the Church's theologians had failed to think through the implications of evolution for metaphysics and theology. In August of the same year, Pope Pius XII's encyclical *Humani Generis* was published. The encyclical cautiously endorsed an evolution of physical forms, but insisted that the soul is directly created by God. John Haught avers that the encyclical's limited acceptance of evolution "may have been in response to Pierre Teilhard de Chardin. . . ."[36] Teilhard may indeed have been on target.[37]

Teilhard sent a partial response to the encyclical to Rome titled "Monogenism and Monophyletism: An Essential Distinction."[38] Teilhard argued that science debates the question of monophyletism versus polyphyletism (i.e., single vs. multiple evolutionary branches giving rise to humans). Science cannot *directly* address the hypothesis of monogenism (i.e. human origins from an individual Adam). However, *indirectly*, the scientist can say that all we believe we know about biology renders an individual Adam untenable—e.g., Adam would be *born adult*. Despite this, Teilhard wrote a letter to his Jesuit superior assuring him of his complete fidelity.

As Teilhard had been "exiled" to China in 1926, so now he was pressured to leave France in 1951. He first traveled to Africa, then to South America, and settled in the United States in November of that year. In 1952, a conference on evolution was held at Laval University in Quebec, to which the great evolutionists of the day were invited, with the exception of Teilhard. Of course, by this time Teilhard was well-known as one of the leading Catholic intellectuals, and certainly the leading Jesuit, who unequivocally defended evolution. The failure to invite Teilhard could hardly be construed as an oversight, but was more likely intended to marginalize his ideas. Teilhard wrote, "These Catholic-scientific events are touching as displays of good will; but a little ridiculous—a desperate attempt to seem as though they are in the lead, without taking one step forward." He concluded that they are "Catholic games."[39]

In these final years, Teilhard remained active, traveling across the United States as well as to South Africa and South America. He made his final trip to France in the summer of 1954. Arrangements had been made by François Russo for Teilhard to give a public presentation on Africa. No sooner was the talk announced than Rome sent word that Teilhard was to return to America at once. Teilhard managed to visit the Lascaux caves with Leroy before leaving France for the last time.

In early 1955, Teilhard declined an invitation from Jean Piveteau to speak at the Sorbonne. A little later in the year, Rome took the precaution of denying him permission to attend the symposium. Leroy summed up the situation in these words:

> Teilhard suffered the intransigence of Rome right to the end. Even though his visa worries and his unhealed wounds from his last visit to France had delivered him from wanting to return to Europe again, Rome itself, having heard that a symposium was going to be held in Paris in April, wrote to forbid Teilhard's participation.[40]

At the same time, Teilhard heard that Rome had denied permission to publish a German translation of some of his published scientific articles. Raymond Jouve's foresight in suggesting that Teilhard bequeath his literary legacy to Jeanne Mortier insured that the Church censors would not have the last word. Jouve, who was then serving as an interim editor-in-chief of *Études*, realized that the Church would not permit Teilhard's works to be published. It was he who consulted a canon lawyer to insure that Teilhard would not be breaking his vows by giving Mlle. Mortier charge of his writings upon his death. With Mlle. Mortier's consent, Teilhard unhesitatingly acted on Jouve's suggestion.[41]

After Teilhard's death, the Church, no longer in a position to prevent the publication of his works, twice issued a warning concerning Teilhard's ideas. The following Monitum (warning) was issued by the Sacred Congregation of the Holy Office:

> Several works of Fr. Pierre Teilhard de Chardin, some of which were posthumously published, are being edited and are gaining a good deal of success. Prescinding from a judgment about those points that concern the positive sciences, it is sufficiently clear that the above-mentioned works abound in such ambiguities and indeed even serious errors, as to offend Catholic doctrine.
>
> For this reason, the most eminent and most revered Fathers of the Holy Office exhort all Ordinaries as well as the superiors of Religious institutes, rectors of seminaries and presidents of universities, effectively to protect the minds, particularly of the youth, against the dangers presented by the works of Fr. Teilhard de Chardin and of his followers.
>
> *Given at Rome, from the palace of the Holy Office, on the thirtieth day of June, 1962. SEBASTIANUS MASALA, Notarius*[42]

In the year of the centenary of Teilhard's birth, on July 20, 1981, the Holy See reiterated the Monitum. Thanks to Pope John Paul II, the Church now embraces evolution and scientific reasoning in a way that some would have thought unlikely. This new openness, however, has not meant a rethinking of Teilhard's case (as it has with the Galileo case)—the reiteration of the 1962 Monitum is proof of that.[43]

GOING UNDERGROUND: *UN MAQUISARD ET SES CLANDESTINS*

To maintain the delicate balance between Church loyalty and individual integrity, Teilhard found it necessary to be a *maquisard* (a member of the

Resistance).[44] In June 1950, he wrote to Leroy, "As someone said recently (jokingly, but seriously), thinking freely in the Church these days means going underground. Come to think of it, that is what I've been doing for thirty years."[45] What does Teilhard mean by this? The most obvious meaning of "going underground" is that Teilhard insured a steady production of *clandestins*. But it can also mean that he came to present his ideas in ways that he thought would meet the demands of the orthodox. In the works that he most wished to see published, he claimed not to be venturing into the fields of philosophy and metaphysics, but only to be extending scientific inquiry in its widest sense to its most parsimonious conclusions. From time to time he suggested that his views, appearances notwithstanding, might be transcribed into the more traditional categories of Thomistic metaphysics.[46] On the other hand, when he was not writing with an eye to satisfy the censors, he was consistently critical of Thomism.

At first, being a *Maquisard* was not necessary. Teilhard's writings prior to 1925 are less guarded in questioning traditional Church teaching. His wartime essays reflect this incautious inquiry. In 1917, he spoke freely of a metaphysic of Creative Union.[47] Note that it is metaphysic, not empirical science or "hyperphysics," of which he speaks. That same year he called the concept of pure nothingness "an empty concept, a pseudo-idea" and said that the only meaning to be given to physical nothingness is pure multitude.[48] From the pure multitude, he argued, God brings order. Later, in 1920, he used the expression "Creative Transformation" as an "act *sui generis* which *makes use* of a pre-existent created being and builds it up into a *completely* new being."[49] These ideas bring Teilhard into direct conflict with the concept of creation ex nihilo, according to which God's act of creation is one that uses no pre-existing material. The traditional idea of creation is that there is nothing, apart from God, antecedent to the divine creative act.[50] The traditional idea also says that God's creative act brings time into existence.[51] Thus, the creative act is eternal. Teilhard's view, on the other hand, seems to put God within time, or to posit a temporal side to God. For Teilhard, God's primary act of creation is to bring unity from disorganized and chaotic multitude.

Teilhard makes no systematic study of the divine attributes, but he was never comfortable with the idea that God was free not to create. In 1935, he explained to Mgr. Bruno de Solage that the idea of an "*absolutely free* creation" is an "absurd thing" that is difficult to harmonize with the existence and importance of "Creation-Incarnation-Redemption." Teilhard continues: "God must create in order to complete himself in something outside of himself."[52] It is true that he preserves divine transcendence by speaking of God—this, in 1946—as subsisting "in himself, independent of time and space."[53] He is equally clear, however, that the universe adds an essential aspect to God that is not already contained in divine transcendence. In the 1944 essay "Centrology," Teilhard speaks of Omega as "partially transcendent [of the conditions of time and space] . . . partially independent of the evolution that culminates in it." This partial transcendence is "one aspect" of Omega, the other being its emergence in the course of evolution.[54] The following year he spoke of God as "completely other" than the world but "unable to dispense with it." He explains that this concept involves a "re-definition of being."[55] He concludes by saying, *We need a metaphysics based on the creative function and maximalist demands of union.*"[56]

In his twilight years, Teilhard returns to these themes but his criticisms of Thomism are even more evident. He wrote to Leroy in 1953 that

> the Thomist notion of the Absolute Contingency of the Universe (in other words, of God's absolute "liberty" to create or not to create) has the triple and incurable weakness of rendering the Cross absurd, the Pleroma vain, and Work on Man's part in advancing the world in and around him quite insipid.[57]

Or again, he speaks of the "brutal metaphysical notion of *Ens a se* [that] dangerously devalues 'participated being.' . . ."[58] Teilhard is here speaking about his 1953 essay, "The Contingence of the Universe and Man's Zest for Survival," where he advises that we forget about *Ens a se* (Being in itself) and Ens ab alio (Being existing by another) and affirm "a strictly bilateral and complementary relationship between the world and God." According to the Thomistic metaphysic of being, on the contrary, creatures are really related to God but there is no real relation in God to the creatures.[59] Against this Thomistic view, Teilhard returns to the theme of his earliest writings, and urges replacing "a metaphysics of *Esse* [to be] by a metaphysics of Unire [to unite] (or of *Uniri* [to be united])."[60]

Teilhard understood that the metaphysics of creative union has consequences for the concept of divine power. The traditional concept of creation entails that God is able to bring any being into existence "from scratch" without any developmental process. As we have already noted, Teilhard wrote in 1950 that the Adam of the scholastic theologians "must have been *born* adult."[61]

In 1920, Teilhard said of this idea that it is "not only puerile, it belittles both God and ourselves—not to mention that it is the source of the most serious objections against Providence."[62] Although the scholastic theologians, Teilhard observes, are always ready to introduce the absolute power of God, he argues that God is no more able to create apart from a developmental process than God is able to make a square circle, perform an evil act, or make something past never to have existed.[63] Teilhard is reminding the reader that Thomas denied God's ability to do the logically impossible, alter the past, or to act in ways that contradict the divine goodness.[64] Omnipotence, he explained in 1933, "must no longer be understood by us in the sense of an instantaneous act but as a process or movement of synthesis"; and this concept of the divine creative act, he clarifies, applies to "every conceivable world."[65] Teilhard imagined what he called a creativity of an evolutionary type, "God *making things make themselves.*"[66]

Teilhard read Henri Bergson's *Creative Evolution* (1911) as a student at Hastings (1910-12). The Church was to put *Creative Evolution* on the Index of Prohibited Books in 1914. Nevertheless, Teilhard knew that Bergson considered evolution to be a creative process. In 1942, Teilhard said more precisely that evolution is "the expression of creation."[67] As Donald Gray notes, Teilhard replaced Bergson's *evolution créatrice* (creative evolution) with creation évolutive (evolutionary creation).[68] Teilhard also learned from Bergson to question the idea of pure nothingness. It was only a brief step for Teilhard to think of divine creativity itself in evolutionary terms. Teilhard resisted Bergson's idea that evolution is without direction; for Teilhard, evolution has direction towards increasing complexity-consciousness, and eventually towards the ultimate form of complexity, Omega-Point or God-Omega. The idea of the complexity of God is also contrary to the theology that was dominant in Teilhard's day. According to this theology, God is without parts of any kind, completely simple.[69] Teilhard, however, would come to speak of the "complexity of God."[70] Connecting the two themes of creative union and divine complexity, Teilhard says, "There is, ultimately, *no unity, without unification.*" In contrast to a unity of singularity, Teilhard embraced a "unity of complexity."[71]

The "unity of complexity" is a corollary of the fact that nature presents itself to our gaze as *an organic whole* rather than as disconnected bits of matter that happen to fall into complex patterns of arrangement. Teilhard argued in the strongest terms that the various parts of nature are interdependent. Nature, he said in 1920, presents itself to the most casual inspection as a unity of forms—for example, there are resemblances between humans and monkeys, crabs and crayfish, and cats and leopards. The scholastic philosophers followed Aristotle in seeing no essential ordering of life-forms, except in terms of a scale of value. For scholasticism, the blueprint of the world is fixed eternally in the mind of God; the deity could create a fully formed man, having no childhood, appearing before all other animal life, as related in Genesis. Teilhard characterizes this form of order as a "*logical relay* existing in the divine thought," and refers to the underlying theory as *logicism* (logicisme). The alternative to logicism is physicism (physicisme) according to which the links in the sequence of biological forms lay down the necessary conditions for their successors, and are activated by "*the play of a specific physical agent.*" Thus, the progression of life is a process of development in which later stages cannot precede earlier ones. The proponent of physicism holds, for example, that "Neither the horse, nor man, nor the first moneran could appear sooner or later than they in fact did."[72]

Whether logicism or physicism is true, one is confronted with the variety of species distributed spatially across the globe and temporally in the fossil record. The question is whether a divine fiat is required for some of these changes, or whether mechanisms within matter prepare the way for each change.

> We must choose: Either there is evolution or there is intrusion. Either, in the order of appearances, living things pave the way for and introduce each other physically and this is true transformism with all of its historical and biological consequences. Or, the diverse living forms arise in isolation (that is to say, without a created precursor), there are no offshoots or phyla, and it is necessary to revert *immediately* to the intervention of an extra cosmic intelligence in order to account for the resemblances that exist among organized beings; and this is to admit pure logicism, with all of its improbabilities.[73]

This passage makes clear that transformism and evolution are the same in Teilhard's vocabulary. What is at issue for Teilhard is not specific Darwinian mechanisms or the permutations of genetic selection; rather, it is *the metaphysical inadequacy of logicism*. It is in this context that we should understand Teilhard's repeated insistence that evolution is not so much a theory as it is a precondition for the acceptability of any theory.[74]

We noted above that the Church did not categorically reject the scientific theory of evolution. Nor is this the aspect of Teilhard's ideas that prevented the publication of his works; after all, he published many articles on scientific topics with no objections from Rome, enough to fill ten volumes.[75] That it is less the scientific theory of evolution that interested Teilhard and more its metaphysical ramifications is evidenced by the fact that he so rarely mentions Darwin. When he mentions Darwin, it is often in the same breath with mention of Lamarck, or it is a question of Darwin as the founder of Darwinism which, for Teilhard, is only of historical interest. The real issue for Teilhard is not Darwinian evolution, but developmental transformation as a metaphysical category. I have no quarrel with Gray's characterization that Teilhard's objective was a resolution of the traditional philosophical problem of the one and the many.[76] Teilhard's metaphysic of creative union and his reflections on nature as an organic whole are arguably his rethinking of traditional Christian ideas in light of the developmental categories that evolution makes inevitable.

The differences between Teilhard's evolutionary metaphysics and the dominant views of the Church prior to Vatican II, with special reference to Thomistic thought, are summarized in the table found on page 82. The references to the works of Thomas Aquinas are as follows:

ST = Summa Theologiae; **SCG** = Summa Contra Gentiles.

Hyperphysics as a New Metaphysics

After the "crisis of obedience" Teilhard presented his views not as metaphysics, but as scientific or as an extension of scientific ideas. In the preface to *The Human Phenomenon* he says that the book, to be properly understood, must be read "exclusively as a scientific study." Again, he warns, "I have carefully and deliberately avoided venturing into that profound domain of being at all times."[77] Of course, "the domain of being" is another way of speaking of the domain of metaphysics as traditionally understood. Finally, he says:

> It is impossible to attempt a general scientific interpretation of the universe without *seeming* to intend to explain it right to the end. But only take a closer look at it, and you will see that this "hyperphysics" still is not metaphysics.[78]

As his struggles with Rome made it increasingly apparent that he would live to see none of his more philosophical works published, he returned to his earlier fascination with the metaphysics of creative transformation. In 1948, he completed the essay, "Comment je vois" (translated as "My Fundamental Vision"), which concludes with an explicitly metaphysical reconstruction of his views.[79]

It must be granted that the form of metaphysics most familiar to Teilhard and to which he had been introduced as a student at Hastings was metaphysics

Catholic Teaching and Dominant Views Expressed Prior to Vatican II (with special reference to Thomas Aquinas)	Teilhard's Evolutionary Metaphysics
Metaphysics of Being (Thomas Aquinas, *On Being and Essence*)	Metaphysics of Creative Union (*Writings in Time of War*, 151-76; *Toward the Future*, 192-99)
Divine creation as creation *ex nihilo* (ST I, Q. 45)	Divine creation as unifying the multiple or the multitude; physical nothingness as a pseudo-idea (*Writings in Time of War*, 95)
God in no sense has need of the created order; relations from God to the world are real but relations from the world to God are rational (ST I, Q 13, a.7; SCG II, 12).	Teilhard affirms a "strictly bilateral and complementary relationship between the world and God" (*Christianity and Evolution*, 226). "God must create in order to complete himself in something outside himself" (*Lettres Intimes*, 296).
Power of God extends to the logically possible—it is in God's power to bring about any state of affairs that is not logically contradictory (ST I, Q. 25, a.3 and a.4; cf. ST I, Q. 49, a. 2).	God's power necessarily occurs within a developmental context—not everything that is logically possible is possible for God to do. God does not so much make as to make things make themselves (*Christianity and Evolution*, 28).
Simplicity of God (ST I, Q 3, a.7)	Complexity of God (*Human Energy*, 68)
Adam and Eve as historical. This proposition depends upon the traditional concept of divine power.	There was no historical Adam conceived as a human who was "born adult" (*Christianity and Evolution*, 210).
Original Sin is the human condition traceable to the Garden of Eden and Adam's sin.	Sin and suffering are the inevitable by-products of cosmic evolution.
Christ's salvific event is geocentric. Christ was an earthling. Thus, theologians speculated whether, supposing extraterrestrials to exist, Christ's death saved them or whether they are naturally sinless because they are not descendents of Adam.	A plurality of inhabited worlds is the greater probability which the Christian worldview must satisfy—this without "unthinkable" ideas such as galaxies not affected by original sin or a terrestrial redemption affecting all galaxies (*Letters From My Friend*, 171-72).

considered as a science of being itself. According to this model, metaphysics deals with the primary cause of being, while science is left to deal with secondary causes (indeed, Teilhard sometimes uses this distinction). Teilhard did not have the temperament or interest for this kind of inquiry. In 1919, he wrote to his cousin:

> I'm less concerned than [my friends] are with the metaphysical side of things, with what might have been or might not have been, with the abstract conditions of existence: all that seems to me inevitably misleading or shaky.[80]

We have already seen, however, that Teilhard also came to rethink the traditional concept of being in terms of a metaphysics of union, but he drew his axioms for this metaphysics not from "the abstract conditions of existence," but from an examination of the age-long developmental processes that make up the evolutionary past.

Teilhard's reservations about traditional metaphysics notwithstanding, he was willing to broaden the meaning of metaphysics to include his own method of inquiry. In a letter to Henri de Lubac in 1934, Teilhard wrote:

> I mistrust metaphysics (in the usual sense of the word), because I smell a geometry in it. But I am ready to recognize another sort of metaphysics which would really be a hyper-physics,—or a hyper-biology.[81]

Teilhard is willing to consider hyperphysics as a different sort of metaphysics, presumably one that is more empirical and subject to revision—in short, fallible and non-dogmatic. In light of this qualification, his 1946 essay "Centrology" can be read as a type of open-ended metaphysic. Echoing his reservations about the "smell" of geometry in metaphysics, he says that he is offering, "an essay in universal explanation—not an *a priori* geometric synthesis starting from some definition of 'being,' but an experiential law of recurrence which can be checked in the phenomenal field and can appropriately be extrapolated into the totality of space and time." Finally, "It is not an abstract metaphysics, but a realist ultraphysics of union."[82] This is precisely the type of inquiry that Teilhard already pursued in *The Human Phenomenon*.

Concluding Thoughts

Teilhard's hyperphysics and his metaphysics of creative union are in the same family of ideas as the process thought of Henri Bergson, Alfred North

Whitehead, and Charles Hartshorne. I am not the first to point this out. In 1963, Madeleine Barthélemy-Madaule thoroughly discussed the comparisons of Bergson and Teilhard. Concerning the metaphysics of union, she said, "being as incessantly fused, incessantly increasing itself; the cosmos as creative actuality. All of Teilhardianism is there."[83] Five years later, Ian Barbour argued for reading Teilhard as a process philosopher in the same tradition as Whitehead.[84] In his introduction to the English translation of Teilhard's *The Heart of Matter*, N. M. Wildiers pointed out that Teilhard "turned away from scholasticism because its categories had become ill-adapted to describe the world as it appears today." He mentioned Barbour's work as showing "a certain convergence between the thought of Teilhard and Whitehead."[85]

Teilhard also seems to have realized the impossibility of insulating his views about the scope of science from its metaphysical implications. The last paper he wrote, "Research, Work and Worship," addresses the problem. Throughout his entire adult life, he says, he had been warned by authority, "Go quietly ahead with your scientific work without getting involved in philosophy or theology. . . ." Drawing, however, from fifty years of experience "living in the heart of the problem," he maintained that this attitude is "psychologically unfeasible and, what is more, directly opposed to the greater glory of God."[86] If the conclusion of this paper is correct, then Teilhard realized what the censors had understood all along—try as he might to present his views as "hyperphysics" (or sometimes "ultraphysics"), his extensions of scientific inquiry were *unavoidably metaphysical*, and that his views were not compatible with the Thomistic philosophy in terms of which Church teaching was expressed. In my view, what Teilhard understood that his critics did not is that the new wine of evolutionary thinking cannot be carried in the old wine skins of Thomism.

Notes

1. Professor of Philosophy, Department of Social Sciences, Pittsburg State University, Pittsburg, KS 66762.
2. Mary Lukas and Ellen Lukas, *Teilhard: The Man, the Priest, the Scientist* (Garden City, NY: Doubleday and Company, 1977), 94.
3. Pierre Teilhard de Chardin, *Lettres Intimes de Teilhard de Chardin à Auguste Valensin, Bruno de Solages, et Henri de Lubac 1919-1955*, introduction et notes par Henri de Lubac (Paris: Aubier Montaigne, 1972), 123, n. 2.
4. Paul Grenet, *Teilhard de Chardin: The Man and His Theories* (New York: Paul S. Erikson, Inc., 1966), 112.
5. Pierre Teilhard de Chardin, *Lettres à Jeanne Mortier* (Paris: Édition du Seuil, 1984), 75-78.
6. Amir D. Aczel's account of Teilhard's relations with Rome is detailed and insightful. See

his book *The Jesuit and the Skull: Teilhard de Chardin, Evolution, and the Search for Peking Man* (New York: Riverhead Books, 2007). My narrative contradicts nothing in Aczel. I highlight important aspects of Teilhard's reception prior to his posthumous fame which Aczel omits, but which are not directly relevant to the story Aczel is telling.

7. The English translation, Pierre Teilhard de Chardin, *Writings in Time of War*, trans. René Hague (New York: Harper & Row Publishers, 1968), omits seven of the essays included in the French edition; the missing essays are collected in Pierre Teilhard de Chardin, *Hymn of the Universe*, trans. Simon Bartholomew (New York: Harper & Row, Publishers, 1961), and Pierre Teilhard de Chardin, *The Heart of Matter*, trans. René Hague (New York: Harcourt Brace Jovanovich, Inc., 1978).

8. Pierre Teilhard de Chardin, *Christianity and Evolution*, trans. René Hague (New York: Harcourt Brace Jovanovich, 1971), 45-55.

9. Lukas and Lukas, *Teilhard*, 91.

10. Ursula King, *Spirit of Fire: The Life and Vision of Teilhard de Chardin* (Maryknoll, NY: Orbis Books, 1996), 107.

11. Lukas and Lukas, *Teilhard*, 93.

12. Teilhard de Chardin, *Lettres Intimes*, 132.

13. Pierre Teilhard de Chardin, *Letters to Léontine Zanta*, trans. Bernard Wall (New York: Harper & Row, 1969), 76, 98, 105.

14. Lukas and Lukas, *Teilhard*, 262.

15. Pierre Teilhard de Chardin, *Letters From My Friend Teilhard de Chardin 1948-1955* (New York: Paulist Press, 1980), 37. Mary Lukas and Ellen Lukas humorously capture a Teilhardian interpretation of the episode: "The priests shook hands, then stood together for a few moments, nodding across a gulf of seven hundred years, and chatted about Auvergne." Lukas and Lukas, Teilhard, 272.

16. Teilhard de Chardin, *Letters to Léontine Zanta*, 110.

17. Piltdown was revealed as a hoax in 1953. For most of Teilhard's life, however, his name could be associated with this "find" as a mark of professional achievement. Stephen Jay Gould implicated Teilhard as one of the hoaxers in an article in *Natural History* (March 1979). Articles agreeing and disagreeing with Gould are available online: http://www.clarku.edu/~piltdown/pp_map.html. Gould's accusations against Teilhard are entirely circumstantial. They falter, in my view, on the question of motive, but there are also crucial missteps in Gould's chain of reasoning that exonerate Teilhard. See chap. 9 of John Evangelist Walsh, *Unraveling Piltdown* (New York: Random House, 1996).

18. *Newsweek*, 27 March 1937, 30-31. Teilhard mentioned a photograph that appeared in *Life*. See Thomas M. King, S. J., and Mary Wood Gilbert, eds., *The Letters of Teilhard de Chardin and Lucile Swan* (Scranton, PA: University of Scranton Press, 2001), 82. I suspect that he was referring to the photograph in *Newsweek* since I have found no such photo in *Life*. Teilhard also says that a reporter from a Toronto newspaper interviewed him (Ibid., 74). I have yet to find such an interview. There is, however, a curious item in *The Toronto Daily Star*, Monday, 22 March 1937, 10. Msgr. Michael Cline of the Holy Name Church was reported as "quoting from a Protestant Bible" to substantiate his disagreement with what Teilhard said in Philadelphia the day before concerning the evolutionary origins of human beings. According to Msgr. Cline, Teilhard's opinion is open to "challenge and denial like that of any other adventurer in the field of science." He added that God did not create man until "the house of this world was completed and furnished for his residence."

19. King and Wood, *The Letters of Teilhard and Lucile Swan*, 78.

20. Ibid., 86.

21. Teilhard de Chardin, *Letters From My Friend*, 62-63.

22. André Billy, "Un grand poète à demi clandestin," *Le Figaro Littéraire*, 5 Août 1950.

23. Teilhard de Chardin, *Letters From My Friend*, 381, 62.

24. Teilhard says that the author was Louis Jugnet, a high school philosophy teacher at Toulouse (Teilhard de Chardin, *Letters From My Friend*, 58). Teilhard may have guessed that Jugnet was the author because one of Jugnet's books is advertised on the back cover as being "in the same collection." Mortier, however, says that she learned that the author was Lefèvre (Teilhard de Chardin, *Lettres à Jeanne Mortier*, 64). This makes sense, for as Billy notes in his article, *Pensée Catholique* was unfriendly to Teilhard's ideas, and it was the same publisher that issued *L'Evolution Rédemptrice*.

25. *L'Evolution Rédemptrice du P. Teilhard de Chardin* (Paris: Librairie du Cèdre, 1950), 67.

26. Ibid., 77.

27. Ibid., 164.

28. Pierre Teilhard de Chardin, "Review of *L'Evolution rédemptrice du P. Teilhard de Chardin,*" in Nichole et Karl Schmitz-Moormann, eds., *L'Œuvre Scientifique* 10 (Olten/Freiburg-im-Breisgau: Walter Verlag, 1971): 4290.

29. Louis Cognet, *Le Père Teilhard de Chardin, et la pensée contemporaine* (Paris: Au Portulan, chez Flammarion, 1952), 11.

30. Ibid., 125.

31. Ibid,, 87.

32. Teilhard de Chardin, *Letters From My Friend*, 131.

33. Ibid., 130.

34. Teilhard de Chardin, *Lettres à Jeanne Mortier*, 104.

35. Teilhard de Chardin, *Letters From My Friend*, 39.

36. John Haught, "Evolution, in Nature and Catholic Thought," in Maureen Fiedler and Linda Rabben, eds., *Rome Has Spoken* (New York: Crossroad Publishing, 1998), 178-85, 180.

37. There may have been others. The month before the encyclical was released, "five of Fourvière's most eminent theology professors . . . were all aware that they were about to be ordered to leave their professorial chairs" (Lukas and Lukas, 284-85). There were also tensions between the Vatican and some French worker-priests inspired by Marxism—the worker-priests were eventually recalled by Rome in 1953, putting an end to their activities.

38. Teilhard de Chardin, *Christianity and Evolution*, 209-11.

39. Teilhard de Chardin, *Letters From My Friend*, 144.

40. Ibid., 211.

41. Lukas and Lukas, *Teilhard*, 296-98.

42. http://www.ourladyswarriors.org/dissent/cdfchard.htm.

43. See Pope John Paul II's three addresses concerning science and Christianity, given in 1979-80, reprinted in Roland Mushat Frye, ed., *Is God a Creationist? The Religious Case Against Creation-Science* (New York: Charles Scribner's Sons, 1983), 141-54.

44. Lukas and Lukas, *Teilhard*, 283.

45. Teilhard de Chardin, *Letters From My Friend*, 56.

46. Pierre Teilhard de Chardin, *Human Energy*, trans. J. M. Cohen (London: William Collins Sons & Co, 1969), 12, 70; Grenet, 112.

47. Teilhard de Chardin, *Writings in Time of War*, 151-76.

48. Ibid., 95.

49. Teilhard de Chardin, *Christianity and Evolution*, 22.

50. ST I, Q. 45. When citing references from Thomas Aquinas, I use ST for *Summa Theologiae* (followed by volume and question and article, if needed), and SCG for *Summa Contra Gentiles* (followed by volume, chapter and paragraph).

51. SCG II, 19, 7.

52. Teilhard used the exclusive language of his time, but he could effortlessly use feminine images of deity. See Teilhard de Chardin, *Letters to Léontine Zanta*, 86; Teilhard de Chardin, *Lettres Intimes*, 296.

53. Pierre Teilhard de Chardin, *Activation of Energy*, trans. René Hague (New York: Harcourt Brace Jovanovich, 1970), 146.

54. Ibid., 112-13.

55. Pierre Teilhard de Chardin, *Science and Christ*, trans. René Hague (New York: Harper & Row Publishers, 1968), 182.

56. Ibid., 186.

57. Teilhard de Chardin, *Letters From My Friend*, 166.

58. Ibid., 170.

59. ST I, Q 13, a.7; SCG II, 12.

60. Teilhard de Chardin, *Christianity and Evolution*, 226-27.

61. Ibid., 210.

62. Ibid., 31.

63. Ibid., 33, cf. 83.

64. ST I, Q. 25, a.3 and a.4; ST I, Q. 49, a.2.

65. Teilhard de Chardin, *Christianity and Evolution*, 82-83.

66. Pierre Teilhard de Chardin, *The Vision of the Past*, trans. J. M. Cohen (New York and Evanston: Harper & Row Publishers, 1966), 25, 154; cf. Teilhard de Chardin, *Christianity and Evolution*, 28.

67. Teilhard de Chardin, The Vision of the Past, 231.

68. Donald P. Gray. *The One and the Many: Teilhard de Chardin's Vision of Unity* (New York: Herder and Herder, 1969), 28.

69. ST I, Q 3, a.7.

70. Teilhard de Chardin, *Human Energy*, 68.

71. Teilhard de Chardin, *Science and Christ*, 184.

72. Teilhard de Chardin, *Heart of Matter*, 110.

73. Against the anonymous author of *L'Evolution rédemptrice* (62), Teilhard thought it wrong to accept micro-evolution (evolution within a species) but deny macro-evolution (evolution between species). See Pierre Teilhard de Chardin, *The Appearance of Man*, trans. J. M. Cohen (New York: Harper & Row, 1965), 218, 226; Teilhard de Chardin, *Heart of Matter*, 112-13.

74. Pierre Teilhard de Chardin, *The Human Phenomenon*, trans. Sarah Appleton-Weber (Brighton: Sussex Academic Press, 1999), 90, 152; Teilhard de Chardin, *Appearance of Man*, 211; Teilhard de Chardin, *Vision of the Past*, 127; Teilhard de Chardin, *Science and Christ*, 193.

75. Nicole and Karl Schmitz-Moormann, eds., *L'œuvre scientifique, Pierre Teilhard de Chardin* (Olten/Freiburg-im-Breisgau: Walter Verlag, 1971). Teilhard's 1948 summary of his career, written for the Director of the Collège de France when he was offered its

chair of Paleontology, is informative: "Qualifications, Career, Field-Work and Writings of Pierre Teilhard de Chardin" (Teilhard de Chardin, *Heart of Matter*, 157-64, 253-61). In the same volume, see Teilhard's 1950 statement written on the occasion of his admission to the Academy of Sciences: "The Scientific Career of Father Teilhard de Chardin," 152-54.

76. I am not convinced by Gray's claim that Teilhard wished to affirm creation *ex nihilo*. Even were this Teilhard's intention, his doctrine that "to create is to unite" presupposes a preexisting multiplicity, whereas creation *ex nihilo* does not. See Gray, *The One and the Many*, 32.

77. Teilhard de Chardin, *Human Phenomenon*, 1.

78. Ibid., 2.

79. Teilhard de Chardin, *Toward the Future*, 192-99.

80. Pierre Teilhard de Chardin, *The Making of a Mind: Letters from a Soldier-Priest, 1914-1919*, trans. René Hague (New York: Harper & Row, 1965), 302.

81. Teilhard de Chardin, *Lettres Intimes*, 269.

82. Teilhard de Chardin, *Activation of Energy*, 99.

83. Madeleine Barthélemy-Madaule, *Bergson et Teilhard de Chardin* (Paris: Éditions du Seuil, 1963), 53.

84. Ian Barbour, "Five Ways of Reading Teilhard," *The Teilhard Review* 3, no. 1 (summer 1968): 3-20; Ian Barbour, "Teilhard's Process Metaphysics," in Ewert H. Cousins, ed., *Process Theology: Basic Writings* (New York: Newman Press, 1971), 323-50. Originally in *Journal of Religion* 49 (1969): 136-59.

85. Teilhard de Chardin, *Heart of Matter*, 9-10. In "Teilhard and Process Philosophy Redux," *Process Studies* 35, no. 1 (Spring-Summer 2006): 12-42, I argue that Teilhard should be considered one of the founders of modern process metaphysics alongside Alfred North Whitehead and Charles Hartshorne.

86. Teilhard de Chardin, *Science and Christ*, 214.

II

TEILHARD

AESTHETIC APPEAL

TEILHARD, BEAUTY, AND THE ARTS

Thomas M. King, S.J.[1]

During his lifetime, Pierre Teilhard de Chardin was well known as a scientist. He published abundantly on the geology of Asia; much of this writing centered on the evolution of life on Earth. After his death his many religious writings appeared and they too were fundamentally shaped by his work in evolution. Yet, those familiar with his published work might be surprised to read his self-assessment: "It would be more to my purpose to be a shadow of [Richard] Wagner [rather] than a shadow of [Charles] Darwin."[2] What is he telling us?

Another surprise: we have known Teilhard through his theories of evolving life, yet he identifies his mission: "to propagate not exactly a theory, a system, a *Weltanschauung*, but a certain taste, a certain perception of the beauty, the pathos, and the unity of being." To propagate a *perception of beauty*! He explains, "I try to translate the species of calm intoxication produced in me by an awareness of the profound substance of things."[3] He did, indeed, propose a cosmic theory, but he saw it only as a translation of what he had immediately perceived, a beauty of which he could not speak directly. He would take what he knew primarily as "a seeing, a taste, a sort of intuition," and "translate" it into a philosophy. This was not easy: "No matter how clear the vision, how difficult it is to translate it into phrases!"[4] "Phrases" were not his preferred approach: "How I wish I could translate it into music!"[5] he says.

Teilhard tells of being aware of a certain tone, note, or harmony that he compares to "the single note produced by the angel's viol[in] of which St. Francis never wearied."[6] In another context he writes, "All the sounds of created being are fused without being confused, in a single note which dominates and sustains them (that seraphic note, no doubt, which bewitched St. Francis)."[7] Teilhard looked forward to the day when everyone would, like him, be "caught up in the essential music of the world." Yet sometimes he could not hear the music himself: "I sometimes live in the frustrating state of a deaf man straining in his effort to hear a music which he knows to be all around him."[8] Yet in no sense was he a musician. He is quoted as saying, "I am a pure idiot concerning music."[9] Though he often used images of music to explain what he was about, other forms of art would do: "I need an outlet and have no aptitude for music or poetry or novel writing. I have tried philosophic literary essays."[10] In short, his preferred way of expressing what he found would have been music and not the essays that made him famous.

During World War I, Teilhard wrote to his cousin Marguerite that his particular destiny was "the fulfilment of the Beautiful and the Good." He continues, "I must live only to develop a *spirituality in immediacy.*" Immediacy! The beautiful is not an abstraction or a theory; it is, like music, a direct or immediate perception. As the passage continues, Teilhard speaks of Christ as a collective entity, but a collective entity that is "immediately apprehended."[11] To understand the apprehension, I propose the following analogy. In one sense we can see only what is physical. So in looking at a friend, you see eyes, nose, hands, etc. And in seeing these you say, "I have seen my friend." Yet all you see are physical features that seem to render your friend (whose essence is not really visible) immediately perceptible. In fact, your friend is the unity animating these features. For Teilhard, each part of creation serves as a feature of Christ that renders him visible; so he speaks of Christ as "Soul of the World," that which animates everything. Just as your friend is perceptible through the constellation of individual features, so Christ is seen through the many aspects of the world. Through them, the world becomes diaphanous and we see Christ as "creation in person"; Christ is "immediately apprehended."[12] Teilhard's aim, then, is to show others how to perceive Christ in all of creation.

A few months after suggesting these ideas in a letter, Teilhard developed them more fully in an essay entitled "The Universal Element." He writes, "The Universal Element makes the transcendent immediate; it unifies, by differentiating, the Multiple."[13] Christ is the Universal who appears within every Element, much as your friend appears in every feature (eyes, hands, etc.). In one sense you do not "see" the person at all. Yet the person is "perceived" as the soul that animates the features. So, Teilhard claims, "Christ appears";[14] the world has made him visible; he is the unifying element that animates everything. Teilhard told of this in surprising phrases: God is "perceived by our eyes"; we have a "perception of the divine spread everywhere"; "Christ appears"; "The whole impact of things . . . brings a contact with Christ, one feels in them the touch of Christ's hand."[15] The ability to see the person of Christ in all the elements of creation and know in them his touch constitutes Teilhard's "spirituality in immediacy."

Perhaps we think of Teilhard as presenting a cosmology or a contemporary rendition of the theology of St. Paul. But his central aim was not to present a cosmology or theology; his writings were (in his words) "only to develop a spirituality in immediacy," that is, a spirituality of perception.[16] So, "Cosmic Life," his first essay, was introduced as a way "to make men see"; *The Divine Milieu* was written as "a way of teaching how to *see*";[17] *The Phenomenon of Man* was composed as "an attempt to see and make others *see*."[18] If we regard these as great theoretical works, we could be missing what Teilhard is saying. He wanted to lead us to a simple perception, to the note played by the angel's violin heard by St. Francis, and to what he was hearing himself.

A First Point: When telling of Francis and the musical note, Teilhard explained, "All the sounds of created being are fused without being confused, in a single note which sustains and dominates them."[19] Likewise, you could say concerning your friend's multiple features (eyes, hands, etc.) that the features light up with meaning when they are seen as "my friend"—that is, as a single someone who "sustains and dominates" what is visible. The features are unified, yet they are not confused or blurred together. So for Teilhard, the Universal Element "unifies by differentiating the multiple." In this phrase, written in 1919, we recognize an anticipation of the statement that he would use abundantly in his later writings, "union differentiates." This 1919 phrase, together with the phrase, "fused without being confused,"[20] tells of a perception. In recognizing our friend's voice on the phone, for instance, we grasp the meaning behind every nuance of that voice. We hear the person behind the voice; this is union differentiating. Teilhard would lead us to experience the world in a similar way, to see it as Christ. He warns, "the Church will perish if it does not get away from the artificial world of verbal theology."[21] So he had no intention of adding to this verbal theology. Instead, he wanted us to see.

A Second Point: Teilhard's message does not stop with the perception of Christ, that is, with me as subject perceiving Christ as object. Rather, Teilhard tells of a type of perception that draws me out of myself and into what is perceived: this is the perception of beauty. In perceiving the beautiful, I identify with what I see or hear and, thereby, I lose some of my autonomy. Teilhard speaks of the goadings of sense beauties penetrating our hearts and making our life *flow outwards*; by the goadings of beauty, one is no longer an isolated self. He writes, sense beauties "took possession of me and bore me away," and "the world invaded my being and drew it back into itself," "it drew me out of myself."[22] We all have a tendency to withdraw into solitude and isolation, to give in to the "temptation of matter." Yet, "each one of our emotions, *the more it is aesthetic,* the more it tends to break up our autonomy."[23] The aesthetic emotion is our response to the beautiful. This emotion draws us from our isolation and into what we see or hear. Beautiful music, for instance, draws us into the sound.

A novel can draw us out of ourselves and into the life of another. In seeing a film, we identify with the beautiful faces on the screen, but we soon lose interest if their characters do not show a deeper beauty. To engage us more deeply, to evoke an aesthetic emotion, their relationships and deeds must be beautiful. If we do not feel the identification, we return to our solitude. But beauty acts to involve us in the world beyond ourselves, and the process continues. So does our knowledge of Jesus. Artists have shown him with a beautiful face. Then, we come to see him having a beautiful teaching. Christ can be seen as an all-around beautiful *human being,* but *for many people that is as far as it goes.* This restricted image of Christ that Teilhard saw prevalent in the Church results in a whole set of "non-believers" who see Christ only as a fine human being. Teilhard writes, for such people "Christ does not appear sufficiently beautiful, sufficiently divine."[24] The fullness of his beauty can be seen only when one comes to see him as "Soul of the World," a Soul shining through the beauties of Earth that constitute his features, Christ clothed with the beauties of Earth. In him, "we shall discover where all the beauties [of the universe] flow together."[25] Only thus can anyone speak to him as follows, "You who gather into your exuberant unity every beauty. . . . In truth you are my Lord and my God."[26]

In seeing the beautiful, we can no longer think of our selves as isolated units perceiving an objective world, for the goadings of beauty have drawn us out of ourselves. For some time, the one sensitive to Beauty will look "to the marvels of art to provide him with that exaltation which will give access to the sphere" beyond the self, but happy is the one who will not shrink from a passionate questioning of the Muses concerning God.[27] By such questioning, we come to see where beauty leads. Teilhard would have us pass beyond all limited beauties. For there is a trail of beauties (from beautiful bodies to beautiful souls, etc.); we are drawn to seek beauties ever more comprehensive. This trail will eventually lead us to Christ the Lord. He writes, "When it was given to me to see where the dazzling trail of particular beauties and partial harmonies was leading, I recognized it was all coming to a single point, on a Person, your Person. Jesus!"[28]

Teilhard told of contemporary pagans standing on the Acropolis blaming "the Gospel for having disfigured the world, and they mourn for beauty."[29] They would claim that appeal to the beauty of Christ, the individual human, cancels the beauties of earth; but Teilhard argues that, if we see Christ as Lord of the universe, this is no longer the case. "The scattered charms of the universe give one a glimpse of the Beauty that would unite them all and bring them to their fullness."[30] Each beauty demands of us a surrender. We have surrendered to the music; we have surrendered to the novel (these are "the scattered charms" that draw us out), but ultimately our joy is in "surrendering to a beauty greater than man, the rapture of being possessed."[31] To surrender to this ultimate Beauty is to come wholly out of ourselves. A perception of sense-beauty starts the process; to it we surrender some of our autonomy; this continues until we surrender to ultimate Beauty and are fully enraptured.

Teilhard elucidates the way to surrender in his essay, "The Eternal Feminine." Here the Feminine speaks and identifies herself as "the beauty running through the world, to make it associate in ordered groups: the ideal held up before the world to make it ascend."[32] The feminine voice tells of its work. "I instilled even into the atoms, into the fathomless depths of the infinitesimal, a vague but obstinate yearning to emerge from the solitude of their nothingness and to hold fast to something outside of themselves."[33] Feminine beauty has drawn the atoms out of themselves. But not only the atoms. Beauty has the same effect on God, for God too has passed out of himself. The Feminine claims, "If God were able to emerge from himself, he had first to lay a pathway of desire before his feet, he had to spread before himself the sweet savor of beauty."[34] The beauty that drew God forth was the Virgin Mary; she drew God into her womb. Again, it was "by aesthetics" that God first proceeded out of himself and set the world in motion.

Teilhard was a highly introverted person and spoke of what, during his early life, was a somewhat self-centered and self-enclosed interior life.[35] His cousin Marguerite (a first cousin once removed) played a significant role in drawing him out of himself. She was the inspiration that moved him to write. Teilhard sent his first essays to her. Mindful of her, he wrote "The Eternal Feminine." Feminine Beauty had drawn the infinite God out of himself; it drew the atoms out of themselves, and it drew the introverted Teilhard out of himself and into the turmoil of life.

But, for Teilhard, beauty was found even in the horrors of the First World War. He wrote, "The supreme beauty of a war like this . . . is to furnish men the occasion of casting themselves, with all the energy of body and soul, into a final sacrifice in a work of evolutionary extent."[36] During the war, moral beauty was calling men out of themselves into an act of sacrifice. Teilhard realized that War could release in a soldier a spring of "moral beauty."[37] Yet this was not what he found while he was "in a section of non-combatants"; instead, he found "so little moral beauty" and was bothered by the soldiers' "selfish, bourgeois," and irreligious ways.[38] Beauty was found only when they acted for a goal outside themselves. Beauty draws one away from selfishness and into a common work. And by our selfless work, the beauty of Earth increases. We are to build the Earth, that is, build a suitable Body for Christ. To do this we are to develop science and improved social systems without which "the beauty and perfection of the mystical Body would never be realized."[39] "In one single movement . . . nature grows in beauty and the Body of Christ reaches its full development."[40] Such is "the fulfilment of the Beautiful" that Teilhard had seen as his destiny.[41] Finally, Beauty will draw us totally out of ourselves and into what we perceive. In our surrender to beauty, we are passive; our surrender is "the highest and at the same time the most complete of our passivities of growth."[42]

In his wartime letters to Marguerite, Teilhard acknowledges the value of music and poetry since they "cosmicize" the soul yet do not simply lead to pantheism: "All they do is to arouse the soul in a general way to the search for the most Beautiful."[43] But aside from such passing references, there was only one occasion when he dealt directly with the work of the artist/poet/musician. In Paris in 1939, Teilhard was asked to speak at a luncheon arranged by the

"Centre d'Etudes des Problèmes Humains." He titled his talk, "The Function of Art as an Expression of Human Energy."[44] This short essay briefly touches many points, and I suspect it takes several readings to grasp what he is saying. (I suspect that many attending the luncheon were confused.) I would like to reflect on this essay.

In "The Function of Art," Teilhard explains that art has value that is more than "Art for the sake of art." Rather, art has a role to play in the evolution of life; that is, "Art for the sake of evolution." At the present phase of evolution, Teilhard sees an excess of psychic energy available. He calls it an excess, for it is an energy not immediately concerned with survival. Some of this excess has found an outlet in science and philosophy, activities that serve evolution: science gives humans a constantly increasing source of power while philosophy shows the direction along which we should advance. But sometimes, the excess of human energy is used to produce art. Do the arts advance evolution? And, more specifically, an evolution directed to a world that will be animated by a single Soul? Teilhard asks, "Is art simply an expenditure and dissipation, an escape of human energy? Its characteristic being, as it is sometimes said, that it serves no purpose? Or is the contrary true, that this apparent uselessness hides the secret of its practical efficiency?"[45] He concludes that art, far from being a luxury or a parasite of evolution, has an important role to play. In fact, art benefits evolution in three ways:

First, "Art serves to give the over-plus of life which boils up within us the first elementary degree of consistence."[46] This boiling up is "initially completely internal," but then it "begins to be realized objectively for all of us." That is, the artist takes what he or she knows privately and externalizes it for all to see. What is within must be "expressed in a significant act, in a gesture, in a dance, a song, or a cry." These provide a body to the private awareness and in some way materialize it. Yet the materialization is seen as the completion of the inner awareness.

Teilhard expressed this in explaining what he saw as his mission: "translating as faithfully as possible what I hear murmuring in me like a voice or a song which are not me, but of the world in me."[47] Here the source of the "song" is "the world in me." It is the world he has come to know, his universe.[48] His writings enable others to see his world. This is what each artist must do: present the world that is singing within. Then it is no longer one's self, but the earth acting through one.[49] The earth within Teilhard was clamoring for a voice.

In writing a personal statement of faith, he says, "As I proceeded I felt that something greater than myself was working its way into me."[50] It was this greater something that seemed to write the essay. These phrases tell of an inner awareness that he would verbalize. Essays were his way to "materialize" what he found. He did not want credit for his ideas, for he did not see himself as their author. How could he? He was simply giving the world a voice.

Some reflections on his first point: In speaking of a need to share what he found, he can be seen as entering into the long Christian debate between contemplation and action. The purely contemplative tradition would tell of one entering ever more deeply into contemplation itself. St. Bernard, a monk of the eleventh century, would claim the monk should always prefer contemplation to acting in the world. But Bernard also tells of some monks finding in the contemplation itself an obligation to proclaim what one has found.[51] This was clearly the case with Teilhard. He felt obliged to get his message out into the public square.

But apart from contemplation-and-action in the monastic tradition, one might consider the claim of Otto Rank, a psychiatrist and long-time co-worker with and disciple of Freud. Rank developed an extensive theory of art and spoke of the neurotic individual as an *artiste manqué*, that is, a person who has gone half way to being an artist. Such a person has come upon a luminous vision, a private world, but, being unable to express it publicly, the visionary is more or less drowned in the vision. Such a one lives in a private world. But, if one can take the inner vision and translate it into some material form, one is then an artist, a musician, a poet, or even an author of literary essays. One is no longer an *artiste manqué*. This understanding has given rise to the term, "troubled genius." The novelist Flaubert was such, and he has reflected on the difference between madness and genius. He tells of some children acutely sensitive to music, but who find their sensitivity only causes them shattered nerves and extreme suffering: "These are not the future Mozarts." Instead, they are captivated and consumed by a wondrous awareness; they are neurotics, *artistes manqués*. Many such people obtain some deliverance by articulating their world to a psychiatrist. Others can be delivered if they have a skill in music, poetry, philosophy, etc. This connects their world with the public world. The connection is the work of art. So Teilhard heard a celestial music and "materialized" it in a series of essays. Friends appreciated his essays, but, to his deep frustration, the Church prevented their publication. But also—to his frustration—he found himself an idiot in regards to music.

Teilhard's second point concerning art and evolution is that, in the act of giving the inner impulse a sensible form, the artist to some degree intellectualizes the impulse. Here he warns that the artist should not try to introduce a doctrine or thesis into the artwork, for it is the intuition and not the intellect that should dominate. If the work truly issues from the depths of one's being with the richness of musical harmony, it will be refracted in the minds of the hearers or observers. Here Teilhard speaks of art as the *first* body and *first* face of the spiritual energy within. For, "more primordial than any idea, beauty will be manifest as the herald and generator of ideas."[52] That is, ideas should arise from the beauty and not beauty from the ideas. This sequence was exemplified when he explained his continued attachment to Catholicism:

> Believe me, when one has penetrated to this axis of the Christian attitude, the ritual, disciplinary and theological encrustations matter little more than musical or acoustical theories matter to the enjoyment of a beautiful piece of music. Truly, there is a Christian note which makes the whole World vibrate like an immense gong, in the divine Christ. This note is unique and universal and in it alone consists the Gospel. Only it is real (happily).[53]

Musical theories are secondary; they are of value only if they elucidate the music. So rituals and theology are only reflections of what is primary, and that is the Christian note. This is what he would have us hear, to directly intuit the music. Art is primary, while theories are only verbal attempts to articulate what the artist has discovered. So Teilhard would sooner work in the shadow of Wagner than in the shadow of Darwin.

A reflection on the second point: That beauty should generate ideas is not new to the philosophic tradition. It is found in Plato's *Symposium*. There, Socrates tells of receiving instructions on love (eros) from a wise woman instructor. This woman tells of men who become pregnant when, at a certain age, they desire to give birth in both body and soul. According to her, in the presence of the ugly, the pregnant one contracts, shrivels up, and turns away. But in the presence of the beautiful, he opens out and is able to beget and bear fruit. So Beauty is called "the goddess of parturition who presides at birth."[54] Socrates is told that a love of beauty is really a "love of generation and birth in beauty." Generation and birth give mortals a type of immortality, for people live on in their children. "Those who are pregnant in the body only betake themselves to women and beget children."[55] But there is another giving-birth proper to the soul, one that gives birth to "wisdom and virtue in general." But that is not all. Poets and artists or any one producing original work is said to need the Beautiful in order to give birth. People seek beauty to beget offspring and thus relieve the soul of its inner burden. This is true even if the beautiful one is not present:

> . . . at the touch of the beautiful which is ever present to his memory, even when absent, he brings forth that which was conceived long before, and in company with [the beautiful one] tends that which he brings forth; and they are married by a far nearer tie and have a closer friendship than those who beget mortal children.[56]

To give birth to a work of art, the lover and beloved are not to embrace physically. Instead, Socrates explains, "Their happiness depends upon their self-control: If the better elements of the mind which leads to order and philosophy prevail, then they pass their life here in happiness and harmony." When the time of their death arrives, they are light and winged for flight.[57]

In this context, one thinks of Teilhard during the First World War. Shortly before being drafted, he met his cousin Marguerite in Paris. For the first time he was awakened to eros, but no sooner had love awakened than they were separated by his military service. Throughout his wartime Journals, he wrote an abundance of short notations trying to understand "the Feminine." Inspired by Marguerite, he writes in "The Eternal Feminine," "The true fertility is the fertility that brings beings together in the engendering of spirit."[58] And again, as in Plato, love becomes spiritual by the exercise of restraint and absence; but it is a love that eventually raises one to heaven. Teilhard dedicates "The Eternal Feminine" to Beatrice, the feminine ideal that inspired Dante. Dante saw Beatrice briefly on six occasions, but they never touched. He called her "the glorious lady of my mind." Having written several poems in her honor, Dante decided not to write of her again until he could do so more suitably. Many years later he would write *The Divine Comedy* (She died before he began writing). Here he tells of a journey to the inferno, through purgatorio, and then meeting Beatrice at the gate of Paradiso. Teilhard, by dedicating his essay to Beatrice, acknowledges the feminine beauty that inspired his own work.

Teilhard wrote *The Phenomenon of Man* under the inspiration of another woman, Lucile Swan. Lucile has told of making many suggestions to him, and added that she was flattered to hear him speak of the manuscript as "our work." The writing was entirely his, but the inspiration was Lucile. He would later explain that he knew no form of self-development without a feminine eye turned on him.[59]

Teilhard offered a third reason for judging art to be necessary for evolution. Art personalizes the energy of evolution. Here Teilhard allows that though science involves personal insight, the scientist's originality is soon swallowed up in the universality of scientific conclusions; it then belongs to everybody and nobody; the personal element has disappeared into the collective creation ("science") to which one has devoted one's self. On the other hand, the artist, precisely because the artist lives by the imagination, can counter-balance the cancellation of the worker by the work. Teilhard writes, "The more the world is rationalized and mechanized, the more it needs 'poets' as the ferment within its personality and perspective."[60]

Teilhard speaks of this third point as the most important, but I am not aware of any other place where he encourages people to personalize what they produce. That is, Teilhard would often urge that we universalize our thinking, but personalizing our thinking was ignored, other than in this singular essay.

I first read Teilhard in 1962 when I was in the seminary. A friend and fellow seminarian kept telling me to read Teilhard. I said, "Yes," not really meaning it. Then one morning I found my friend had placed a copy of *The Divine Milieu* on my desk. I picked it up mildly curious thinking I would look through it for five minutes and then proceed with other work. But the prose resonated with me as no other prose had done. I kept on reading at a great pace without understanding, but I could not stop. I do not usually read that way. I finished the work in one sitting. Why did I keep reading what I did not understand? The best answer I can give is that in reading I heard a tone or a musical note; it was much like the angel's violin heard by St. Francis. So I kept reading.

I suspect many of us are like that. We find it difficult to explain many of his texts, but there is something about his prose that gets through to us and makes our world sing.

Notes

1. At his death in June 2009, Father King was Professor of Theology, Georgetown University, Washington, DC.
2. Pierre Teilhard de Chardin, *Letters to Two Friends, 1926-1952*, ed. Ruth Nanda Anshan, trans. Helen Weaver (New York: World Publishing, 1969), 59.
3. Ibid., 59.

4. Pierre Teilhard de Chardin, *Lettres à Jeanne Mortier* (Paris: Editions de Seuil, 1984), 25.

5. Teilhard de Chardin, *Letters to Two Friends*, 59.

6. Teilhard de Chardin, *Writings in Time of War*, trans. René Hague (New York: Harper & Row, 1968), 520.

7. Pierre Teilhard de Chardin, *The Divine Milieu*, trans. Bernard Wall (New York: Harper & Row, First Harper Torchbook edition, 1965), 120.

8. Teilhard de Chardin, *Letters to Two Friends*, 40.

9. Dominique Wang, *A Pekin avec Teilhard de Chardin: 1939-1946* (Paris: R. Laffont, 1981), 84.

10. Pierre Teilhard de Chardin, *Towards the Future*, trans. René Hague (New York: Harcourt Brace Jovanovich, 1975), 43. See Teilhard de Chardin, *Divine Milieu*, 59.

11. Pierre Teilhard de Chardin, *The Making of a Mind: Letters from a Soldier-Priest, 1914-1919*, trans. René Hague (New York: Harper & Row, 1965), 241.

12. Ibid.

13. Teilhard de Chardin, *Writings in Time of War*, 301.

14. Ibid., 246.

15. Ibid., 246, 178.

16. Teilhard de Chardin, *Making of a Mind*, 241.

17. Teilhard de Chardin, *Divine Milieu*, 46.

18. Pierre Teilhard de Chardin, *The Phenomenon of Man*, trans. Bernard Wall (New York: Harper & Row, 1957), 31.

19. Teilhard de Chardin, *Divine Milieu*, 120.

20. Ibid., 120.

21. Pierre Teilhard de Chardin, *Lettres à Auguste Valensin, Bruno de Solages, et Henri de Lubac*, introduction et notes par Henri de Lubac (Paris: Editions Aubier-Montaigne, 1972), 182.

22. Teilhard de Chardin, *Writings in Time of War*, 117.

23. Ibid., 118.

24. Pierre Teilhard de Chardin, *Journal*, Tome I, texte intégral publié par Nicole et Karl Schmitz-Moorman (Paris: Fayard, 1975), 252.

25. Teilhard de Chardin, *Divine Milieu*, 115.

26. Pierre Teilhard de Chardin, *The Heart of Matter*, trans. René Hague (New York: Harcourt Brace Jovanovich, 1978), 132.

27. Teilhard de Chardin, *Writings in Time of War*, 119.

28. Ibid., 146.

29. Ibid., 198.

30. Teilhard de Chardin, *Toward the Future*, 49.

31. Teilhard de Chardin, *Writings in Time of War*, 131.

32. Ibid., 192.

33. Ibid., 193.

34. Ibid., 200.

35. Teilhard de Chardin, *Heart of Matter*, 52.

36. Teilhard de Chardin, *Journal*, 61.

37. Teilhard de Chardin, *Writings in Time of War*, 284.

38. Teilhard de Chardin, *Making of a Mind*, 55.

39. Teilhard de Chardin, *Writings in Time of War*, 64.

40. Ibid., 62.

41. Teilhard de Chardin, *Making of a Mind*, 241.
42. Teilhard de Chardin, *Divine Milieu*, 131.
43. Teilhard de Chardin, *Making of a Mind*, 97.
44. Teilhard de Chardin, *Toward the Future*, 88-91.
45. Ibid., 89.
46. Ibid.
47. Teilhard de Chardin, *Letters to Two Friends*, 44.
48. Two of his essays are titled, "*Mon Univers*."
49. Teilhard de Chardin, *Letters to Two Friends*, 73.
50. Pierre Teilhard de Chardin, *Christianity and Evolution*, trans. René Hague (New York: Harcourt Brace Jovanovich, 1971), 130.
51. Thomas Merton, *Merton on Saint Bernard* (Kalamazoo, MI: Cistercian Publications, 1980), 76.
52. Teilhard de Chardin, *Toward the Future*, 90.
53. Teilhard de Chardin, *Letters to Two Friends*, 30-31.
54. Plato, *The Dialogues of Plato, Volume I* (New York: Random House, 1892), 331.
55. Ibid., 333.
56. Ibid.
57. Ibid., 259.
58. Teilhard de Chardin, *Writings in Time of War*, 117.
59. Teilhard de Chardin, *Heart of Matter*, 59.
60. Teilhard de Chardin, *Toward the Future*, 90.

THE TRUTH OF THE
TEILHARDIAN VISION

John D. Ryan[1]

The truth that Teilhard pursues in his religious writing is neither purely scientific nor psychological truth, nor is it even purely socio-historical or theological truth. It is rather a *religious truth*.[2] In order to arrive at religious truth, he constructs a theopoiesis,[3] a conception and expression of the meaning of human-life-and-God which arises from the creative imagination, from the deepest level of the mind, as it seeks to find, out of its own resources, and especially its creativity, the ultimate meaning of its existence. I begin with two preliminary observations.

First, Teilhard spoke of this work as his vision. He introduces *Le phénomène humain* with the premise that seeing is at the center of spiritual life, that we become more fully human in accord with what we see.[4] One of his more important late works (1948) bears the title, "My Fundamental Vision."[5] Such seeing, moreover, in line with the main currents of religious thought of the past two centuries, beginning with Schleiermacher, but foreshadowed in Pascal a century and a half earlier, is always subjective. As Teilhard repeatedly affirms of his own thought, it is his; it is personal. But for that very reason it is more than a single person's vision. "Humanity is essentially the same in all of us," he declared in his 1934 essay, "How I believe." "It is through that which is most incommunicably personal in us that we make contact with the universal."[6]

Second, many have loved Teilhard's vision. For those who discover him, Teilhard takes on something close to vital importance.[7] What accounts for its magnetism? What draws people to him, or to an extended Teilhardian vision, with the passion it does? What is most important in this case is: what does this response suggest about the *truth* of his work?

These observations bear directly upon the topic I wish to pursue. In a profusion of writings, Teilhard reformulated the meaning of Christianity in evolutionary terms. Many have responded with the eagerness of an experience of enlightenment. But, what grounds the legitimacy, provides the validity of the truth found there?

The path to answering this question is not difficult to discern. It consists in following his language and the movements of his thought as he tells his story. To accomplish this task, one could use almost any of Teilhard's texts.

In "My Fundamental Vision," a major, relatively late essay (1948), Teilhard describes his *Weltanschauung* (his world) as built of conceptions provided by modern sciences, with its structure constituted by "a cluster of axial lines of progression."[8] Those "lines" are Unification, according to which the initial scattering into multiplicity of the universe turns back upon itself forming an ever greater unity; Centration, according to which all of its elements as they unify become increasingly centered; and Spiritualization, the outcome of the ever greater unifying and centering. As a consequence of progression along these lines, human life continually surpasses what it has achieved before. It is "forced by reasons that are cosmic in scale and urgency gradually to transcend . . . every limit," every prior boundary, political, economic, even spiritual.[9]

These axial lines are likewise the lines upon which the future will form. The more human life "interpenetrates," that is, the more human cultures come together and contribute to each other, "the more it continually raises the psychic temperature of the noosphere," that is, the more it creates further unification and centeredness of consciousness throughout the earth.[10]

The cosmic evolutionary process which develops along these lines of progression occurs in four great steps. The first is the *involution* of everything into ever-greater complexity. It is "in the direction of consciousness and reflection, that life's current always flows, so that one may say that, for the stuff of the cosmos, its higher form of existence and its final state of equilibrium is in *being thought*."[11] Following this current, this "process of complexification and centration of the cosmic stuff upon itself" allows us to recognize "the correlative rise in interiorization (that is, of psychism) in the world."[12]

Evolution advances only by "endlessly feeling its way." Nevertheless, we have to see life—and therefore thought itself—as a force which is everywhere and at all times contained under pressure—and which, accordingly, is only waiting for a favorable opportunity to emerge: and once emerged, to carry its constructive processes (and with them, its interiorization) right through to the end.[13]

The second step, again in accordance with Teilhard's cluster of axial lines, is the breakthrough into self-consciousness or *reflection*. With the crossing into self-consciousness, "something completely new appears"; a higher order of being emerges. "It is no exaggeration to say that the appearance of thought completely renewed the face of the earth."[14]

The third step is the continued elevation of the human by *socialization*, a process that apes the original compression of matter into greater complexities. At the end of the Paleolithic Age, after the earlier dispersion of human life around the globe, "a movement of re-involution or convergence emerges and grows more pronounced." This compression, or convergence of human life has become "the main terrestrial axis of evolution," moving human life in continual self-transcendence towards unification.[15]

The fourth step: All of this points to the progressive genesis of what I have called a 'noosphere'—the pan-terrestrial organism in which . . . a resurgence of evolution (itself now become reflective) is striving to carry the stuff of the universe towards the higher conditions of a planetary higher-reflection.[16]

The end towards which this pan-terrestrial organism is striving, a future of "unimaginably enormous . . . distances to which we will have traveled after some hundreds of thousands of years," is "Christ/Omega." It is an end Teilhard projects first by extending the lines of evolution through a sweeping view of the past into the present and on into an immensely extended future. He sees the process of evolution as such fulfilling itself in a unification, "Omega." Simultaneously, he sees this fulfillment from his Christian perspective as the advent of the complete "Christ."

A small portion of the language that Teilhard uses here is straightforward. For instance, when he speaks of human life continually surpassing what it has achieved before, and that therefore it is "forced by reasons that are cosmic in scale and urgency gradually to transcend . . . every limit," we recognize words we can take literally. And when he speaks of "the cosmic evolutionary process," or describes the second step as the breakthrough into self-consciousness or *reflection,* and adds, "something completely new appears," we again meet a direct statement. In defining the third step as the continuation of evolution through socialization, he once again speaks directly. But much of his language is figurative.

And so we have: "A cluster of axial lines of progression"; "involution"; the more human life "interpenetrates ... the more it raises the psychic temperature of the noosphere"; "a 'noosphere'—the pan-terrestrial organism"; "in the direction of consciousness and reflection life's current always flows"; evolution advances by "endlessly feeling its way"; "we have to see life—and therefore thought itself—as a force which is everywhere and at all times contained under pressure—and ... is only waiting for a favorable opportunity to emerge"; a future of "unimaginably enormous . . . distances to which we will have traveled after some hundreds of thousands of years"; the terminus towards which this pan-terrestrial organism is striving, is "Christ/Omega."

Figurative language, predominantly metaphoric language, permeates Teilhard's story in all of its versions. However, I would assert that, for Teilhard, figurative language is primary, not embellishment. It provides the foundational elements of his vision.

The term, "vision," expresses a unified meaning which a person develops, an understanding that embraces many parts drawn into a whole, a synthesis of multiple elements. It comes to be through language—words, sentences, complete essays—through the construction of meanings in words. It is vision occurring, as Plato first put it, in "the mind's eye."[17] And it occurs likewise in those who have come to share in that same eye. "Vision" is a trop, a metaphor by which one names and characterizes what one cannot capture directly, but by which nevertheless one communicates with others, and they in turn with others still.[18]

Two of Teilhard's most dramatic expressions, "The Heart of Matter" and "The Christic," not only bear out the centrality of his figurative language. They also make evident the way his mind functioned in creating his vision, as they also show that his vision grew from profound inner experiences, experiences of the kind that normally break forth poetically.

In the very term, "heart of matter," opposites are overlaid. But not arbitrarily. The term comes as the product of "a direct psychological experience" of a source of life at the core of what we normally consider dead. He declares further, "the World gradually caught fire for me, burst into flames. . . ."[19] And so his famous words, jamming together vivid images:

Crimson gleams of Matter, gliding imperceptibly into the gold of Spirit, ulti-
mately to become transformed into the incandescence of a Universe that is
Person—and through all this there blows . . . a zephyr of Union—and of the
Feminine . . . the Divine radiating from the depths of a blazing Matter.[20]

Not only is there a chain of images here, but the laying over and seeing
together of one image, or one set of meanings, upon another. This basic feature
of his thought, a process of joining together and overlaying, recurs again and
again. Its primary instance, providing the fundamental dynamic whereby his
vision came to be, is the union of the scientific and the religious traditions *tout
court* in his consciousness, the merging, in his words, of his "'pagan' ego" and his
"Christian ego."[21] The source of his vision, in other words, is creativity, a making
by the power of imagination.

This imaginative making in religious matters, this theopoiesis, becomes the
primary mode of bringing together the evolving world and Christ. As
Teilhard understood it, the trajectory of evolution as such must be to reach, irreversibly, ever beyond itself in a unifying process to higher levels of life. It must
thereby come to a completion, "Omega." Nevertheless, this Omega "remains by
nature conjectural, it remains a postulate."[22] But what do we discover, he asks,
if we "first suspect and then accept as proved that the *Christ of Revelation* is
none other than the *Omega of Evolution*?" What, in other words, can result if
one can bring together a (secular) telos-ordered universe and the meaning of
Christ one has developed through a deep personal participation in the Christian
tradition, and especially the Pauline Christ of Colossians 1, he in whom "all
things hold together"?[23]

"Forthwith, we both see with our minds and feel with our hearts that the
experiential Universe is once and for all activized and plenified." We can see
"above us" a "way out," a divine light at the end of the evolutionary process.
Through the joining of the humanistically conceived Universe and a contemporary "neo-Christianity," we can see Christ at its summit "and so feel its
absorbing magnetic attraction." "We are in a World whose peak certainly opens
out in *Christo Jesu*." And what comes to us from that peak "is the radiance of a
love." We are offered, as he often says elsewhere, a culmination worthy of
worship.[24] And so, in truth, "it is Christ . . . who saves."[25]

How, we might pause to ask, did Teilhard come to this grand conception?
He frequently states that this thought formed within him. It was not directly

his doing; rather, he was the locus within which this new vision emerged. I would translate this by saying again that his thought is the product of the poetic imagination at work in him, his vision the work of poiesis, its truth "religious truth."

There is a major consequence imbedded in all of this. Teilhard's vision expands the meanings of God and of Christ, even transforms them, or, better still, recreates them. And, in the process of coming to his vision, its nature as a poiesis is further borne out.

A Transformed Meaning of God

Teilhard allows that Christianity "still to some degree provides a *shelter* for the 'modern soul,'" but laments that "it no longer *clothes* it, nor *satisfies* it, nor *leads* it. Something has gone wrong."[26] Therefore he asks, "What is it we are looking for?" It is a question "asked on all sides." What is missing, what people are seeking, is something "whose manifest existence has been haunting me for what will soon be half a century. I mean the rise (irresistible and yet still unrecognized) over the horizon of what one might call a God (*the* God) of evolution."[27] In other words, what is missing is a religious truth adequate to sustain the modern spirit and provide a fitting object of worship.

Once the universe is recognized as a cosmogenesis and no longer a finished cosmos, "the Author of all things" can no longer be seen as in the past. That God, creator of a cosmos, stood outside the creation, and, as Lawgiver, spoke from a place apart. According to Teilhard, in an evolving world, "God is not conceivable (either structurally or dynamically) except in so far as he coincides with . . . the centre of convergence of cosmogenesis."[28] Only a God immanent to it and ahead of it will suffice.[29] "Where, then, shall we find such a God? And who will at last give evolution *its own* God?"[30]

As the outcome of what promises to be an extensive "new mysticism," the God of evolution comes to be the Universal Christ. This God grows in the mind of all who are "alive to the reality of the cosmic movement of complexity-consciousness which produces us." What is to be seen in this growth of the mind is "a most revealing correspondence between . . . the two confronting Omegas: that postulated by modern science, and that experienced by Christian mysticism."[31]

Humankind has reached a time and a situation at which the ends as seen by science and by Christian beliefs "are undoubtedly on the point of reacting upon one another in human consciousness, and finally of *being synthesized.*"[32] Minds draw them together. In that synthesis of the cosmic trajectory of evolution with the Christian heritage, the meaning of Christ expands to suffuse the cosmic, and the cosmic is permeated by the amorizing power of Christ, that is, it becomes divinely loveable. A religious truth emerges adequate to sustain the modern spirit and provide an object of worship. With this, the meaning of God comes to coincide with the enlarged meaning of Christ. Christ becomes "the ultimate summit (that is, the only possible God) of an evolution definitively recognized as a movement of convergence."[33]

Here God and the fuller Christ become one. Nevertheless, God as the creative source, as the "Father," remains as well, but dwells in a certain obscurity. One expression of this comes in the Foreword to *The Phenomenon of Man.* "I doubt there is a more decisive moment for a thinking being," Teilhard says, "than when the scales fall from his eyes and he discovers that he is not an isolated unit lost in the cosmic solitudes, and realizes that a universal will to live converges and is hominized in him."[34]

At the same time, the more explicit sense of God as creator that continues in Teilhard is extended and re-formed. As for Whitehead, God's own self *becomes* in the "creative advance" of the universe, and specifically, in the continuing progress of human evolution. On the one hand, as Teilhard describes his personal development, it was always the same God who was operative in his consciousness. Whether "from the depths of the cosmic future," or "from the heights of heaven," it was *"always the same God,* who was calling me." At first, it was *"the traditional God of the Above."* But in time, a sense of *"a God of the Ahead,"* "appeared athwart" that God. What resulted from this was a re-imagining of God by the superimposition of "those two images so that they form *one.*"[35]

One consequence of this superimposition is that it becomes possible to see God at once as both transcendent and immanent. "God" is that which forms and transforms the world "from the depths of matter to the peaks of Spirit." And simultaneously, and this is what most moved Teilhard, "the World must inevitably and to the same degree 'endomorphize' God"—it must absorb and embody God, bring God into matter.[36] In this, God "in some way 'transforms himself' as he incorporates us." Consequently, not only is human life and matter itself penetrated by God; likewise matter and human life discloses and completes God "ever more fully."[37]

Multiple Meanings of "Christ"

Teilhard notes that "Christian tradition is unanimous" in recognizing "that there is more in the total Christ than Man and God. There is also He who, in his 'theandric' being, gathers up the whole of Creation: *in quo omnia constant.*"[38] Then, he says, if this understanding of Christ is laid upon the apex of evolution, thus creating for evolution a religious meaning in accordance with the potentialities of Christianity, it both infuses the meaning of evolution with a new life (the vivifying life that seeing it in terms of Christ can give it), and it expands the meaning of Christ to the limits of evolution.[39]

Teilhard's early appreciation of Christ's extended significance was prompted by his encounter with the cult of the "Sacred Heart." This, his mother's central devotion, manifested to him "the immersion of the Divine in the Corporeal."[40]

> The moment I saw a mysterious patch of crimson and gold delineated in the very centre of the savior's breast, I found what I was looking for. . . . It was an astounding release. . . . the whole physical and spiritual reality of Christ was visibly condensed for me into a well-defined, compact object from which all accidental and restrictive particularity disappeared: the first approach of a Christic beyond Christ.[41]

The experience of "crimson and gold at the saviour's breast," *of divine love in matter*, meant that under the symbol of the "Sacred Heart," the divine would take on "the form, the consistence and the properties of an ENERGY, of a FIRE." This divine energy, moreover, could extend itself into everything. Insofar, that is, as it was open to being universalized in human minds, "it could in future force its way into and so *amorize*, the cosmic Milieu in which I was . . . engaged in making my home" (emphasis added).[42]

From here (this encounter with the Sacred Heart had come well before his formal study of theology), the expanded meaning of Christ, or "the Christic," would unfold. This Christ came to be seen as the culmination of evolution, its ultimate summit and locus of convergence. Christ becomes thereby the "Prime Mover of the evolutive movement of complexity-consciousness." In this Christ, "all things hold together," not as St. Paul must have understood it, but in the modern frame of cosmic evolution. From the peak of evolution, this Christ, attracts to himself humanity and the material universe because what emanates from that peak is "the radiance of a love." This Christ allows us to "see with our minds and feel with our hearts that the experiential Universe is once and for all activized and plenified."[43]

But what might be said of the ontological status of Christ so understood? When apprehended in these ways, Christ becomes of cosmic import in historical fact because this Christ now informs human minds. This Christ provides their religious meaning and structures their lives. This Christ becomes, for a leading wave of Christians in the second half of the twentieth century and into the twenty-first, *the* Christ of faith. And so it becomes correct to say that Cosmogenesis culminates in "the Christogenesis which every Christian venerates." And it becomes correct to say that, if the universe, "as the facts make certain," forms "a sort of biological 'vortex' dynamically centered upon itself," then at its peak "Christ, effortlessly and without distortion, becomes literally and with unprecedented realism, the *Pantocrator*."[44] And so we have as historical realities, because we have come to see, "the universalized Christ," the "Christified Universe," "Christ-Omega," a "Divine Milieu," the whole of evolution transformed "*in Christo Jesu*," an "ultra-Christianity" to meet the needs of the "ultra human," etc.

CONCLUSIONS

1. By virtue of his figurative language and the processes of his thought, Teilhard's vision of God and of human existence in relation to God, his truth, is a product of mind's creative power, of the mind's capacity to make meanings, of imagination. However, it is not the product of Teilhard's mind alone. For Teilhard already participated in the meanings of God and Christ generated from the same source, that is, mind's poiesis, by those who earlier came to understand God and Christ in the ways he, and Christians generally, have inherited. The poiesis whereby these meanings are produced, therefore, is at once individual and collective.

2. From their very nature, Teilhard's truths are religious truths. Religious truths, as already stated,[45] are comprehensive meanings humans live by, meanings that provide the fundamental structure of our selves (our "souls"), meanings that shape our desires and guide our actions. They bring together conceptions of life, the world, its destiny and one's place within it, into a meaningful whole: a story with a beginning, a middle, and an end, and so a comprehensive meaning of individual and collective life. They do not state *what is*. Instead, they always retain a mythic quality. Teilhard's Christ/Christic at the end of time—the God

of evolution—is not someone that is now *there*, or will be, as we project it. It is a vision created by the personal and interpersonal (social) imagination, emerging at this moment in time, and the product of a very long history: a vision which allows us to see our lives as having an ultimate importance in a world with a compelling destiny. It offers a glimpse of the divine, a fresh and culturally appropriate window into the meaning of God. To open such windows, to provide such glimpses, that is, to create religious truths, is the function of theopoiesis.

3.   Many in the past fifty years have responded to Teilhard's truth with a certain eagerness, out of a hunger which it satisfies, with a passion, with what can only be described, finally, as a desire for a great good. Why? Because, it opened for them a view of life that makes sense in the universe in which they now find themselves. It is a dramatically different universe from that of the first century, and of most centuries since. As Teilhard said, we require "a God of evolution," a God who holds ultimate meaning in an evolving universe and on an earth which is rife with difficulties and energized by longings for betterment, a world in which sin and grace are everywhere. In sum, people in the most technically and culturally developed part of the world (to echo Teilhard's words) require a religious truth that coheres with the world as they otherwise know it.[46] Offered one, they spring to it.

4.   People's passionate response to Teilhard is not only a clue to the nature of its truth. It is central. The truth of his vision lies, finally, at the base of all the other ideas offered to support it, in its capacity for being loved: in its capacity for meeting the fundamental desire—the ontological need—of the human person for infinite good. It connects us conceptually with what Tillich calls our "ultimate concern," allowing us to see it, momentarily, in a concretized form, and so to live in accord with it.

5.   Teilhard's is an open-ended truth. It does not take its finite form as the reality itself; it is not idolatrous. This follows from its character as personal and inter-personal, and as an achievement of poiesis: it is a witness to an understanding, always rooted in already recognized understandings, and always to be participated in by others. As such, and as is all religious truth, it can never be absolute, or final.

This accords with Teilhard's own, explicitly stated sense of truth. For Teilhard, truth is not a matter of reaching "a definitive framework" within which all of the world may be organized, but of drawing out "lines of penetration through which we can see a still unexplored immensity of the real opening up for us."[47] Truth enables us to see more deeply and comprehensively into what is ever-unfolding. Its "essential criterion" and its "specific mark" is its "power of developing indefinitely . . . in such a way as to form a positively constructed whole in which the parts support and complement one another ever more effectively."[48] Truth, in sum, is an event, a creative coming-to-be whereby consciousness is extended, or modified, or transformed.

6.   Because religious truths are the products of poiesis, hence open-ended, never-finished, they must always be open to the kind of re-formation and transformation that Teilhard gave birth to. Indeed, religious truth must be continuously re-created in every age, by religious leaders, preachers, theologians, and in every person (even when the language remains the same), if it is to continue to live. In this light, one can comprehend not only the legitimacy but also the necessity of work such as Teilhard's. It is essential to the continued re-appropriation of a religious tradition.

7.   To participate in Teilhard's truth, then, is not to follow the words and thus understand what he said, but to see (and now understand) the world and one's self through what he said.

8.   The fundamental issue for Teilhard, put simply, is this: How can our past understandings of God and Christ relate to our present understandings of the world? The answer, also put simply, is: re-discover, or re-create, or create anew the meanings of God and Christ. And so we can say, simply again, that Teilhard has given to those who respond to him a truth whereby they comprehend their world and themselves, and so structure their lives and support their hope.

9.   From all of this it seems to me, and even more so as I spend time with it, that Teilhard's grand vision is itself an elaborate metaphor, a magnificent trop which leads us to see beyond the depictable—beyond the name to the named—and to thereby unite in will, or faith, with it.

Notes

1.   Psychotherapist, retired Professor of Philosophy and Religious Studies, Stony Brook University.

2.   By religious truths I understand those comprehensive meanings of the world, one's place in it, and one's self, which people, together and sometimes singly, have come to. As such they structure people's lives and give form to their souls. They arise from many sources. And, so far as these meanings are shared, they form the basis of religious communities. They are born of an awareness that life and the desire for an absolute good—an ultimate "salvation"—was unsatisfactory and incomplete. Religious truths are always informed by

this awareness and desire, whether consciously present or not; it is this characteristic which distinguishes them as religious.

3.   Stanley Romaine Hopper, "The 'Eclipse of God' and Existential Mistrust," in R. Melvin Keiser and Tony Stoneburner, eds., *The Way of Transfiguration: Religious Imagination as Theopoiesis* (Louisville, KY: Westminster/John Knox Press, 1992).

4.   Here we find him saying, ". . . we might say that the whole of life lies in that verb," to which he adds, "to see or perish is the very condition laid upon everything that makes up the universe." Pierre Teilhard de Chardin, *The Phenomenon of Man*, trans. Bernard Wall (New York: Harper & Row, 1959), 31.

5.   Pierre Teilhard de Chardin, *Toward the Future*, trans. René Hague (New York: Harcourt Brace Jovanovich, 1975), 164-208.

6.   Pierre Teilhard de Chardin, *Christianity and Evolution*, trans. René Hague (New York: Harcourt Brace Jovanovich, 1969), 97-98.

7.   It was this kind of love, for example, which fueled Sarah Appleton-Weber's determination to provide a new translation of *Le phénomène humain*.

8.   Teilhard de Chardin, *Toward the Future*, 165.

10.   Ibid.

11.   Ibid., 165.

12.   Ibid., 168.

13.   Ibid., 170.

14.   Ibid., 172 n.

15.   Ibid., 179.

16.   Ibid., 180.

17.   Plato, *Republic*. Bk. VII.

18.   Perhaps one might argue that such strong displays of metaphor are not the underpinnings of his vision; that more sober argument forms its structure. But I would submit that they do, and that argument serves to give it a superstructure which rises from the foundations, and is itself always an alloy of logic and poiesis, with poiesis the primary component. He says as much himself. In "The Heart of Matter," his aim is to describe "a direct psychological experience—with just that amount of hard thinking behind it that will enable it to become intelligible and communicable without losing the objective, indisputable value of a document that reflects life [i.e., his personal experience]." Pierre Teilhard de Chardin, *The Heart of Matter*, trans. René Hague (New York: Harcourt Brace & Company, 1978), 15.

19.   Teilhard de Chardin, *Heart of Matter*, 15.

20.   Ibid., 16.

21.   Ibid., 44.

22.   Ibid., 91.

23.   Col 1:17.

24.   See, for example, "My Fundamental Vision," in Teilhard de Chardin, *Toward the Future*, 189, 204; and "The God of Evolution," in Teilhard de Chardin, *Christianity and Evolution*, 240, 243. "Worship" signifies a total dedication, an absolute love. The issue is finding a "God" that will elicit such dedication—love.

25.   Teilhard de Chardin, *Toward the Future*, 92.

26.   See Henri de Lubac, *Catholicism* (New York: The New American Library. 1964), ix. This issue was commonly recognized. For Henri de Lubac, it was the question that framed his book *Catholicism*, written in the late 1930s. Many have begun to doubt the permanent value of Christianity, he notes. "'How,' they ask in particular, 'can a religion which appar-

ently is uninterested in our terrestrial future and in human fellowship offer an ideal which can still attract the men of today?'"

27. Teilhard de Chardin, *Christianity and Evolution*, 237. It seems no longer even questionable that Christianity has fallen from the place of leadership it once held in the Western world—except inasmuch as our modern, post-enlightenment sense of justice and human rights is rooted in the long history of Christian, and Jewish, developments which formed the Western conscience.

28. Ibid., 239.

29. In a world conceived as a developing organic whole, to imagine and worship God as one whose primary place is outside it fails to provide adequate meaning for sustaining human life.

30. Teilhard de Chardin, *Christianity and Evolution*, 240.

31. Ibid., 242.

32. Ibid., 243.

33. Ibid. If I may over-simplify: Teilhard says, in effect, if you look on it this way, you will see a world which you can love and to which you can devote yourself.

34. Teilhard de Chardin, *The Phenomenon of Man*, 36. But Teilhard's interest is in the evolutionary process and its culmination, and for that, "Christ" becomes the operative carrier of the divine. Minimally, it seems fair to say here that, while he presupposes a meaning of God at the source, he is driven above all by a need to break beyond conceptions of God inadequate to the world as a cosmogenesis.

35. Teilhard de Chardin, *Heart of Matter*, 53. "In the inmost depths of my soul," he confesses, "a struggle, between the God of the Above and a sort of new God of the Ahead was, through structural necessity, being produced by the definitive co-existence and the irresistible meeting in my heart of the Cosmic Sense and the Christic Sense." Teilhard de Chardin, *Heart of Matter*, 45.

36. Ibid., 52-53.

37. Ibid., 53. Historians of theology might argue that Teilhard's re-definition of God was not altogether new. God's transcendence and immanence and a Cosmic Christ have long been recognized. But the dominance Teilhard gives to the "God of the Ahead" in his writings suggests a great change in the meaning God would have for him, and by extension, for anyone who came to share in his view. In effect, he set forth a transformed meaning of God, joined with a greatly extended Christ—all born in response to the newly unfolding understanding of the cosmos as a cosmogenesis, and all expressed as a "vision." It might equally be called a new "story."

38. *Col.* 1:17. On the one side, there is the Jesus of the Gospels; on the other side, the mystical Christ of John, the universal Christ of Paul, etc., and now the Christ who is Omega: by what cunning do we expand from the first to the last? I offer here a brief suggestion as to the process whereby Jesus became "the image of the invisible God," "the firstborn of all creation," of *Col.* 1:15ff., or the Word who was in the beginning of John I. We can briefly schematize the process of the expansion of Christ. In the beginning, Jesus of Nazareth was seen by his disciples as The Messiah. Although this was probably a post-resurrection recognition, it was placed by the authors of the synoptic Gospels at their center. From it, a number of interpretations arose. As Messiah/Christ, Jesus was "Son of God," "only [the one true] Son of God," and most often "Lord." Initially these were synonymous, by and large. But in the first-century world (with its multiple divinities and its semi-divinities

who dwelt in the heavens and passed back and forth between there and the earth), "Son of God" quickly and easily became also a pre-existent divine son who came to earth from heaven, etc. Likewise, Jesus as Christ was also seen as the incarnation of the Word (John), and "the image of the invisible God, the first-born over all creation," etc., thus attaining cosmic significance. The expansion of the meaning of Jesus seen to be the Christ was not without great controversy. Its orthodox settlement (for the Western Church) came in the Council of Chalcedon. Even so, theological thought continued to play upon the affirmations of the human-cosmic-divine meaning in Christ through the centuries. Upon its basis in tradition, and his own Christ-centered spiritual development, Teilhard could come to see Christ as the informing power and term of evolution. The cunning by which it occurred? The capacity to make meanings.

39. See Teilhard de Chardin, *Christianity and Evolution*, 242-43.
40. Teilhard de Chardin, *Heart of Matter*, 44.
41. Ibid., 43.
42. Ibid., 44. Teilhard's words are, "*and so, in as much as it was patient of being universalized, it could in future force its way into and so amorize. . . .*"
43. Ibid., 92.
44. Ibid., 94.
45. See n. 1.
46. Teilhard's statement: "Christianity . . . is decidedly and obviously losing its reputation with the most influential and most progressive portion of mankind and ceasing to appeal to it." Teilhard de Chardin, *Christianity and Evolution*, 237.
47. Teilhard de Chardin, *Toward the Future*, 164.
48. Ibid., 165.

TEILHARD'S PHYSICS IMAGERY

KATHLEEN DUFFY, S.S.J.[1]

Teilhard was not a physicist, although, early in his life, he did have a strong desire to become one. Rather, as a scientist, he is best known for his work in paleontology, geology, and geobiology. Yet, he was always fascinated by the content of the physics curriculum that, as a young Jesuit, he taught to high school students in Cairo. Throughout his life, he continued to follow break-throughs in physics, and eventually attempted a synthesis that he called hyperphysics, a new and broader kind of physics that would allow for the presence of mind. His effort to see things connected and as part of a single whole consumed him. And he dedicated his life to leading others to what he called that "naturally advantageous panoramic point"[2] where all is one.

I maintain that one of Teilhard's greatest contributions is the way he teaches us how to see. And scientists, who wrestle with matter, who search the heavens through their telescopes, who unravel DNA, who explore the potential of superstring theory, and who discover order in chaotic systems, come to know the cosmos in an intimate way, and thus find themselves at an auspicious point from which to probe the mind and heart of God. In order to teach the art of seeing, Teilhard integrates the language of physics with the language of mysticism. He sprinkles his writings with images involving optics, acoustics, thermodynamics, relativity, and quantum mechanics. The dynamics of the evolutionary process become major input for his theology, his spirituality, his understanding of himself as a human person. As he comments in his biographical essay, "The Heart of Matter," written five years before his death,

> I find it difficult to express how much I feel at home in precisely this world of electrons, nuclei, waves, and what a sense of plenitude and comfort it gives me. . . . It was surely there that I met those very "archetypes" which . . . I still use, even when I come to the Christic itself, when I try to express for my own satisfaction precisely what I mean.[3]

Teilhard's love for the cosmos, particularly for Earth, is contagious. His scientific imagery embeds us firmly within the cosmos. It encourages us to let "the great breath of the universe"[4] insinuate itself in us.

Teilhard shows us a universe that is creative. He notes how, from the beginning, elementary particles have been weaving the spacetime fabric of the cosmos, experiencing significant phase changes, as they transform from atoms into molecules, from amino acids into living organisms, from sentient life into thought, from one critical point to another, constructing forms that exhibit novelty and increasing complexity. For Teilhard, Earth is alive, a "great breathing body . . . [that] rises and sinks."[5] He images the emergence of the noosphere, that intricate web of thought that covers our Earth, as a phase transition, and considers it as one of two major critical points in cosmic history.[7]

Having looked long and hard at Mother Earth,[8] Teilhard, the scientist, believes deeply in science. But this does not keep him from asking questions about the limits to science as it is practiced. For instance, he wants to know whether science has "ever bothered . . . to look at the world except from the outside of things."[9] He says,

> . . . everywhere in the stuff of the universe there necessarily exists an internal conscious face lining the external "material" face, habitually the only one considered by science. Can we go further and define the rules according to which this second, most often hidden, face comes to shine through?[10]

For Teilhard, spirit and matter are not separate entities. Rather, like the poles of a spectrum or the waves and particles of quantum mechanics, they represent two ways of interacting with the Really Real. What is most moving about Teilhard's descriptions is the way he connects the emergence that we experience in matter with its complement in spirit. What happens in the vastness of the universe has its counterpart in the depths of our being. As we begin to explore the cosmos with him, we sense his love for the spiritual power of matter.

Like the physicists who construct a picture of reality from superstrings, elementary particles, and electromagnetic waves and fields that are invisible to the eye, Teilhard makes use of scientific images as a bridge to unify the material and spiritual aspects of reality and to point to the relational character of the Divine. He uses optics to show how the divine presence permeates the cosmos; acoustics, to illustrate how the divine communicates with us; field theory, to depict divine action; and thermodynamics, to depict our transformation into God. Written in the language of science, these images teach not only the scientist but all of us how to see. Below, I attempt to illustrate Teilhard's technique by weaving together some of the images of light, sound, attraction, and transformation that are found scattered throughout his religious essays.

DIVINE PRESENCE:

Just as light always "eludes ... our grasp,"[11] so it is difficult for us to comprehend the Divine presence that surrounds us. Yet, for those who know how to see, "something is gleaming at the heart of matter,"[12] within "the crystalline transparency of beings."[13] Its perception "begins ... with a diffused radiance which haloes every beauty,"[14] and "like those translucent materials which a light within them can illuminate as a whole, the world appears ... bathed in an interior light."[15] Capable of scattering, reorganizing, and energizing, the divine presence totally pervades matter, transforming it from within.[16] And "like sunlight in the fragments of a broken mirror,"[17] the Divine is reflected everywhere so that the center from which it radiates becomes difficult at times to locate.[18] In its radiance, "all elements of psychological life ... become more colored, more intense,"[19] and those "things that characterize the structure and general progress of the universe are clarified and come into sharper focus."[20]

DIVINE COMMUNICATION:

Embedded within the very fibers of the space-time tapestry, at a level below even that of the modern-day superstring, at the very heart of matter, Divine Energy pulsates.[21] By arousing a "resonance that lies muted in the depth of every human,"[22] the Divine draws us out of ourselves into a wider harmony, into a richer spiritual rhythm.[23] "Indeed, we are called by the music of the universe to reply, each with [our] own pure and incommunicable harmonic."[24] Sometimes, we are "caught up in the essential music of the world."[25] At other times, "the very core of [our] beings vibrates in response ... sounding a unique note of expansion and happiness."[26] At these moments, we are drawn to desire the radiance engendered by the synthesis of all elements of the world.[27] The least of our desires and efforts can cause the marrow of the universe to vibrate.[28]

DIVINE ACTION:

"The layers of divine action . . . come to us impregnated with . . . organic energies."[29] From the future, an attractive force, "more irresistible [than] and just as universal as that imposed on the heavenly bodies,"[30] "maintains us in the field of his presence,"[31] and allures creation towards novel patterns of beauty. Like the pull of a magnet or the force of gravity, "the forward drive [is] inseparable from this intoxicating . . . cosmos that carries us along and asserts itself in the mind of each one of us."[32] The Divine summons us away from multiplicity towards the Omega Point, that "center of convergence"[33] where all will be one. "The whole of the world's psychism gravitates towards [this] single centre."[34] This center is "a transcendent Reality." The nearer we approach, the more we "feel its absorbing magnetic attractions"[35] over us and the more receptive our powers become to the Divine attraction.[36] "Through the force of his magnetism . . . [the Divine] establishes again at the heart of the world the harmony of all endeavours and the convergence of all beings."[37] The Divine "snatch[es] us away from our pettinesses and impel[s] us imperiously towards a widening of our vision, towards the renunciation of cherished pleasures, towards the desire for ever more spiritual beauty."[38] Being itself begins to draw us and to intoxicate us.[39] The universe responds, as if to gravity, by "falling forwards—in the direction of Spirit."[40]

TRANSFORMATION:

"Today . . . the world we live in is drifting, as far as the eye can reach, under the pull of two combined opposite currents, each equally irreversible: entropy and life."[41] It is the "product of two processes . . . the process of arrangement . . . [which] produces infinite variety . . . [and the process of] 'dis-arrangement' ([or] Entropy) . . . [which is] constantly [dissipating] Energy."[42] Because deep within "the substance of the cosmos [there is] a primordial disposition . . . for self-arrangement,"[43] "no organic . . . being . . . appear[s] in a completely finished state."[44] Rather, each one seems to us to be "resting upon an endless series of earlier states" so that "the mere organic combination of a number of elements inevitably brings about the *emergence* in nature of something completely new."[45] "And the result of this structural torsion is an increase . . . of consciousness."[46]

"It is not only by a continual augmentation of the number of its members, but also by a continual augmentation of their zone of individual activity . . . [that] humanity . . . is . . . subject to an enormous pressure—a pressure that is continually accumulating by an interplay of its own."[47] "Life is always under pressure everywhere; and . . . where it has reached an appreciable breakthrough, nothing can ever stop it from pushing to the maximum the process from which it has come."[48] "Each additional degree of tightening . . . has the effect of exalting the expansion of each element a little more."[49] "As happens with the eddies in a river . . . birth is accompanied by a more far-reaching movement which not only carries [us] along beyond [ourselves] but is also, in some way, the actual cause of [our] emergence."[50] The evolutionary process we experience is "not [a] gentle drift towards equilibrium and rest, but [an] irresistible 'Vortex' which spins into itself."[51] Like "a fantastic molecular swarm . . . surging up like smoke from [an] explosion . . . [it] whirls us around in its tornado!"[52] "From time to time [powerful] currents collide with one another in formidable crises which cause them to seethe and foam in their efforts to establish their equilibrium." Like a macroscopic quantum system whose molecules at low temperature begin to act coherently, it "gradually . . . extend[s] the radius of its zone of influence over the Earth."[54] "The physical influence of every human being, once restricted to several kilometers, now extends for hundreds of miles."[55] "The swarming of the multitudes and . . . the flow of the cosmic current [make] the petty well-being of [one's] own person . . . cease to appear . . . the central concern of the universe."[56]

"God exerts pressure, in us and upon us—through the intermediary of all the powers of heaven, earth and hell—only in the act of forming and consummating Christ who saves and super-animates the world."[57] Our generation is gradually "awakening to consciousness of a movement which is cosmic in breadth and organicity: a movement which, whether we welcome it or not, is drawing us, through the relentless building up in our minds of a common *Weltanschauung* [or world view], towards some 'ultra-human' lying ahead in time."[58] We must, then, "orientate our being in the flux of things";[59] we must plunge boldly into the vast current of things and see whither its flow is carrying us."[60]

CONCLUSION:

Teilhard's words have the power to move us because they are so rooted in the fabric of the cosmos, in the dynamic processes at work within our psyches, our bodies, our societies, our Earth. They ring true to the fundamental nature of the cosmos. They act as a bridge, connecting spirit and matter, our inner and outer worlds, in a single image. They situate us within the cosmic becoming by calling us "consciously to share in the great work that goes on within it."[61] Thus, our spirits acquire a new dimension and begin to resonate with the divine dream of a humanity grown capable of consciously assuming its place in Earth's evolution. [62]

Notes

1. Professor of Physics, Chestnut Hill College, Philadelphia, PA 19118.

2. Pierre Teilhard de Chardin, *The Human Phenomenon*, trans. Sarah Appleton-Weber (Portland, OR: Sussex Academic Press, 1999), 4.

3. Pierre Teilhard de Chardin, *The Heart of Matter*, trans. René Hague (New York: Harcourt Brace Jovanovich, Inc., 1978), 23.

4. Pierre Teilhard de Chardin, *The Divine Milieu*, trans. Sion Cowell (Portland, OR: Sussex Academic Press, 2005), 30.

5. Pierre Teilhard de Chardin, *Writings in Time of War*, trans. René Hague (New York: Harper & Row, Publishers, 1967), 157.

6. Teilhard de Chardin, *Human Phenomenon*, 59.

7. See Pierre Teilhard de Chardin, *Human Energy*, trans. J. M. Cohen (New York: Harcourt Brace Jovanovich, 1969), 160.

8. Pierre Teilhard de Chardin, *The Future of Man*, trans. Norman Denny (New York: Harper & Row, Publishers, 1964), 154.

9. Teilhard de Chardin, *Human Phenomenon*, 26.

10. Ibid., 26.

11. Teilhard de Chardin, *Divine Milieu*, 74.

12. Pierre Teilhard de Chardin, *Journal*, Tome I, texte intégral publié par Nicole et Karl Schmitz-Moormann (Paris: Fayard, 1975), 13.

13. Teilhard de Chardin, *Divine Milieu*, 31.

14. Ibid., 91.

15. Ibid., 92.

16. Ibid., 79.

17. Ibid., 75.

18. Ibid., 78.

19. Ibid., 91.

20. Pierre Teilhard de Chardin, *Toward the Future*, trans. René Hague (New York: Harcourt Brace Jovanovich, Inc., 1975), 190.

21. Teilhard de Chardin, *Human Energy*, 123.

22. Teilhard de Chardin, *Writings in Time of War*, 101.

23. Ibid., 117.

24. Teilhard de Chardin, *Human Energy*, 150.

25. Teilhard de Chardin, *Writings in Time of War*, 101.

26. Pierre Teilhard de Chardin, *Hymn of the Universe*, trans. Simon Bartholomew (New York: Harper & Row, Publishers, 1961), 46.

27. Teilhard de Chardin, *Divine Milieu*, 93.

28. Ibid., 76.

29. Ibid., 84.

30. Pierre Teilhard de Chardin, *Letters to Two Friends*, 1926-1952, ed. Ruth Nanda Anshen, trans. Helen Weaver (New York: The New American Library, 1967), 107.

31. Teilhard de Chardin, *Divine Milieu*, 84.
32. Teilhard de Chardin, *Writings in Time of War*, 17.
33. Teilhard de Chardin, *Letters to Two Friends*, 107.
34. Teilhard de Chardin, *Writings in Time of War*, 158.
35. Teilhard de Chardin, *Heart of Matter*, 92.
36. Teilhard de Chardin, *Divine Milieu*, 102.
37. Teilhard de Chardin, *Writings in Time of War*, 106.
38. Teilhard de Chardin, *Divine Milieu*, 69.
39. Ibid., 91.
40. Teilhard de Chardin, *Heart of Matter*, 28.
41. Pierre Teilhard de Chardin, *Christianity and Evolution* (New York: Harcourt Brace Jovanovich, Inc., 1969), 109.
42. Teilhard de Chardin, *Heart of Matter*, 84.
43. Ibid., 33.
44. Pierre Teilhard de Chardin, *Science and Christ* (New York: Harper & Row, Publishers, 1968), 26.
45. Pierre Teilhard de Chardin, *Activation of Energy* (New York: Harcourt Brace Jovanovich, Inc., 1970), 131-32.
46. Teilhard de Chardin, *Heart of Matter*, 33.
47. Teilhard de Chardin, *Human Phenomenon*, 170.
48. Ibid., 217.
49. Ibid., 170.
50. Teilhard de Chardin, *Writings in Time of War*, 22.
51. Teilhard de Chardin, *Heart of Matter*, 33.
52. Ibid., 56.
53. Teilhard de Chardin, *Writings in Time of War*, 222.
54. Teilhard de Chardin, *Human Phenomenon*, 169.
55. Ibid., 169.
56. Teilhard de Chardin, *Writings in Time of War*, 42.
57. Teilhard de Chardin, *Divine Milieu*, 84.
58. Teilhard de Chardin, *Christianity and Evolution*, 238.
59. Teilhard de Chardin, *Divine Milieu*, 68.
60. Teilhard de Chardin, *Writings in Time of War*, 28.
61. Ibid., 32.
62. Teilhard de Chardin, *Human Energy*, 123.

REDEEMED BY BEAUTY:
TEILHARD AS POET

WILLIAM FALLA[1]

INTRODUCTION

Some of Teilhard's critics have labeled his style as too poetic. This label strikes me as being somewhat superficially dismissive of his work, allowing one to avoid confronting its deeper meaning. Coming as it did during the heyday of logical positivism and language philosophy, this discomfort with Teilhard's language, especially with works such as *The Human Phenomenon* that seek to bridge science and religion, is understandable. It is also symptomatic of a larger twentieth-century issue—the general devaluing of aesthetics as a discipline—one that has significant epistemological validity.

Unlike these critics, I suggest that, as theology, Teilhard's work stands well within the theological spectrum of early to mid-twentieth century Catholic theology, especially as it came to be defined by Erich Przywara and Joseph Marechal. More than that, however, I argue that Teilhard's "poetic style" was in fact required by the task that he assumed for himself, that of communicating a new vision, a vision that celebrates the conjunction of science and religion.

There are many ways to understand and explain how this conjunction might work and to analyze the attempts that have been made. One that has been historically under-represented is the aesthetic as it is manifested when the act (creativity) and the form (beauty) of art-making cohere.

Creativity is not something imposed from without as if by some alien invader, but arises instead from the very nature of the human. In fact, Jean-Pierre

Changeux notes, "if we look at the discoveries of what are soon to be made in the neurosciences, it seems reasonable to suppose that creativity results from epigenetic combination at the level of the evolution of individual thought, involving the highest cognitive and/or affective representations."[2] And, since, as Paul Ricoeur states, "Creativity covers vast domains that include the arts, sciences, ethics and politics";[3] creativity is at the heart of human endeavor.

In Fyodor Dostoyevsky's *The Idiot*, Prince Myshkin claims, "the world will be redeemed by beauty." If, as I have suggested, there is coherence between creativity and beauty, one can posit that there is a real connection between this claim and the work of Teilhard.

Prior to writing *The Idiot*, Dostoyevsky was transfixed and profoundly moved by Hans Holbein the Younger's "The Entombment of Christ," a painting noted for its graphic starkness. Yet, rather than let the awfulness of Golgotha take him down the path to Neitzchean nihilism, Holbein experienced within this expression of tragedy a sign of hope.[4] Both in the awfulness of Golgotha and in the everyday chaotic nature of life itself with its many irrational and unsystematic elements, scientists and theologians have encountered not only the mystery of life, but also, surprisingly, a source of redemption and hope. As Einstein once noted, "The most beautiful thing we can experience is the mysterious. It is the source of all true art and science."[5]

What then of aesthetics or, more precisely, theological aesthetics within a Christian context? Furthermore, how does theological aesthetics fit into the task of Catholic theology/philosophy before and during the career of Teilhard de Chardin?

THEOLOGICAL AESTHETICS

John de Gruchy defines theological aesthetics as the reflection on the beauty (and I would add the creativity) that from the perspective of faith saves.[6] Its roots can be traced to a question that was occupying Christian theology and particularly Catholic theology during the late nineteenth and early twentieth centuries—how to describe transcendence within immanence. Two important Catholic figures in this movement were Erich Przywara, S.J., and Joseph Marechal, S.J. However, in this paper, I will focus on the work of Erich Przywara (1889-1972) because of his influence on the field of theological aesthetics and his congruency with the life and work of Teilhard. Although Przywara was Teilhard's contemporary, there is no evidence that they ever interacted, despite the fact that both their thought and their lives are eerily similar. In fact, Karl Rahner notes that both Jesuits, Przywara and Teilhard, were solitary pioneers involved in the dialogue between faith and science and independent minds in a time of ecclesiastical condemnation.[7] In addition, in their writing, both display a poetic bent—Teilhard, implicitly, while Przywara explicitly, with two published works of poetry.

At the time of his ordination when Przywara began to formulate his thought, German Catholicism was struggling to articulate a positive appreciation of modernity as manifested in contemporary science, philosophy, and art.[8] For Przywara, discovering a means to take the absolute seriously, seeing the transcendent within it, and maintaining the integrity of both became a lifelong task. To the question: how do we receive (see) the transcendent within our concrete situation,[9] he answered that there is a dynamic tension set up between the concreteness of the message (the revelation of Jesus Christ) and that of the medium (things of the world) that is a property of reality itself and not of our perception of it. This dynamic tension Przywara labels as analogous thinking, his analogy of being or *analogia entis*. Furthermore, analogous thinking is for him aesthetic in nature since it is the means by which the transcendent is made visible in the immanent.[10] How all this is articulated or explained forms the basis for his major work, *Analogia Entis*. Beyond its congruency with Teilhard's work and its importance in its own right, Przywara's *analogia entis* also greatly influenced the work of two major twentieth-century Catholic theologians, Karl Rahner and Hans Urs von Balthasar. In fact, it laid the foundation for Balthasar's monumental work on theological aesthetics, *The Glory of the Lord*.

For Balthasar, beauty is one of the three classic transcendentals along with truth and goodness. It is "the manner in which God's goodness (*bonum*) gives itself and is expressed by God and understood by man as the truth (*verum*)."[11] Thus, beauty is not that which pleases but that which comes to be known through revelation.[12] Furthermore, Balthasar argues that such beauty is evident in both nature and art.[13] He also maintains that the three transcendentals are interrelated so that the neglect of beauty leads to the diminishment of the other two.[14] Here, one can see that beauty, and therefore aesthetics, has epistemological as well as axiological content. It is in its revelatory nature that beauty teaches.

It might seem that the above discussion applies to the visual arts alone, but such is not the case. Balthasar describes life as a stage or a theater, and discusses the need for what he calls "theo-dramatics." This connection is articulated by de Gruchy who, referring to our faith lives, notes, "That is why theological aesthetics flows directly into theological dramatics and becomes the point at which it relates directly to human and social transformation and therefore to Christian formation and the mission of the Church in the world."[15]

Karl Rahner, in his article "Theology and the Arts," takes this one step further. In speaking of the literary arts, he writes, "For by the very nature of the case these 'verbal arts' are closely related to theology, which also comes to expression in word."[16] For Rahner, this relationship is not accidental but far more intentional. "If theology is not identified *a priori* with verbal theology but is understood as man's total self-expression insofar as this is borne by God's self-communication, then religious phenomena in the arts are themselves a moment within theology taken in its totality."[17] As with Balthasar, this relationship arises for Rahner from the transcendental nature of the enterprise. Like Balthasar, Rahner sees the failure to foster this relationship and the so-called poetic theology to be a defect of contemporary theology.[18] Rahner outlines three characteristics of "poetic theology" that would apply both to the artist and to the theologian as artist in pursuit of "poetic theology." First, the theologian as an artist would proclaim what is eternal in truth, in love, and in humanity's endless quest and boundless desire. Second, the absolute particularity of the artist's work would become one with what is eternal in his or her proclamation. Finally, the observer would begin to see in the work the very infinity and incomprehensibility of God.[19] Not only is this kind of theology revelatory but, as "art," it is also transformative, since by its nature art seeks to transform reality as well as the viewer who truly engages it. It is against this background that I now examine Teilhard's work and his "aesthetic," an aesthetic that appears more implicit than explicit.

TEILHARD'S AESTHETICS

Teilhard once wrote to Lucile Swan: "Your art is, I think, a sacred thread which if followed will lead you to the light that is yours."[20] This, in fact, is what happened to Teilhard himself when he gazed at a picture of Jesus offering his heart to humanity. He describes this encounter in "The Picture," the opening portion of one of his most poetic pieces, "Christ in the World of Matter." He writes,

It was as though the planes that marked off the figure of Christ from the world surrounding it were melting into a single vibrant surface whereon all demarcations vanished. . . . I perceived that the vibrant atmosphere which surrounded Christ like an aureole was no longer confined to a narrow space about him, but radiated outwards to infinity.[21]

For Teilhard, art, like science and all human endeavors that are imbued with the Spirit and Energy of Christ, is transformative not simply for the individual but for the cosmos as well. In an address entitled "The Function of Art," he concludes: "art represents the area of furthest advance around man's growing energy, the area in which nascent truths condense, take on their first form, and become animate, before they are definitively formulated and assimilated."[22] As such, Teilhard maintains that human energy, which is a manifestation of the Spirit of Christ and displayed in art, becomes a force for change and for transformation in the world.

Furthermore, like Balthasar and Rahner, Teilhard saw beauty, natural and created, as reflective of divine beauty. Although beauty is not Christ himself, nonetheless, it is the driving force that impels a person to seek God. Teilhard remarks, "There is supreme art in the fish, the bird, the antelope."[23] But there is also beauty created by humans. "In art there is . . . the freedom and even the imaginative fancy, which is characteristic of an ebullition of energy in its native form."[24] In "The Picture," he writes,

Yet that beauty (of Christ) was something I divined rather than perceived; for whenever I tried to pierce through the coverings of inferior beauties which hid it from me, at once other beauties rose up before me and formed another veil over the true beauty even while kindling my desire for it and giving me a foretaste of it.[25]

In short, beauty has the power to reveal and to motivate, that is, to transform one towards Christ.[26] Nevertheless, as revelatory of God/Christ, the aesthetic (beauty) maintains a transcendental quality and with it a connection to the true and the good, with the good referring to the end, beauty to the form, and truth to the fact that it imitates the divine exemplar—what Teilhard calls the Christic.

Moreover, it can be said that while scientists such as Dirac and Einstein have articulated the value of the aesthetic for science, and theologians such as Balthasar and Rahner have noted its value for theology, Teilhard envisioned its value for both science and theology and in some ways attempted to unify them through art. As I have argued elsewhere, in his dialogue between science and religion, Teilhard attempted to keep both disciplines on equal footing.[27] This forced him into a new and little explored area where few have gone before. In turn, he used forms and language that are often unfamiliar to both science and religion.

Examples of this can be found in three of Teilhard's short essays: "The Mass on the World," "Christ in the World of Matter," and "The Spiritual Power of Matter." Here, Teilhard is at his poetic best. In "Mass on the World," Teilhard's creativity is focused on both the form and content of the Mass, that is, in its very nature, an artistic medium. As John de Gruchy notes, "After all, liturgy at its best is a creative work of art in and through which we are able to discern the redemptive beauty of God."[28] The term, "creative," points to the organic nature of the Mass or Liturgy, reflecting what Rahner calls the union of the historical particularity of the faithful and the eternality of the essential message. According to Geoffrey Wainwright, liturgy is the place where one's vision of the faith becomes sharpest.[29] Here the ancient doctrine of "*lex orandi, lex credendi*" (loosely translated: what one prays, one believes), with its propensity for interplay between worship and doctrine, gives Teilhard an opportunity to express in both form and content his theological vision. His altering of the Mass, the holy reenacting of the Pascal mystery, is more than a simple pragmatic exercise imposed by the exigencies of his isolation. It is instead a carefully crafted expression of Teilhard's vision of Christ's redemptive activity in the world—a world defined in part by science. In it, one catches a glimpse of the transformative and revelatory nature of the vision that was his. It is a vision clearly anchored in both the material and the spiritual, and one that clearly exemplifies the three characteristics of Rahner's poetic theology.

In "Christ in the World of Matter," Teilhard writes three stories in the style of the mystic R. H. Benson, and presents his thought in the form of three nouvelles. Then, in "The Spiritual Power of Matter," he begins with an encounter with the "Thing" and ends it with a "Hymn to Matter." In all of these, the style is that of fiction and the use of language, lush.

Teilhard's use of lush poetic language that is often highly metaphorical in nature raised many difficulties for him, especially in the face of logical positivism. Yet, as Gerald Vann suggests in his Introduction to *Hymn of the Universe*, Teilhard's language arose in no small measure from his task. "The aim of scientific literature is to provide exactly defined and unambiguous statements about reality; that of poetic language, to communicate reality itself, as expressed by means of image, evocation . . . and the ambivalence of paradox, of symbol."[30]

This is exactly what we see, for instance, in *Hymn of the Universe* and in *The Human Phenomenon* when Teilhard introduces what might be called his "metascience." In these works, Teilhard expresses a new and radical vision for the world that involves the integration of science and religion. He posits a different way of seeing both Christ's relationship to the world and Christ's action in the world. In many ways, he creates a world unlike any other, and thus he is faced with one for which there is no common descriptive language. He is therefore forced into the extravagance of analogical language, a situation not unknown in either science or religion.[31] Ricoeur and his students, Gerhart and Russell, suggest that what happens here is not simply description, but new understandings.[32] By holding two fields of knowledge in tension, it becomes possible for new understanding to arise in an area that was heretofore opaque to description, much less to understanding.

This in my estimation is what Teilhard is doing. Rather than a detriment, then, his language is essential for moving his reader to the level of understanding that he desires and for effecting the transformation that he envisions. He is trying to present a vision of the world where the material and the spiritual are equal partners in informing that vision. He refuses to collapse one into the other. In other words, he does not describe his science in terms of his faith, or his faith in terms of his science. Rather, he carves out a new area, where a new and highly metaphorical language is used to describe God's redemptive activity in the material world that he loved. He uses the language of the poet.

As Adelaida warmly notes in Dostoyevsky's *The Idiot*, "Such beauty is power. With such beauty one can turn the world upside down."[33] That, I maintain, is exactly what Teilhard wanted to do and what he did do in his attempt to facilitate the redemption of the cosmos.

Notes

1. Adjunct Professor of Philosophy, Moravian College, Bethlehem, PA 18018; Minister, St. John's United Church of Christ Mickleys, Whitehall, PA 18052.
2. Jean-Pierre Changeux and Paul Ricoeur, *What Makes Us Think* (Princeton: Princeton University Press, 2002), 240.
3. Ibid., 241.
4. John de Gruchy, *Christianity, Art and Transformation* (New York: Cambridge University Press, 2001), 101.

5. Albert Einstein, *Ideas and Opinions* (New York: Modern Library, 1994), 11.
6. De Gruchy, *Christianity, Art and Transformation*, 101.
7. Thomas O'Meara, *Erich Przywara, S.J.* (Notre Dame: University of Notre Dame Press, 2002), 141.
8. Ibid., 17.
9. James Zeitz, "Przywara and Balthasar on Analogy," *The Thomist 52* (1988): 475.
10. Ibid.
11. De Gruchy, *Christianity, Art and Transformation*, 104.
12. Ibid., 104.
13. Ibid.
14. Ibid., 105.
15. Ibid., 128.
16. Karl Rahner, "Theology and the Arts," *Thought* 57, no. 224 (March 1982): 24.
17. Ibid., 25.
18. Ibid.
19. Ibid., 29.
20. Thomas M. King, *Teilhard's Mass: Approaches to "The Mass on the World"* (New York: Paulist Press, 2005), 139.
21. Pierre Teilhard de Chardin, *Hymn of the Universe*, trans. Simon Bartholomew (New York: Harper Colophon, 1961), 43.
22. Pierre Teilhard de Chardin, *Toward the Future*, trans. René Hague (London: William Collins Sons & Co, 1975), 90.
23. Ibid., 88.
24. Ibid., 89.
25. Teilhard de Chardin, *Hymn of the Universe*, 45.
26. A cautionary note is in order here. Although Teilhard's work is similar in tone to Balthasar and Rahner, it must be noted that the chasm between God and nature experienced by Balthasar and Rahner is not so great for Teilhard.
27. William Falla, "Evolution and Faith: The Study of a Dialogue" (Th.D. thesis, Lutheran School of Theology at Chicago, 1993).
28. De Gruchy, *Christianity, Art and Transformation*, 239.
29. Geoffrey Wainwright, *Doxology* (New York: Oxford University Press, 1980), 3.
30. Teilhard de Chardin, *Hymn of the Universe*, 9.
31. For instance, we see the terms "quarks" used in physics or the use of metaphors such as "life after death" in religion.
32. Mary Gerhart and Alan Russell, *The Metaphoric Process* (Dallas: TCU Press, 1984).
33. De Gruchy, *Christianity, Art and Transformation*, 97.

III

TEILHARD

IN DIALOGUE

TOWARD A GOD FOR EVOLUTION: A DIALOGUE BETWEEN TEILHARD AND ARTHUR PEACOCKE

GLORIA L. SCHAAB, S.S.J.[2]

INTRODUCTION

In his 1953 essay, "The God of Evolution," Teilhard wrote,

> We still hear it said that the fact that we now see the universe not as a cosmos but henceforth as a cosmogenesis in no way affects the idea we used to be able to form of the Author of all things. "As though it made any difference to God," is a common objection, "whether he creates instantaneously or evolutively."

In response to this claim, Teilhard asserts,

> While, in the case of a static world, the creator (the efficient cause) is still, on any theory, *structurally* independent of his work, and in consequence, without any definable basis to his immanence—in the case of a world which is by nature evolutive, the contrary is true: God is not conceivable (either structurally or dynamically) except in so far as he coincides with (as a sort of "formal" cause) but without being lost in, the center of convergence of cosmogenesis (Teilhard's italics).[2]

Teilhard then goes on to ask, "Where shall we find such a God? And who will at last give evolution its own God?"[3] Some forty years later, Anglican biochemist and theologian Arthur Peacocke raised a similar issue. In his own quest to explore how evolutionary science might influence Christian theology,

Peacocke suggests that attention to the evolving cosmos of which God is the creator impels theologians and believers alike "to reckon with ... God's relation to a continuously developing world," which implies "a continuously changing relation of God to the world."[4]

Fundamentally, what Teilhard and Peacocke each call for is the recognition that, in an evolving universe, one can no longer conceive of the Creator or of creation solely in terms of a single act at a moment long past. Rather, speaking of God as Creator must refer to a perennial relation of God to the world. As Teilhard explains, "God exercises an overall activity in the universe (providence) which cannot be reduced to, though it is co-extensive with the sum total of elementary activities" that the sciences observe in the evolution of the universe.[5] In other words, God creates continuously through the very processes that God built into creation "in the beginning," from the "primordial flaring forth"[6] of the universe to this very moment in time. Because of this ongoing creative activity, God must be understood not only as original Creator, but also as continuous Creator of the universe.

So how might one speak of this God for evolution? I intend to suggest one way of speaking by following a particular example of divine creativity in the cosmos, the creative interplay of chance and law in the process of cosmic evolution. I examine Teilhard's notion of this creative interplay, which he terms *tâtonnement* or "groping," and do so in dialogue with the insights of Arthur Peacocke on the operation of chance in the universe. I then explore what both Teilhard and Peacocke view as the unavoidable by-product of such a groping evolutionary process—the pervasiveness of pain, suffering, and death in the cosmos that often accompanies the emergence of new life. Having come that far, I propose, with Teilhard and Peacocke, that the God for evolution that we seek is none other than the God of Jesus Christ, the God revealed paradigmatically in the paschal mystery of the cross and resurrection.

The Operation of Chance in an Evolving Universe

Scientific observations suggest that evolving life forms display both a remarkable continuity and a surprising uniqueness in relation to the forms that precede them. The continuity in life forms results largely from the operation of natural laws, such as those of reproduction and heredity. However, time and again, organisms of increasing uniqueness and particularity emerge that cannot be explained in terms of the forms or matter from which they proceed. This has led scientists to propose that evolutionary development unfolds not only through the guidance of natural law, but also through the impact of chance occurrence.[7] Examples of such chance events would include the mutation of DNA in an organism and the interaction of that organism with its environment. To the regularity of law in the evolutionary process, therefore, the operation of chance adds randomness, a randomness that frequently results in kaleidoscopic diversity. According to Peacocke, the play of chance operates within the framework of law to elicit the potential that the universe has possessed from the beginning.

This process of eliciting cosmic potential through chance is what Teilhard termed *tâtonnement* or "groping." For Teilhard, however, *tâtonnement* is not mere chance, but "directed chance," directed by God immanent in the cosmos itself.[8] Admittedly, the idea of "directed chance" seems somewhat of an oxymoron. Nonetheless, the concept is reminiscent of the response of chaos theorist Joseph Ford to Albert Einstein's famous question of whether God plays dice with the universe. According to Ford, "God plays dice with the universe. But they're loaded dice. And the main objective of physics now is to find out by what rules were they loaded and how can we use them for our own ends."[9] Peacocke in turn amplifies Ford's reply by suggesting that the dice are "loaded" in favor of the emergence of new life. In Teilhard's own elaboration of the notion of directed chance, he explains, "The divine action . . . cannot limit itself to enclosing and molding individual natures from outside. In order to fully dominate them, it must have a hold on their innermost life."[10] God creates "by partially immersing himself in things, by becoming 'element,' and, then, from this vantage point in the heart of matter, assuming the control and leadership of what we now call evolution."[11] Hence, God enters into the very life of the cosmos; "every quark, every particle, every aspect of matter and energy is connected to God's desire and hope for the world."[12]

Peacocke uses a musical metaphor for this immanent mode of creation by God through chance, envisioning God as the Great Improvisor of the cosmic fugue. Expanding his metaphor, Peacocke suggests that, in musical composition, "there is an elaboration of simpler units according to, often conventional, rules intermingled with much spontaneity, surprise even." After "beginning with an arrangement of notes in an apparently simple subject," God as composer "elaborates and expands it into a fugue by a variety of devices of fragmentation, augmentation, and reassociation. . . . Thus might the Creator be imagined to enable to be unfolded the potentialities of the universe which he himself has given it."[13] If one were to inquire as to the whereabouts of the composer in such a composition, one could suggest that the composer was immanent in the music itself. According to Peacocke, "This very closely models . . . God's immanence in creation and God's self-communication in and through what he is creating."[14] Despite the creative potential of this image, commentators have nonetheless criticized it for over-harmonizing the process of creation through chance. However, neither Peacocke nor Teilhard attempts such harmonization. Teilhard anticipated Peacocke's own thinking when he wrote, "For the Almighty, to create is no small matter: it is no picnic but an adventure, a risk, a battle, to which he commits himself unreservedly."[15] Moreover, it is an adventure, a risk, and a battle which God enters into gropingly, "step by step by dint of billionfold trial and error" in order to unite the world organically to Godself.[16]

THE UBIQUITY OF PAIN, SUFFERING, AND DEATH IN THE UNIVERSE

Teilhard's description of evolution as a risky and embattled process signals the presence of what Teilhard calls the shadow side of the creative process. While creation through the interplay of chance and law elicits a kaleidoscopic diversity of life forms, this process also results in a pervasiveness of pain, suffering, and death in the cosmos and its creatures. From Peacocke's perspective, pain, suffering, and death in the universe are necessary conditions both for the survival of life and for the transition of life to novel and emergent forms. According to Peacocke, the emergence of new forms and patterns within a finite universe can occur only when the death of old forms and patterns make way for them. Thus, Peacocke observes,

> There is a kind of *structural* logic about the inevitability of living organisms dying and of preying on each other for we cannot conceive, in a lawful nonmagical universe, of any way whereby immense variety of developing, biological, structural complexity might appear, except by utilizing structures already existing, either by way of modification (as in biological evolution) or of incorporation (as in feeding) (Peacocke's italics).[17]

For Teilhard, however, the presence of pain, suffering, and death is not just structurally logical in an evolving universe, but statistically necessary. To comprehend this claim, one must grasp Teilhard's understanding of what it means to create. For Teilhard, the primordial nature of matter is multiple and unorganized. Through the evolutionary processes in which God is immanent, the multiple is unified and organized, converging gradually toward unity in God. Therefore, Teilhard suggests, "if to create is to unite (evolutively, gradually), then God cannot create without evil appearing as a shadow."[18] According to Teilhard, pain, suffering, and death in an evolving universe are woven into the creative process itself. They are not solely experiences that sentient beings inflict upon one another by necessity or by choice. Rather, they are inherent aspects of a universe in the process of unification and transformation toward God. In Teilhard's words,

> By virtue of the very structure of the nothingness over which God leans, in order to create he can proceed *in only one way*. He must under his attractive influence arrange and unify little by little. . . . But what is the inevitable counterpart of the complete success which is obtained by following a process of this type? Is it not the payment of a certain amount of waste? It involves disharmony or physical decomposition in the pre-living, suffering in the living, and sin in the domain of liberty.

Free as it is, creation "cannot progress toward unity without giving rise to… some evil here or there and that *by statistical necessity*" (Teilhard's italics).[19] To concretize his claim, Teilhard invites us to consider our own human experience.

> Right up to its reflective zones we have seen the world proceeding by means of groping and chance. Under this headline alone—even up to the human level on which chance is most controlled—how many failures have there been for one success, how many days of misery for one hour's joy, how many sins for a solitary saint? . . . Statistically, at every degree of evolution we find evil always and everywhere, forming and reforming implacably around us.[20]

Hence, Teilhard suggests, so long as disorder, disunity, and disorganization endure within the creative movement toward God, so long do pain, suffering, and death endure as inherent, inescapable elements of the process.

At this point, one might question whether the outcome is worth the cost. Yet, for both Teilhard and Peacocke, it is the ultimate outcome, rather than the proximate cost, that is significant; it is the general movement of evolution toward fullness of life rather than the particular false starts and blind alleys that is vital. For Peacocke, the ultimate end that justifies the means is the emergence of freely responsive persons in the cosmos. He conjectures that God had an "overarching intention" in this regard that makes the risks of the cosmic process worth taking. He suggests that there was and is "some fundamental way of God being God which allows God's relationship" with human persons "to be valued by God over other forms of matter."[21] Clearly such a statement betrays an anthropocentrism that is not altogether absent from Teilhard's own evolutionary view of humanity as the privileged axis of evolution.[22] Nevertheless, there is no need for Peacocke's hypothesis when viewed from a Teilhardian perspective. Teilhard does not focus attention on some overarching divine intent, but on the free process of evolution itself. He asserts that "physical suffering and moral transgression are inevitably introduced into the world not because of some deficiency in the creative act but by the very structure of participated being" *in fieri*, in the process of becoming. However, confronted by the scandalous by-products of this process, Teilhard himself is compelled to ask, "Is the game worth the candle?" His answer: "Everything depends on the final value and beatitude of the universe."[23]

THE GOD FOR EVOLUTION AND THE PASCHAL MYSTERY OF CHRIST

In view of the insights of these two scholars concerning pain, suffering, and death in a groping universe, we return to the question with which we began: How might one speak of a God for evolution? What kind of God is this who bears the pain, suffering, and death of the cosmos out of love? What kind of God is this whose mode of creativity brings forth new life from the midst of suffering and death? Where shall we find this God for evolution for whom Teilhard so poignantly longed? Based on Teilhard's and Peacocke's theological insights, I would submit that the God for evolution is none other than the God of Jesus Christ, paradigmatically revealed in the paschal mystery of the cross and resurrection.

Confronted with the reality of pain, suffering, and death that lead nonetheless to the life of the world, both Teilhard and Peacocke are seized by a singular conviction. They see in the general evolution of the universe a reflection of the creative and unifying energy that raised Jesus Christ from the dead to risen life in union with God. This paschal mystery dramatically discloses to them the infinite creativity of divine Love that ultimately overcomes finite pain, suffering, and death. This realization, in fact, redeems the mystery of the Cross for Teilhard. "If," Teilhard maintains, the Cross is to reign over an earth that has suddenly awoken to consciousness of a biological movement drawing it ahead, then at all costs and as soon as possible, it must (if it is to co-exist with human nature which it claims to save) present itself to us as a sign, not merely of "escape," but of progress. It must have for us not merely a purifying but a *driving* brilliance.[24]

Seen in the context of cosmogenesis, the Cross took on "greater breadth and dynamism" for Teilhard. No longer solely a symbol of "the dark retrogressive side of the universe," the paschal mystery of cross and resurrection becomes "the symbol of progress and victory won through mistakes, disappointments, and hard work."[25]

Projected upon the evolutive universe, the Cross assumes a new importance and beauty.... Christ is he who structurally in himself, and for all of us, overcomes the resistance to unification offered by the multiple, the resistance to the rise of spirit inherent in matter. Christ is he who bears the burden, constructionally inevitable, of every sort of creation. He is the symbol and sign-in-action of progress.[26]

Based on his respective revisioning of the paschal mystery from an evolutionary perspective, Peacocke grasps a further insight, one that concerns the very nature of God in relation to this evolving and suffering universe.

If Jesus is indeed the self-expression of God in a human person, then the tragedy of his actual human life can be seen as a drawing back of the curtain to unveil a God suffering in and with the sufferings of created humanity and so, by natural extension, with those of all creation.

From this perspective, "The cry of dereliction [of Jesus on the cross] can be seen as an expression of the anguish of God" in a suffering cosmos.[27]

Nevertheless, informed by a Christian evolutionary understanding, we are led with Teilhard and Peacocke to the conviction that suffering and death need not have the last word. Rather, in the light of the paschal mystery of Jesus Christ, pain, suffering, and death are enveloped within the transforming and unifying synergy of the Triune God. Within this theological understanding, the God for evolution neither wills nor prevents the pain, suffering, and death of a free cosmos and a free humanity anymore than God willed or prevented the cross of Jesus Christ. However, neither does God intend that such pain, suffering, and death endure or triumph. Rather, God ceaselessly and powerfully conceives new life in, with, and under the travail of the cosmos, even as God raised Christ to new life from the dead. How does God accomplish this? God does so by liberative and transformative acts that reveal, in the words of the Christian liturgy, that life is changed not ended, and that new and abundant life can emerge from the most deleterious events in creation and its creatures. Informed by the evolutionary theology of Arthur Peacocke, the illuminating insights of Pierre Teilhard de Chardin, and their relentless pursuit of the God for evolution, we may be assured that the unifying and transforming creativity of the God of Jesus Christ gives us such a God for evolution, and that this God quickens creation and its creatures inexorably toward one mind, one heart, in and through Christ.

Notes

1. Assistant Professor of Theology, Department of Theology and Philosophy, Barry University, Miami Shores, FL, 33161.
2. Pierre Teilhard de Chardin, *Christianity and Evolution*, trans. René Hague (New York: Harcourt Brace Jovanovich, 1971), 239.
3. Ibid., 240.
4. Arthur Peacocke, *Theology for a Scientific Age: Being and Becoming: Natural, Divine and Human*, rev. and exp. (Minneapolis: Augsburg Fortress, 1993), 100-101.
5. Teilhard de Chardin, *Christianity and Evolution*, 35, n. 6.
6. See Brian Swimme and Thomas Berry, *The Universe Story: From the Primordial Flaring Forth to the Ecozoic Era: A Celebration of the Unfolding of the Cosmos* (San Francisco: HarperSanFrancisco, 1994).
7. The notion of chance in biological evolution applies to different situations in the evolutionary process. It may apply to a situation in which there is an ignorance concerning the variables involved in a particular outcome. It may also refer to the interaction of two or more unrelated causal chains that interact to produce a novel effect. Finally, it may describe the outcomes of events governed by quantum theory, e.g. the Heisenberg theory of uncertainty, which suggests that events at the quantum level of systems are unpredictable in principle.
8. See Theodosius Dobzhansky, "Teilhard de Chardin and the Orientation of Evolution: A Critical Essay," *Zygon: The Journal of Religion and Science 3* (1968): 242-58. Theodosius Dobzhansky directly disputes this notion. According to Dobzhansky, what directs the operation of chance is not God, but the anti-chance process of natural selection.
9. James Gleick, *Chaos: Making a New Science* (New York: Penguin Books, 1987), 314.
10. Teilhard de Chardin, *Christianity and Evolution*, 27.
11. Pierre Teilhard de Chardin, *The Phenomenon of Man*, trans. Bernard Wall (New York: Harper & Row, 1959), 294.
12. Jeffrey C. Pugh, *Entertaining the Triune Mystery: God, Science, and the Space Between* (Harrisburg, PA: Trinity, 2003), 53.
13. Peacocke, *Theology for a Scientific Age*, 174-75.
14. Ibid., 176.

15. Teilhard de Chardin, *Christianity and Evolution*, 85.

16. Teilhard de Chardin, *The Phenomenon of Man*, 302.

17. Arthur Peacocke, "The Challenge and Stimulus of the Epic of Evolution to Theology," in Stephen Dick, ed., *Many Worlds* (Philadelphia: Templeton Foundation Press, 2000), 88-117, at 106.

18. Teilhard de Chardin, *Christianity and Evolution*, 134.

19. Pierre Teilhard de Chardin, "Comment Je Vois," in Georges Crespy, *From Science to Theology: An Essay on Teilhard de Chardin*, trans. George H. Shriver (New York: Abingdon Press, 1968), 99.

20. Teilhard de Chardin, *The Phenomenon of Man*, 311-12.

21. Arthur Peacocke, *Creation and the World of Science* (Oxford: Clarendon, 1979), 197.

22. It must be noted that Peacocke later amends this anthropocentric perspective. In *Paths from Science Towards God: The End of all our Exploring* (Oxford: Oneworld, 2001), 87, he suggests that God risks the natural evils of cosmic creation because "God purposes to bring about a greater good thereby, that is, the kaleidoscope of living creatures, delighting their Creator, and eventually free-willing, loving persons who also have the possibility of communion with God and with each other."

23. Teilhard de Chardin, *Christianity and Evolution*, 196.

24. Ibid., 217.

25. Ibid., 163.

26. Ibid., 85.

27. Arthur Peacocke, "The Cost of New Life," in John Polkinghorne, ed., *The Work of Love: Creation as Kenosis* (Grand Rapids, MI: Eerdmans. 2001), 21-42, at 42.

TEILHARD AND JOHN STEWART:
A METAPHYSICS OF THE FUTURE

HUGH MCELWAIN[1]

My first encounter with Teilhard occurred in the fall of 1959. I had just returned from Rome, having completed my doctoral work in theology, to teach my first course, a graduate course in the theology of creation (then referred to as *De deo creante et elevante*). It was obvious even then that some module in the course would have to deal with the "theory" of evolution. The only guidance at the time came from the somewhat ambiguous teaching in the encyclical *Humani Generis*. Whatever the reality of evolution previous to the human presence, according to this document, it would be absolutely necessary to posit direct divine intervention in the case of the human "soul." Further, there was no way that polygenism could be possible, since the doctrine of original sin postulates a single first couple, or monogeneism.[2]

About the same time—to my great surprise—while scanning a news item about a conference being held at the University of Chicago to mark the centennial of the *Origin of Species*, I came across a reference to this Jesuit (only recently deceased) and his book titled *Le phénomène humain*. Needless to say, I was taken aback, given the disposition of the Magisterium of the Church at that time toward the "theory" of evolution. Out of curiosity, as much as any other motivation, I eventually acquired a copy of *The Phenomenon of Man* (as the French was then translated). Frankly, after attempting to wade through the text, I rather cursorily dismissed it as too complex for me and, it seemed, for my students. Nonetheless, I put it on the reserved shelf in the library, commenting that it was certainly worth noting that here was a Catholic priest who was clearly an evolutionist.

At some point during the semester, I decided to have another look at the *Phenomenon*, especially the epilogue that had earlier caught my attention. As it turned out, the book was gone from the reserved shelf. The librarian informed me that the rector of the seminary had taken it out of circulation because of a *monitum* (warning) from the Holy Office (since known as the Congregation of Doctrine). As one might have suspected, this gesture by the rector deeply disturbed me. Not only that, but I then became intensely curious, and immersed myself passionately into Teilhard's writings (my initial understanding of his thought coming first from *The Divine Milieu* and *The Future of Man*). His vision of the evolving universe literally "blew my mind" (a phrase not in vogue at that time).

Even though I have not written much on Teilhard in recent years, his vision has had a pervasive influence on all my theological studies and research over the last forty-some years. Only recently have I begun to recapture the excitement I experienced when I first encountered him. One of the significant moments in this renewed enthusiasm was my reading of *Evolution's Arrow* by John Stewart and his later article, "The Evolutionary Significance of Spiritual Development."[3] The same kind of visionary aura found in Teilhard's work characterized Stewart's writings for me. Even though it was evident that this was a biologist at work, Stewart stimulated the deeper questions of meaning, purpose, and destiny that Teilhard had elicited. True, the pervasive presence of the mystical that characterized Teilhard's interpretation of the scientific phenomenon is not immediately evident in Stewart's work. And yet the keen sense of destiny and the corresponding human responsibility for the evolutionary future is deeply imbedded in Stewart's approach.

It is interesting to note that both Teilhard and Stewart—even though separated by a gap of a half-century—faced a similar barrier within their own scientific communities because of their affirmation that evolution possesses an inherent purpose or direction. Listen to Teilhard anticipating the reaction of his professional colleagues as he answers the challenge to show evolution's directionality:

> Asked whether life is going anywhere . . . nine biologists out of ten will today
> say no, even passionately. . . . As I shall show, mankind in its march is marking
> time at the moment because men's minds are reluctant to recognize that

evolution has a precise orientation and a privileged axis. . . . I believe I can see a direction and a line of progress for life, a line and a direction which are in fact so well marked that I am convinced their reality will be universally admitted by the science of tomorrow.[4]

Teilhard offered this prophecy over fifty years ago. And yet there have continued to be strong voices criticizing the notion of direction/progress. One of the most well known among these is Stephen J. Gould, who, with specific reference to Teilhard, wrote: "Perhaps the problem with all these *visions* . . . is our penchant for building comprehensive and all-encompassing systems in the first place. Maybe they just don't work."[5] Now fifty years later, one hears the same kind of exchange between John Stewart and his critics. Stewart says, "I will argue that evolution has direction, and that the direction is progressive. I will also show that this direction is important in answering the fundamental question of how we should live our lives. . . ."[6] Then, almost echoing Teilhard's earlier "prophecy," Stewart writes:

Our ability to assess objectively whether evolution progresses does not mean the issue is free of controversy. Evolutionists do not currently agree on whether evolution is progressive. Most believe it is not. The view that evolution is progressive and that humans are now at the leading edge of evolution on this planet is not supported by most evolutionary thinkers. A major task of this book *will be to show that they are wrong* (emphasis added).[7]

My objective in this study is to compare Teilhard and Stewart regarding their notion of the direction, purpose, and progress of evolution. My approach is to look first at each author and briefly summarize the comprehensive thesis of each regarding evolution and its forward/upward direction. Secondly, I highlight the place of religion/spirituality in the each author's vision of evolution's direction and purpose. Finally, I explore with both authors how humans, communally and individually, not only become conscious of the direction of evolution, but also use this awareness to guide their own evolution and to contribute to the next steps in the evolution of life on Earth.

THE VISION OF TEILHARD

Here, I will only accentuate the broad lines of Teilhard's thought. Perhaps the best term to use to describe his overall perspective is *cosmogenesis*, that is, literally, the genesis of the cosmos. Cosmogenesis is further divided into four broad evolutionary epochs: geogenesis, the development of the planet; biogenesis, the origin and evolution of life; noogenesis, human evolution; and Christogenesis, the future.

There are also several underlying principles or driving forces behind cosmogenesis. Teilhard termed its most comprehensive principle "complexity consciousness." Simply stated, what time added to process was complexity; complexity in turn produced increased consciousness. The principle of complexification leading to consciousness is accompanied by a second principle, namely, that all energy is psychic in nature. But, adds Teilhard, in each particular element, this fundamental energy is divided into two distinct components: a *tangential energy*, which links the element with all others of the same order, and a *radial energy*, which draws it towards ever greater complexity and centricity—in other words, forwards.[8] This movement through complexification toward increasing consciousness reaches a unique moment with the appearance of humans, with whom consciousness becomes reflexive. Humans not only know; they know what/that they know. Teilhard calls this phase of evolution noogenesis, that is, the emergence of mind (*nous* in Greek). In the noogenetic phase, Teilhard further distinguishes four significant phenomena, namely, hominization, socialization, personalization, and survival or superlife (*survie*).

HOMINIZATION

My synonym for the Teilhardian neologism, hominization, is "peopling of the planet." The general sense implied here is that humans emerged in the evolutionary process as the end-term of a continuous and complex development that can be traced to the origin of life itself. The advantages of this model and its accompanying images are essentially two. First, the traditional story of the special creation of the first human, from which is derived the myth of superiority, is reversed. The image of hominization relates the human group to the earth, from which we have emerged, as indeed has all life. Second, the myth of homocentricity (anthropocentrism) is also open to reinterpretation. Through the image of hominization, the earth is seen as the matrix or womb of human existence, the support system, as it were, for everything human. The interrelatedness of the human with all the components of our ecosystem is captured in this image. Uniqueness is derived not from a special divine intervention (itself a rich metaphor), nor from some other a-cosmic independence, but rather from the place of the human *in* nature. As Teilhard notes, humanity *is* evolution become conscious of itself.[9] To paraphrase, humanity is nature arrived at its reflective, self-conscious level.

SOCIALIZATION

Teilhard makes the point emphatically that "Socialization is not an epiphenomenon in the sphere of reflective life, but the essential phenomenon of hominization."[10] To put it another way, the correlative of hominization is socialization, which Teilhard understands as the unification of humans on Earth. This fact is self–evident, since there comes a point in time when the peopling of the planet, because of convergence and compression due to populating a closed surface, leads to the very issue of human survival. This is the central thrust of socialization: humankind living together in unity and harmony, simply because the alternative threatens human survival itself. Species survival at the human level is a relatively new human concern, since only recently has humankind been able to imagine its own extinction.

One of the advantages of this model of socialization is that it describes the human as primarily a relational being, thereby rejecting the metaphor of rugged individualism as well as self-definition totally and completely from within. The sense of relatedness also helps to extend the concept of belonging already implicit in the hominizing process. Humankind not only belongs to the larger ecosystem of which it is part, but also belongs to each fellow human being, across all barriers—racial, sexual, economic, geographical, national, and age. As Heidegger might put it, the human is a being-*in*-the-world-*with* others.

PERSONALIZATION

The third phase of the human phenomenon in Teilhard's thought is what he calls personalization. This is the process that leads to unification within the human community (socialization). He insists that unification (convergence, synthesis) at the human level cannot happen in any haphazard way, but that such union or unity must simultaneously preserve and enhance the uniqueness (self) of each person in the union. His most common description of this reality is that "union differentiates."[11] Thus the concise Teilhardian axiom, "Love alone is capable of uniting living beings in such a way as to complete and fulfill them, for it alone takes them and joins them by that which is deepest in themselves."[12] And so he coins the term "amorization." Amorization, in short, is the process through which personalization must take place if it is to be true unity (unification) and not merely uniformity.

Teilhard's evolutionary model places the human group *within* the flow of evolution. To speak about uniqueness in this sense is to assume the unique trust and responsibility for the unfolding of this process that humanity must assume because of its unique qualities of reflection, language, and freedom. With the appearance of the human, things no longer simply happen (in the Darwinian sense); humanity now participates in the process—for better or for worse—in an increasingly significant manner. Cooperation and co-creation are expected, although not guaranteed. At best, as Teilhard notes, it is a "groping toward the future." And it is this vision of a collective humankind, greater than the sum of its parts, characterized by a super-consciousness, that leads to a new domain of psychical expansion, the construction of a spirit of the earth—the hyperpersonal—Omega.

THE "FUTURE": A PERSONALIZING UNIVERSE

This fourth sequence in the noogenetic evolutionary phase represents something novel in Teilhard's vision, since he has now stepped beyond the realm of phenomenon, or objectivity, the provable, and into metaphysics. The following passage offers his insight into this transition:

> Once he has been brought to accept the reality of a Noogenesis, the believer in this World will find himself compelled to allow increasing room, in his vision of the future, for the values of personalization and transcendency. Of Personalization, because a Universe in process of psychic concentration is *identical* with a Universe that is acquiring a personality. And a transcendency, because the ultimate stage of "cosmic" personalization, if it is to be supremely consistent and unifying, cannot be conceived otherwise than as having emerged by its summit from the elements it super-personalizes as it unites them to itself.[13]

This reflection of Teilhard on the seemingly inevitable future of personalization leads him to one of the more controversial aspects of his vision, namely, the *Omega*, "the birth of some single centre from the convergent beams of millions of elementary centers dispersed over the surface of the thinking earth."[14] The focus of love (amorization), therefore, is the Omega Point, a "*source* of love and the *object* of love at the summit of the world above our heads."[15]

As a kind of final synthesis to this metaphysical answer to the future of man, Teilhard fuses the notion of amorization and Omega with his own Christian revelation, resulting in what he has termed *Christogenesis*. Teilhard proposes a summary account of this connection:

. . . Under the combined influence of men's thoughts and aspirations, the universe around us is seen to be knit together and convulsed by a vast movement of convergence. . . . modern cosmogony is taking the form of a cosmogenesis (or rather a psycho- or noo-genesis) at the term of which we can distinguish a supreme focus of personalizing personality. Who can fail to see the support, the reinforcement, the stimulus which this discovery of the physical pole of universal synthesis contributes to our view of revelation? Just suppose we *identify* (at least in his "natural" aspect) the cosmic Christ of faith with the Omega Point of science: then everything in our outlook is clarified and broadened, and falls into harmony. . . .[16]

I would like to conclude this brief introduction to Teilhard with some reflections from perhaps the most insightful contemporary theologian of evolution, John Haught:

What Teilhard seemed to be looking for is what we might call a "metaphysics of the future." "Metaphysics" is a term philosophers use to refer to the general vision of reality that one holds to be true. As Teilhard acknowledged explicitly, our religious thought has been dominated by a metaphysics of esse (or "being") that has obscured the obvious fact of nature's constant "becoming" and its perpetual movement toward the future. . . . Teilhard called his proposed alternative a "metaphysics of *unire*," that is, a conception of reality in which all things are drawn perpetually toward deeper coherence by an ultimate force of attraction, abstractly identified as Omega, and conceived of as an essentially *future* reality. Evolution seems to require a divine source of being that resides not in a timeless present located somewhere "up above," but in the future, essentially "up ahead," as the goal of the world still in the making.

The term "God" in this revised metaphysics must once again mean for us, as it did for many of our biblical forbears, the transcendent future horizon that draws an entire universe, and not just human history, toward an unfathomable fulfillment yet to be realized.[17]

EVOLUTION'S ARROW: THE VISION OF JOHN STEWART

In *Evolution's Arrow,* John Stewart uses the methods, tools, and findings of science to demonstrate that the evolution of life is not an aimless and random process, but directional. Life is headed somewhere, and this fact has implications for humanity. Stewart begins his compelling interpretation of the evolutionary story with several critical assumptions. First, the emergence of organisms who are conscious of the direction of evolution is one of the most important steps in the evolution of life on any planet. Second, things either evolve without having any knowledge of the direction of evolution, or they can guide their evolution by forming a picture of how evolution is likely to unfold in the future. Third, on Earth the organism that appears likely to take this significant evolutionary step is the human. However, we humans need to develop a comprehensive understanding of the direction of evolution and of the implications of this direction for humanity.[18]

Given these assumptions, Stewart proceeds to develop his thesis. He begins by demonstrating that evolution has a direction and that that direction is progressive, at least in evolutionary terms; that is, "evolution is progressive in the sense that it produces increasing cooperation amongst living processes. Further, evolution moves to greater cooperation by discovering ways to build cooperative organizations out of components that are self-interested."[19] Thus, when elementary particles cooperate, atoms can exist. When atoms cooperate, molecules can exist. When molecules cooperate, cells can exist. When cells cooperate, plant and animal life can exist. As Stewart sums it up, "We are cooperators that are made of cooperators that are made of cooperators and so on. It is cooperation all the way down."[20] What is obvious is that this sequence has direction. Thus, the same evolutionary forces that drove the expansion of cooperative organization in the past can be expected to continue to do so.

Now, in Stewart's view, to exploit the benefits of cooperation effectively, groups of entities must evolve the ability to discover the most useful forms of cooperation and to modify them as conditions change. And, in fact, processes that adapt and evolve organisms have gotten progressively better at discovering such effective forms of cooperation amongst the living processes that make up the organisms. In other words, evolution itself evolves, and living processes get smarter at evolving. One of the first such processes to emerge was gene-based natural selection. Progressive evolution has improved the ability of the genetic evolutionary mechanism itself to adapt organisms. The genetic mechanism uses trial-and-error to search for better adaptation.[21]

However, as Stewart notes, improvements in the genetic evolutionary mechanism can go only so far in enhancing the ability of the organism to adapt and evolve. An organism can experiment with change and discover better adaptation only when it reproduces, since evolution operates only across generations. It cannot search for improvements during its lifetime. A key milestone was reached when organisms could communicate with each other about adaptive improvements they had discovered during their lifetimes. Adaptive discoveries no longer died with the individual who made them. They could be passed on to others, and a culture of adaptive improvements could be developed. On this planet, only humans and human societies have evolved this capacity to a high level.[22]

But the most important and far-reaching advance in adaptability is the capacity for mental modeling. An organism capable of mental modeling can imagine how its environment will unfold in the future, and how its actions will affect the future. To an extent, it can predict the future. Such an organism is able to try out possible actions mentally, select the one that promises to produce the best possible results in its mental models, and only then try it out in practice. Such organisms will not only become aware of the direction of evolution; they will also become aware that their increasing awareness of the direction is itself a significant step in evolution. Stewart comments:

> And we are on the threshold of developing the capacity to do something that no other organism on this planet has been able to do: to consciously use our modeling of the direction of evolution to increase our chances of participating successfully in future evolution. We are in the process of developing complex mental models of the direction of evolution. These will show what we will have to do individually and collectively to contribute to the future evolutionary success of humanity.[23]

But, Stewart is quick to note, being able to mentally model our evolutionary future does not mean that *we will want to use* these models to guide our behavior. The challenge is not only having the insight to see what is needed for future evolutionary success, but also having the will to be able to accomplish it. He offers a solution: we must develop the psychological capacity in a real sense to change our own nature.[24] If we succeed in this challenge, we can transcend our biological and socio-cultural past. We also know that only organisms that choose to struggle to develop this psychological capacity are likely to make a significant contribution to the future evolution of life in the universe.

The vital question, then, is how organisms such as ourselves are likely to develop this psychological capacity. First of all, an organism can use its modeling capacity not only to model and manage its external environment, but also to model and control its internal processes of adaptation. It is possible for organisms to develop a capacity for self-management that enables them to revise and modify their previous motivations, beliefs, and objectives. These will be revised and managed so that they support the ultimate objective of future evolutionary success.[25] In all of this, the major focus for Stewart is how cooperative human organization has evolved (the evolution of evolution, as he calls it), and how it is likely to evolve in the future.

The fact is that not only has the scale of cooperative organization expanded rapidly (multi-family bands, tribes, agricultural communities, cities, empires, nation states, and now some global forms of economic and social organizations), but human societies have gotten better at discovering and supporting more effective cooperation and adapting it as circumstances change. Modern human societies can adapt and evolve through internal processes during their lifetime. They are not limited to evolving through competition and natural selection. And yet, Stewart points out, the ability of human cooperative organizations to exploit the benefits of cooperation can be greatly improved. "Guided by this awareness of evolution's arrow, they will go on to form cooperative organizations of larger and larger scale and of greater and greater evolvability."[26]

Matter, energy, and life will be managed on the scale of the organism's solar system and, eventually, its galaxy. The greater the scale of the resources the organism is able to manage, the more likely it will be to adapt to whatever challenges it faces in pursuit of future *evolutionary* success. Concretely, the issue is how modern societies can change to improve their ability to organize cooperation to satisfy the needs of their members. Stewart answers that

> economic markets and governments are the main processes in current societies that support and adapt large-scale cooperation. These processes would produce benefits for all humanity by suppressing conflict and other damaging competition within the society, and by efficiently organizing cooperation to serve the needs and objectives of citizens.[27]

But, he also notes, by themselves these changes would not establish a society that would consciously pursue future *evolutionary* success, since the society would naturally tend to satisfy the needs and objectives of its citizens, *whatever* they may be.

Until its citizens choose to consciously pursue future *evolutionary* success, the society no doubt will continue to serve only the preexisting biological and cultural needs of its members. The enormous power of our emerging technologies (artificial intelligence, genetic engineering, etc.) would not be harnessed to achieve future *evolutionary* success. Instead, shortsighted and flawed evolutionary mechanisms[28] will be used merely to satisfy obsolete desires and values that conflict with future evolutionary needs.[29] Now, this would/could all change once humans become aware of the *direction of evolution* and the capacity to use it to guide their own future evolution. As humans begin consciously to pursue future *evolutionary* success and to learn to bring their personal values in line with this objective, they will produce a planetary society that also pursues *evolutionary* goals. And since this planetary society would manage matter, energy, and life to serve the needs and values of its members, it would also serve their *evolutionary* needs and objectives. The society as a whole would develop plans, strategies, projects, and goals designed to maximize its contribution to the successful evolution of life in the universe.[30]

Stewart concludes his analysis of the direction of evolution and the future of humanity by suggesting what it means to us as individuals here and now. His thought is that a full understanding of evolution and its direction leaves an individual with very limited choices. It is not open to us, for example, to choose to ignore the dictates of evolution. Further, once individuals become aware of the direction of evolution and continue to serve the dictates of past evolution only (both biological and cultural), they are choosing evolutionary failure. On the contrary, individuals who use the direction of evolution to guide their actions also discover a clear answer to one of the central questions of their existence, "What should I do with my life?" It becomes apparent to them that they ought to do what they can to promote the awareness of the direction of evolution amongst others and to develop in themselves and in others the psychological capacity to do what is necessary for *evolutionary* success.[31] They will want to contribute to the formation of a unified, sustainable, cooperative, planetary society. And they will be aware that their actions are contributing to the next great step in the evolution of life on earth—*evolution's arrow*.

In his concluding summation, Stewart boldly asserts that one of the most important steps in the evolution of life on any planet is the emergence of organisms who are conscious of the direction of evolution and who use this awareness to guide their own evolution. The actions of individuals who are living now will help to determine whether we will be the organism that reaches that milestone on earth. In sum, we need to use our intelligence, plans, and intentions to identify where we are going, and to design strategies to get there. Stewart concludes:

> Those of us who acquire awareness will have three general projects: first, we
> will work on ourselves to improve our adaptability and evolvability . . . to
> develop the self-knowledge and psychological skills needed to transcend our

biological and cultural past. . . . Second, we will promote in others a deeper understanding of the evolutionary process. . . . Finally, we will support the formation of a unified and self-actualized planetary society. . . . How successful we are at advancing these projects will determine the significance of our lives.[32]

COMPARISONS BETWEEN TEILHARD AND JOHN STEWART

In discussing the comparisons between the respective visions of Teilhard (especially in *The Human Phenomenon*) and John Stewart (primarily in *Evolution's Arrow*), it seems wise first to highlight those visionary elements that they share. Following this, I will suggest some substantive differences in their very similar evolutionary philosophies.

A SHARED VISION.

Having systematically analyzed the visions of Pierre Teilhard de Chardin and John Stewart, I present a number of areas where I see fairly clear overlapping elements in their approaches to the evolutionary story:

- Evolution has direction or purpose. Both authors, despite often strong opposition from fellow scientists, are unambiguous in their affirmations about directionality in evolution.
- The notion of time, the nearly four billion years of evolutionary development of life on Earth, and the growing complexity in this development (consciousness for Teilhard and cooperation for Stewart) has led to the appearance on Earth of the human species some million or so years ago.
- At this human level, growth in consciousness pursues the line of altruism (love/amorization for Teilhard and cooperation for Stewart).
- The challenge according to both scientists is for the human group to realize progressively the evolvability of evolution itself. By this they mean that humans themselves become aware of evolving. Concretely, humans represent evolution become self-conscious, that is, aware of itself.
- Humans, therefore, must *now* consciously mold the direction of evolution. Future evolvability depends on the unification through cooperation of the human group and in relationship with the entire biotic community.
- The common thread between Teilhard and Stewart is the conviction that the evolutionary future is in human hands. We will either live

together in unity and harmony or we will perish (Teilhard), or, to phrase it slightly differently, the cooperators will inherit the earth (Stewart).

• Finally, both Teilhard and Stewart agree with the generally accepted scientific fact of evolution. However, both also subscribe to what John Haught calls a "Metaphysics of the Future."[33] They are concerned that the implicit metaphysical assumptions that scientists bring with them to the study of life do not blind them to what is really going on in an evolving universe. They both have a sense that the materialistic metaphysics that frames the "scientific" ideas of many modern biologists is simply inadequate to the full reality of evolution.[34]

SIGNIFICANT DIFFERENCES BETWEEN TEILHARD AND STEWART

The discussion of differences must take place in the context of the last point. Both Teilhard and Stewart are interested in what is really going on in an evolving universe and subscribe to a "Metaphysics of the Future." However, they also differ. For instance, Teilhard believes that a metaphysically adequate explanation of any universe in which evolution occurs requires a transcendent focus of attraction to explain the overarching tendency of matter to evolve toward life, mind, and spirit. Since the end term of biological and cultural evolution would be personalization through amorization (union in love), this ultimate force of attraction would be personal, identified by Teilhard as Omega, and conceived as an essentially future reality (emphasis on "omega" rather than "alpha"). Concretely, in Teilhardian terms, evolution seems to require a divine source of being who, as John Haught puts it, "resides not in a timeless present located somewhere 'up above,' but in the future, 'up ahead,' as a goal of the world still in the making."[35] Teilhard never intended this notion of the driving force or the "Omega" (identified with the Creator God of the Christian faith) to be taken as a strictly scientific explanation, but rather as theological metaphysics. Teilhard's metaphysical model would allow *all* of the data of evolution, especially the emergent future, to be included.[36]

In many ways Stewart's evolutionary metaphysics is similar to Teilhard's. Stewart, however, seems not to have any particular theological overlay to his philosophy. He simply indicates the evidence of continuous cooperation at all levels of the evolutionary process. At the biological level, Stewart highlights the particular advance in evolutionary cooperation with the reality of genetic mutation. The next significant advance in cooperation occurred with the possibility of communication, especially with the human organism. Cooperation through communication is followed at the human level by mental modeling.

We use thinking and other mental representations to model the effects of our behavior on our environment. Further, the acquisition of language is a critically important step forward in our ability to construct mental models.

Mental modeling of itself, however, even though it may produce the ideal model for the *evolutionary* future, does not guarantee that humans will respond in such a way as to bring about behavior guaranteeing the evolutionary future. Faced with this apparent stumbling block, Stewart raises the engaging question of evolutionary psychology. He observes that even with mental modeling the evolutionary adaptability of humanity is seriously limited. We do not use this immense capacity offered by mental modeling to pursue evolutionary ends. His main point is that, even though adaptations exist that are superior in evolutionary terms, we spend our lives chasing positive reinforcement from our internal reward system. If humanity is to realize the full evolutionary potential of mental modeling, we will have to free ourselves from our biological and cultural past.[37]

It is precisely at this point that Stewart introduces the notion of spiritual development and its evolutionary significance. To quote him at length:

> But some knowledge about the possibility of psychological development has existed among humans for a very long time. It has long been known that an individual can develop a psychological capacity that will free him somewhat from the dictates of the external events of his life and from his social and biological past—the individual can acquire a mode of consciousness, which gives him some independence from his emotional and physical states. In most cases this knowledge has been developed and passed on as part of a religious or spiritual system of beliefs and practices. The promotion of psychological and spiritual development has been an explicit part of many eastern religions such as Hinduism, Buddhism, and Sufism. And it is at least implicit in many varieties of Christianity. Most of these religions have developed particular practices and activities that are intended to assist psychological and spiritual development. Yoga, prayer, and meditation are well known examples.[38]

Stewart believes that until we humans develop the capacity to free ourselves from our biological and cultural past, our evolutionary adaptability will be seriously constrained. However, realizing our capacity for transforming the psychology of humanity through the practices of spiritual development, it is possible to align our internal reward and motivation system with evolutionary goals. This would enable us to find satisfaction and motivation in whatever adaptations serve these goals by sacrificing what we are for what we can become.

CONCLUSIONS

There are perhaps two general conclusions that characterize the evolutionary stories of Teilhard and Stewart. First, both scientists easily affirm the Darwinian evolutionary process, but refuse to apply the same purely instinctive and deterministic behaviors, as humans populate and begin to affect planetary evolution. Second, both authors move systematically from the physical and biological realms into what we have called the metaphysical with the appearance of humans and the evolutionary future of noogenesis. Human consciousness opens up a direction that is no longer satisfactorily explained by neo-Darwinian principles. We are participating in the evolution of evolution, from unconscious to conscious choice, from natural selection to selection according to human purpose.

We have termed this new reality, demanded by the uniqueness of the human presence, a "metaphysics of the future." The primary critical factor here is the acquisition, with the appearance and continuous evolution of humans, of the ability to project and give direction to our future. More specifically, we must engage in conscious/self-guided evolution and develop an evolutionary path which leads us to the design of a civil society that will sustain and nourish the community of life on earth.

Notes

1. Professor of Theology, Dominican University, River Forest, IL, 60305.
2. Pope Pius XII, *Humani Generis*, 1950. English translation is available at www.papalen-cyclicals.net (see nos. 36-37).
3. John Stewart, *Evolution's Arrow: The Direction of Evolution and the Future of Humanity* (Canberra, Australia: The Chapman Press, 2000); John Stewart, "The Evolutionary Significance of Spiritual Development," *Metanexus online Journal*, (September 2003) at www.metanexus.net/monthly/2003.09.html.
4. Pierre Teilhard de Chardin, *The Phenomenon of Man*, trans. Bernard Wall (New York: Harper & Row, 1961), 141-42.
5. Stephen J. Gould, *Hen's Teeth and Horse's Toes* (New York: Norton, 1983), 250.
6. Stewart, *Evolution's Arrow*, 6-7.
7. Ibid., 8.
8. Teilhard de Chardin, *The Phenomenon of Man*, 65.
9. Ibid., 227. Here Teilhard is quoting Julian Huxley, as he acknowledges.
10. Pierre Teilhard de Chardin, *The Future of Man*, trans. Norman Denny (New York: Doubleday, 1964), 217.
11. Teilhard de Chardin, *The Phenomenon of Man*, 262.
12. Ibid., 265.
13. Teilhard de Chardin, *The Future of Man*, 70-71.

14. Teilhard de Chardin, *The Phenomenon of Man*, 259.

15. Ibid., 267.

16. Pierre Teilhard de Chardin, *Christianity and Evolution* (New York: Harcourt, 1969), 180.

17. John Haught, *God after Darwin: A Theology of Evolution* (Boulder, CO: Westview Press, 2000), 83-84.

18. Stewart, *Evolution's Arrow*, 5-6.

19. Ibid., 9.

20. Ibid., 43.

21. Ibid., 12, and chap. 9.

23. Ibid., 13, and chap. 10.

24. Ibid., 14-17, and chap. 11.

25. Ibid., 17. See also Stewart's related article, "Future Psychological Evolution," *Dynamical Psychology* (online journal) (2001) at http://goertzel.org/dynapsyc.

26. Ibid., 18, and chap. 13.

27. Ibid., 19.

28. See "The Evolutionary Significance of Spiritual Development," 8, where Stewart writes: "We have not yet developed a comprehensive capacity to free ourselves from the dictates of our biological and social past. . . . As a result, the evolutionary adaptability of humanity is seriously limited. We do not use the immense capacity of mental modeling to pursue evolutionary ends. Adaptations exist that are superior in evolutionary terms, we can see that they are superior, but we do not implement them. Instead we spend our lives chasing positive reinforcement from our internal reward system. If humanity is to realize the full evolutionary potential of mental modeling, we will have to free ourselves from our biological and cultural past."

29. Ibid., 19.

30. Ibid., 217.

31. Ibid., 20-21.

32. Ibid., 322.

33. Haught, *God after Darwin*, 83.

34. Ibid.

35. Ibid., 84.

36. Ibid., 83.

37. Stewart, *Evolution's Arrow*, 211.

38. Ibid.

TEILHARD, WHITEHEAD, AND A METAPHYSICS OF INTERSUBJECTIVITY

JOSEPH A. BRACKEN, S.J.[1]

Almost forty years ago, Ian Barbour wrote an article entitled "Teilhard's Process Metaphysics," which was originally published in *The Journal of Religion* and then republished in an anthology on process theology edited by Ewert Cousins.[2] With his customary thoroughness, Barbour compared and contrasted the metaphysical schemes of Teilhard de Chardin and Alfred North Whitehead in seven major areas: reality as temporal process, the "within," freedom and determinism, continuing creation, God and time, the problem of evil, and the future of the world. Without going into detail on each of these themes, I wish in this brief essay to focus on one key difference in the way that Teilhard and Whitehead view the cosmic process, and then indicate how these differences might be unexpectedly complementary in the creation of a third position, namely, a metaphysics of intersubjectivity which, as I see it, neither Teilhard nor Whitehead fully achieved.

The key difference in their approach to reality, as Barbour points out,[3] is that, while Teilhard focuses on the unity of the cosmic process as a whole and its teleological orientation to the Cosmic Christ, Whitehead emphasizes instead the diversity and multiplicity of "actual occasions" as "the final real things of which the world is made up."[4] Furthermore, even though Whitehead concedes that "the growth of a complex structured society [of actual occasions] exemplifies, the general purpose pervading nature,"[5] he anticipates "no integrated cosmic convergence and no final consummation of history" even apart from the Cosmic Christ.[6]

For Whitehead, unlike Teilhard, cosmic process does not mean progress toward a goal predetermined by a Creator God. For him, "God and the World are the contrasted opposites in terms of which Creativity achieves its supreme task of transforming disjoined multiplicity, with its diversities in opposition, into concrescent unity, with its diversities in contrast."[7] The cosmic process is thus infinite, without beginning or end. God and the World are forever in dialectical relationship.

One can certainly attribute this difference in metaphysical vision between Teilhard and Whitehead to their contrasting personal backgrounds and previous training. Teilhard was a Jesuit priest anxious to reconcile his Christian faith and seminary training with the theory of evolution and his studies in paleontology. He was not a professional philosopher of science like Whitehead who was consciously trying to break free of the materialistic determinism characteristic of much of early modern natural science.[8] Whitehead's primary objective was to set up a metaphysical scheme in which novelty and spontaneity would be as much an ongoing feature of physical reality as order and predictability. Hence, how the cosmic process began and where it might end some day were not questions pertinent to his task. What was important was to expose the fallacy in the implicit metaphysics of early modern science whereby reality is composed of inert bits of matter "simply located" in space and time and thus with purely external relations to one another.[9] Instead, as noted above, he stipulated that "the final real things of which the world is made up" are actual occasions or momentary self-constituting subjects of experience with varying degrees of spontaneity depending upon the relative complexity of their self-organization. In this way, he implicitly agreed with Teilhard in the latter's insistence that material things have a "within" as well as a "without," a principle of spontaneity as well as a principle of order,[10] but for quite different reasons. That is, both were opposed to the dualism between spirit and matter in the early modern period, but Teilhard for largely theological reasons and Whitehead for strictly philosophical reasons.

At the beginning of this essay, I mentioned that it might be possible to reconcile these two different process-oriented visions of reality in terms of a third position, namely, a metaphysics of intersubjectivity which neither Teilhard nor Whitehead fully realized in his own work. Intersubjectivity, after all, basically implies a balance between multiplicity and unity, between multiple subjects of experience and the higher-order level of existence and activity that they achieve by their dynamic interaction. On the one hand, in saying that "the final real things of which this world is made up" are actual occasions or momentary self-constituting subjects of experience, Whitehead, provides the necessary plurality of subjects of experience needed for a metaphysics of intersubjectivity. But, as I shall indicate below, he is vague on the ontological status of "societies" as the objective result of all this intersubjective activity. Teilhard, on the other hand, was clearly thinking in intersubjective terms with his notion of the noosphere or collective consciousness of humankind.[11] But he too is vague with respect to the details of his scheme, specifically, how the law of "complexification" works at the inanimate level or even at the pre-human animate level of Nature.[12] Is the "within" of things to be identified with subjectivity, as in Whitehead's scheme, or simply to be accounted for in terms of a distinction between "radial" and "tangential" energy, both of which terms are themselves more suggestive than scientifically descriptive?

Admittedly, intersubjectivity as a theme of scientific investigation is still in its infancy. What seems clear from a historical perspective is that the subjectivity of the individual human being was basically ignored by Plato and Aristotle in the Greco-Roman era and by philosopher/theologians like Thomas Aquinas and John Duns Scotus in medieval times.[13] Their common focus was on objective knowledge of the external world in and through universal forms or essences with little or no attention to the role of the individual human being in that objective world order. Only with Descartes' celebrated "cogito, ergo sum"[14] was there the beginning of a paradigm shift in philosophical reflection from objectivity to subjectivity, from metaphysics to epistemology. But here, too, the key question was still about objectivity, the necessary conditions for certitude in human knowledge. In due time, this passion for objective certitude led to transcendental subjectivity as worked out by Immanuel Kant and the German Idealists. German Idealism, especially at the hands of Hegel, was a speculative triumph. But, as Søren Kierkegaard made clear in his basically autobiographical reflections on faith and reason, systematic philosophical reflection tends to ignore the feelings and desires of the individual in her or his subjectivity.

At the start of the twentieth century, Edmund Husserl in his *Cartesian Meditations* tried to deal with the reality of the (human) Other as truly Other, that is, as not simply a component in one's own self-consciousness, but without much success.[15] Martin Heidegger, with his notion of Mitsein (being-with), and Emmanuel Levinas, with his stipulation of the ontological priority of the Other to the Self, both contributed significantly to the theme of intersubjectivity, without setting forth an appropriate paradigm for its conceptual analysis.[16] As I see it, only Martin Buber, first with his distinction between I-Thou relations and I-It relations, and then with his elusive notion of the "Between" as the intentional space generated in moments of genuine interpersonal exchange, provided the entry-point for thinking through the notion of intersubjectivity as simultaneously involving both subjectivity and objectivity.[17] That is, two or more subjects of experience by their interaction create something other than themselves, not simply Buber's somewhat illusive Between, but a longer-lasting social context (an environment or a community) with a definite structure or law-like character. Such a social context, once constituted, heavily conditions the subsequent behavior of those same subjects of experience and their successors, even as they by their continuing interaction sustain it as a commonly shared reality.

If this preliminary analysis of the notion of intersubjectivity were true or at least plausible, then a combination of the theological insights of Teilhard and the philosophical categories of Whitehead could result in a new understanding of the God-world relationship as a cosmic community of subjects of experience (divine and creaturely) in dynamic interrelationship. That is, from Teilhard one could draw the insight that God is tripersonal rather than unipersonal, hence that God is not an individual subject of experience in ongoing dialectical relationship with created subjects of experience (as in Whitehead's own scheme), but rather a community of divine subjects of experience who make a "space" within their own divine intersubjective field of activity for the emergence of created subjects of experience. Hence, instead of the dualism between God and the world that still exists in Whitehead's scheme,[18] one has in hand a panentheistic understanding of the God-world relationship. The world of creation exists within God, but is still distinct from God in terms of its own creaturely existence and activity.[19]

Then, instead of talking in general terms about the "within" of things, we can say with Whitehead that "the final real things of which the world is made up" are actual occasions or momentary self-constituting[20] subjects of experience. Likewise, we can propose that Teilhard's process of gradual complexification within cosmic evolution is not simply to be attributed to a growth in "radial energy" with its counterpart in new forms of "tangential energy." Rather, with Whitehead, we can claim that growth in complexity is to be explained in terms of progressive growth in the structure and organization of "societies" of actual occasions with a "common element of form" or analogous self-constitution.[20] At the same time, however, to validate Teilhard's claim that the human community and perhaps all of material creation as well is summed up in the cosmic Christ, we should rethink Whitehead's notion of society. It is more than an association of actual occasions with a "common element of form" or closely analogous self-constitution.[21] Rather, a Whiteheadian society is a structured field of activity for its constituent actual occasions. So understood, it nicely serves as the "Between" or the common space for the dynamic interrelation of actual occasions (momentary subjects of experience) from moment to moment.

Whitehead himself, to be sure, did not conceive the God-world relationship or, for that matter, the relations of created actual occasions with one another in terms of intersubjectivity. For him, intersubjectivity was logically impossible, since concrescing actual occasions only "prehend" (on a feeling-level grasp) their predecessors, not their contemporaries. But the predecessors have already lost their subjectivity in becoming "superjects," objective data for their successors. Thus even God cannot prehend created actual occasions except as "superjects," entities lacking in subjectivity. In *Process and Reality*, however, Whitehead referred to societies as "environments" in "layers of social order" limiting the self-constitution of any given set of actual occasions here and now.[22] But he failed to exploit this insight to explain intersubjectivity. For, understood as matching fields of activity for their constituent actual occasions, two Whiteheadian societies can overlap so as to create a common field of activity populated by both sets of concrescing actual occasions. Thus, while the concrescing actual occasions do not directly prehend one another, they prehend the structure of their common field of activity and thereby experience the reality of their ongoing intersubjective relations. You and I, for example, are in Whiteheadian terms very complex structured societies of actual occasions; and yet we enjoy intersubjective relations with one another through sharing a Between or common field of activity in successive moments of consciousness.

Turning once again to Teilhard's vision of the Cosmic Christ as the goal of cosmic evolution, we see how with the aid of this revised notion of a Whiteheadian society we steer clear of pantheism, the absorption of all created reality into the reality of the risen Lord, and affirm instead panentheism, the incorporation of creation as a complex set of created fields of activity into the field of activity proper to Christ and ultimately into the field of activity proper to all three divine persons in their ongoing interrelation. The advantage of the notion of "field" as opposed to the classical understanding of "substance," therefore, is that fields can be layered into one another without losing their individual identity as different fields of activity. Individual substances, on the contrary, inevitably lie outside one another unless one of them is actively assimilated into the other as in the consumption of food by human beings and other animals. Hence, Teilhard's vision of the Cosmic Christ as goal of the evolutionary process makes excellent sense within a field-oriented approach to Whiteheadian societies.

Furthermore, not just human beings but all of physical reality can be thus incorporated into the Cosmic Christ as members of his Mystical Body. Whereas Teilhard in *The Phenomenon of Man* seems to imply that at the end of the world only human beings will survive after the noosphere has detached itself from its material matrix,[23] this neo-Whiteheadian scheme allows for everything to survive, albeit in a transformed state, within the Cosmic Christ as an all-embracing divine-creaturely field of activity. Every thing that exists, after all, is either itself a momentary self-constituting subject of experience, or a society (structured field of activity) for such transient subjects of experience. Hence, if human beings, as a highly complex society of interrelated subjects of experience, can experience resurrection in both body and soul, then all God's creatures can be incorporated into the Mystical Body of Christ and share in the life of the divine community. The intimate interconnection of matter and spirit, after all, is the key insight of both Teilhard and Whitehead. Neither can exist without the other at all the different levels of existence and activity within Nature, from the highest to the lowest.[24]

One final way in which these two metaphysical schemes can be fruitfully compared and combined so as better to mediate between the sometimes conflicting claims of religion and science would be in terms of an explanation for God's specific role in the cosmic process. Both Teilhard and Whitehead agree that God does not suspend the laws of Nature, but instead works within Nature, using Nature's own laws, to achieve the divine purposes for creation. But, whereas Teilhard simply appeals to the cosmic law of complexification/consciousness to argue for the transit from non-life to life to rational life, Whitehead has a more detailed scheme to show how God works with the natural spontaneity of creatures from moment to moment, and yet manages to keep the evolutionary process moving in the direction of divine goals and values for creation. According to Whitehead, God provides to each actual occasion or momentary subject of experience an "initial aim" to guide it in its process of self-constitution.[25] The "initial aim" from God, however, does not impede the natural spontaneity of the finite subject of experience, but rather empowers it to make its own self-constituting decision, albeit with divine assistance, if the actual occasion chooses to follow the divine lead.

Once this decision is made, God incorporates it into what Whitehead calls the divine consequent nature, the divine experience of the world from moment to moment. In this way, God unifies for Himself what might otherwise be a chaotic jumble of independent self-constituting decisions on the part of creatures at any given moment into a coherent unity within the divine experience of the world. Then, out of this renewed experience of the world as a unified reality, God is able to provide a new set of initial aims to the next set of concrescing actual occasions or self-constituting subjects of experience in the ongoing movement of the cosmic process as a whole. Thus, without endangering the spontaneity of individual creatures in making their own self-constituting decisions, God is able to provide purpose and direction to the cosmic process as a whole. God's role in the world of creation, in other words, is not to make things happen in virtue of divine efficient causality, but in more bilateral fashion first to empower creatures to make their own self-constituting decisions and then on God's own part to order those same decisions, into an intelligible whole within the divine experience so as to provide the necessary guidance and direction to creatures for the next moment in the cosmic process.[26]

One can quarrel with details of Whitehead's scheme here. For example, is the unity of the world process from moment to moment to be found only in God's experience of the world, or does the world possess its own objective unity as a finite structured field of activity within the all-encompassing divine field of activity? In terms of my own understanding of the God-world relationship, as sketched above and laid out more in detail elsewhere,[27] I would argue for the latter alternative. But this is clearly secondary to the way an adroit combination of insights from Teilhard and Whitehead can deal with the currently controversial issue of "intelligent design" as set forth by Michael Behe, William Dembski, and others within what is called "creation science" as opposed to Neo-Darwinism, the standard scientific explanation of evolution in terms of natural selection. Relying upon Teilhard and Whitehead, one does not claim with some proponents of natural selection that there is no purpose or direction to the cosmic process. But at the same time one, does not stipulate with Behe,

Dembski, and others that there are instances of "irreducible complexity" within natural processes which require the active intervention of an other-worldly designer (presumably God) in order to make something happen.[28] Rather, with Teilhard and Whitehead, one can argue that God works patiently within natural processes to achieve well-defined goals and values, while all the time respecting the spontaneity of the creatures involved. As Teilhard comments at the conclusion of *The Phenomenon of Man*, "God as providence, [is] directing the universe with loving, watchful care; and God the revealer, [is] communicating himself to man on the level of and through the ways of intelligence."[29] Or, as Whitehead remarks in *Process and Reality*, God "is the poet of the world, with tender patience leading it by his vision of truth, beauty, and goodness."[30] Perhaps we, too, should be more patient and adopt more of a "wait-and see" attitude, as we try to understand how God is at work in the world around us.

Notes

1. Professor Emeritus of Theology, Director Emeritus of the Edward B. Brueggeman Center for Dialogue, Xavier University, Cincinnati, OH 45207.
2. Ian G. Barbour, "Teilhard's Process Metaphysics," *The Journal of Religion* 49 (1969): 136-59; Ewert Cousins, ed., *Process Theology: Basic Writings* (New York: Newman/Paulist Press, 1971), 323-50.
3. Cousins, *Process Theology*, 323, 327.
4. Alfred North Whitehead, *Process and Reality: An Essay in Cosmology*, eds. David Ray Griffin and Donald W. Sherburne (1929; New York: Free Press, 1979), 18.
5. Ibid., 100.
6. Barbour, "Teilhard's Process Metaphysics," 348.
7. Whitehead, *Process and Reality*, 348.
8. See Whitehead's early philosophical work, *Science and the Modern World* (New York: Free Press, 1967), 1-74.
9. Ibid., 57-58.
10. Pierre Teilhard de Chardin, *The Phenomenon of Man*, trans. Bernard Wall (New York: Harper & Row, 1965), 53-66.
11. Ibid., 180-84.
12. Ibid., 48-49, 142-52.
13. In what immediately follows, I will be summarizing the early chapters in my new book entitled *Subjectivity, Objectivity and Intersubjectivity: A New Paradigm for Religion and Science*, (Conshohocken, PA: Templeton Foundation Press, 2009).
14. René Descartes, *Meditations concerning First Philosophy*, II, in René Descartes, *Discourse on Method and Meditations*, trans. Laurence J. Lafleur (Indianapolis, IN: Bobbs-Merrill, 1960), 82.
15. See Edmund Husserl, *Cartesian Meditations*, trans. Dorion Cairns (Dordrecht: Kluwer, 1991), 89-151.
16. See Martin Heidegger, *Being and Time*, trans. John Macquarrie and Edward Robinson

(New York: Harper & Row, 1962), 153-63; Emmanuel Levinas, *Totality and Infinity*, trans. Alphonso Lingis (Pittsburgh, PA: Duquesne University Press, 1969), 39-40.

17. See Martin Buber, *I and Thou*, 2nd ed., trans. Ronald Gregor Smith (New York: Scribner's, 1958), esp. 3-9, 63.

18. See Whitehead, *Process and Reality*, 348: "God and the World are the contrasted opposites etc." Even though it is a dualism within an overarching cosmic process, Whitehead's God-world relationship is still a dualism between quite separate realities.

19. See, for instance, Joseph Bracken, *The Divine Matrix: Creativity as Link between East and West* (Maryknoll, NY: Orbis, 1995), 52-69; Joseph Bracken, *The One in the Many: A Contemporary Reconstruction of the God-World Relationship* (Grand Rapids, MI: Eerdmans, 2001), 109-30.

20. See, for instance, Whitehead's *Process and Reality*, 89-109, where he sketches "The Order of Nature" within his system of metaphysics.

21. Ibid., 34.

22. Ibid., 90.

23. Pierre Teilhard de Chardin, *The Phenomenon of Man*, 285-90.

24. See Joseph A. Bracken, *Christianity and Process Thought: Spirituality for a Changing World* (Philadelphia, Templeton Foundation Press, 2006), esp. 103-15, for further details.

25. Whitehead, *Process and Reality*, 244.

26. Ibid., 350-51.

27. See above, n. 19.

28. See Michael J. Behe, *Darwin's Black Box: The Biochemical Challenge to Evolution* (New York: Free Press, 1996), 39: "By *irreducibly complex*, I mean a single system composed of several well-matched, interacting parts that contribute to the basic function, and where the removal of any one of the parts causes the system to effectively cease functioning." See also William A. Dembski, *Intelligent Design: The Bridge between Science and Theology* (Downers Grove, IL: Intervarsity Press, 1999).

29. Teilhard de Chardin, *The Phenomenon of Man*, 293.

30. Whitehead, *Process and Reality*, 346.

IV

TEILHARD

CONTRIBUTIONS TO SCIENCE
AND TECHNOLOGY

TEILHARD'S SCIENCE

James F. Salmon, S.J.[1]

Speaking of Teilhard de Chardin, 1977 Nobel–laureate in chemistry Ilya Prigogine, notes, "The work he has left has so many aspects that it can be a focus of interest for a wide variety of people including scientists, philosophers and historians."[2] Writing as a chemist, I will focus on two aspects of scientific interest. The first concerns the way scientists have responded to and evaluated the quality of Teilhard's scientific work; the second deals with qualitative and quantitative aspects of evolution that are directly related to his scientific legacy, specifically, to the evolution of information. My thesis is that Teilhard's insights about evolution and his rather ambiguous concept of energy have turned out to have significant scientific relevance.

CRITICS OF TEILHARD'S SCIENTIFIC LEGACY

References to Teilhard and his work, both pro and con, are found throughout the literature. I examine first negative critiques of his insights offered by two well-known biologists. Then I present a brief analysis of his understanding of cosmology.

Teilhard's most devastating evaluation comes from British immunologist Peter Medawar. In a 1961 edition of the journal *Mind*, Medawar reviews the original English translation of *Le phénomène humain* and remarks:

> Yet the greater part of it [the book], I shall show, is nonsense, tricked out by a variety of tedious metaphysical conceits, and its author can be excused of dishonesty only on the grounds that before deceiving others he has taken great pains to deceive himself. *The Phenomenon of Man* cannot be read without a feeling of suffocation, a gasping and flailing around for sense. There is an argument in it, to be sure—a feeble argument, abominably expressed . . . but consider first the style, because it is the style that creates the illusion of content, and which is in some part the cause as well as merely the symptom of Teilhard's alarming apocalyptic seizures.[3]

Medawar continues to argue that Teilhard stands squarely within "a philosophical indoor pastime of German origin which does not seem even by accident (though there is a great deal of it) to have contributed anything of permanent value to the storehouse of human thought." Further, says Medawar, "Teilhard has accordingly resorted to the use of that tipsy euphoric prose-poetry which is one of the more tiresome manifestations of the French spirit."[4] For most people interested in understanding what Teilhard is trying to say, Medawar's rhetoric seems to interfere with any scientific substance in his criticisms.

A second critic of Teilhard's science is the late Stephen J. Gould, known more for his fine literary style than for his contributions as a scientist. In a long essay found in a 1980 volume of *Natural History*, Gould proposes one of his more infamous hypotheses. He first recounts the details of the Piltdown hoax. In 1912, lawyer and antiquary Charles Dawson unearthed a human skull and ape-like jaw fragments along with primitive artifacts at a gravel pit at Piltdown in the south of England. Dawson then proposed that this so-called Piltdown find was the missing link between animals and humans. But in 1952, chemical analyses showed all of the artifacts were of recent date. Gould then argues:

> But I do believe that a conspiracy existed at Piltdown and, for once, the most interesting hypothesis is actually true. I believe that a man [who] later became one of the world's most famous theologians, a cult figure for many years after his death in 1955, knew what Dawson was doing and probably helped in no small way—the French Jesuit priest and paleontologist Pierre Teilhard de Chardin.[5]

Gould was convinced that Teilhard cooperated with the discoverers. So he continues:

> But who among us would or could have come clean in Teilhard's position? Unfortunately intent does not always correlate with effect in our complicated

world—yet I believe that we must judge a man primarily by intent. . . . But I cannot view his [Teilhard's] participation as more than an intended joke that unexpectedly turned to a galling bitterness almost beyond belief. I think that Teilhard suffered for Piltdown throughout his life. I believe that he must have cried inwardly as he watched Smith Woodward and even Boule himself make fools of themselves.[6]

As most Teilhardians had expected, Gould's "belief" was ill placed. A 1996 article in *Nature*, "Box of bones 'clinches' identity of Piltdown palaeontology hoaxer," begins: "A trunk discovered under the roof of London's Natural History Museum appears to have provided vital evidence allowing the Piltdown fraud—one of the most successful hoaxes in scientific history—finally to be put to rest."[7] Gould was wrong. However, I have met people in recent years, who are not aware of the discovery of the real "hoaxer." They are still suspicious of Teilhard. Unfortunately, they base their suspicion on the original publicity given to Gould's false hypothesis.

From the time that Teilhard first visited the site while he was still a student in theology, he was suspicious that the Piltdown find might be someone's hoax. Not having been trained yet as a professional geologist when he visited the site, he made no public comment, but continued to remain skeptical about the Piltdown. After World War I, he wrote an essay, "Le cas de l'homme de Piltdown," which verifies his continued suspicion about the validity of the discovery.[8]

We turn next to Teilhard's cosmology. In 1994, at the annual Cosmos and Creation Conference in Baltimore, the distinguished Polish philosopher of science and cosmologist, Michael Heller, offered a careful evaluation of Teilhard's scientific legacy. Heller compared Teilhard's vision with the observations of the physical universe made by contemporary theoretical astrophysicists. Heller argues that the vision in *The Phenomenon of Man* reflects views of science prevalent during Teilhard's time: the first concerns matter as the stuff of the Universe, and the second deals with the existence of a special energy that accounts for the phenomena of complexification and emergence of consciousness in the Universe. I have written elsewhere about Heller's first observation and will not elaborate here.[9] Although Heller does not discuss Teilhard's well-known proposed law of complexity-consciousness, he questions Teilhard's intuition that there must be a special aspect of energy to explain evolution.[10]

It is interesting to note that the seriousness of the scientific problem of evolution itself and the related issue of subjective unidirectional time did not escape another scientist, Albert Einstein. Philosopher Rudolf Carnap recalls the following:

> Once Einstein said that the problem of the Now worried him seriously. He explained that the experience of the Now means something special for man, something essentially different from the past and future, but that this important difference does not and cannot occur within physics. That this experience cannot be grasped by science seemed to him a matter of painful but inevitable resignation. I remarked that all that occurs objectively can be described in science; on the one hand, the temporal sequence of events is described in physics; and on the other hand, the peculiarities of man's experiences with respect to time, including his different attitude towards past, present, and future, can be described and (in principle) explained in psychology. But Einstein thought that these scientific descriptions cannot possibly satisfy our human needs; that there is something essential about the Now which is just outside of the realm of science.[11]

Thus, for Einstein, as for Teilhard, there was no scientific solution to the subjective experience of unidirectional time. Both were aware of the problem that has waited years for scientific clarification.

Likewise, in 1944, Erwin Schrödinger argued

> that the spread, both in width and depth, of the multifarious branches of knowledge .... has confronted us with quite a dilemma. We .... are only now beginning to acquire reliable material for welding together the sum-total of all that is known into a whole; but, on the other hand, it has become next to impossible for a single mind fully to command more than a small specialized portion of it.[12]

Schrödinger concludes: "I can see no escape from this dilemma . . . than that some of us should venture to embark on a synthesis of facts, and theories . . . at the risk of making fools of ourselves."[13] In the remainder of this paper, I discuss Teilhard's two energies, offer a response to Teilhard's insights about both the qualitative and quantitative features of evolution, and comment on whether history will say that Teilhard actually did make a fool of himself.

QUALITATIVE AND QUANTITATIVE FEATURES OF INFORMATION

Before proceeding to discuss Teilhard's two energies, I focus on one limited aspect of evolution—namely, the evolution of information, both its qualitative and quantitative features. Both features provide us with tools that seem capable of testing the value of Teilhard's scientific legacy.

Teilhard's insistence on the use of a phenomenal and qualitative approach for understanding evolution is found throughout the ten volumes of his scientific papers.[14] In his book, *Theology of Creation in an Evolutionary World*, the late Karl Schmitz-Moormann, who has systematically assembled Teilhard's thought on the role and evolution of information in the physical world,[15] refers to three levels of being or, as Teilhard would prefer, three levels of evolutionary becoming: matter, life, and mind. At the first level, the level of matter, we cannot differentiate information from structure. For example, at the atomic level, we cannot differentiate the information in the atom from the structure of its neutrons, protons, and electrons. Matter can communicate only through forces within its structure. Matter of itself does not seek communication. Its encounters are accidental and mediated through forces that are gravitational, electrical, and magnetic. As structures become more organized and complex, more information is present within the matter. But at this first level of pre-life, matter itself is identical with its information. Matter does not carry information distinguishable from its structure.

The situation changes fundamentally with the appearance of life. At this second level, matter suddenly becomes a carrier of information. Life uses matter to store information symbolically. For example, the DNA structure contains information, but the DNA structure is not the information itself. We can differentiate the molecular structure of the stuff of genes from the information stored in the genes. In other words, what is significant here is that with the coming of life, the structure of the material carrier of information is no longer the information. An essentially immaterial message is read and transferred by material carriers. But the carriers are not the message. Our knowledge of how this cryptic information is used to make blue eyes and gifted artists is an active field of scientific research. As we ascend the evolutionary ladder from prokaryotes and eukaryotes to higher forms of plants and animals, we note that life communicates information through a variety of means, including sound, smell, and mimicry.

On the human level the storage of information acquires a new dimension. Animals can store information in the soma, in the brain, and in the DNA. But beyond sharing this capacity with other animals, humans also store information extra-somatically in libraries and computers, for example. The information does not change with the medium nor can it be deduced from the material used for storage. Schmitz-Moormann offers extensive scientific data that clarify Teilhard's insight into the emergence of information from matter to life and finally to mind.[16] This emergence verifies Teilhard's qualitative approach at clearly differentiated levels of complexity within matter, life, and mind.

THE TWO ENERGIES

No concept seems to have been the subject of greater criticism by members of the physics community than Teilhard's approach to energy. Philosophers of science in general see merit in his effort and try to understand his proposal. Yet, they reject his introduction of a "radial energy" because it was an immeasurable quantity.

The scientific problem that Teilhard faced lies in the area of bioenergetics. How does one organize energy to explain cosmic and biological evolution? We can trace the roots of the paradox to proposals made by naturalists such as Darwin and Wallace about evolution on Earth. At the same time, physicists became aware of a Second Law of Thermodynamics which may be formulated, "It is impossible to construct an engine which will work in a complete cycle, and convert ALL the heat it absorbs from a reservoir into mechanical work." Or, as it is often paraphrased, "there are no machines with perpetual motion," or even "there are no free lunches." In other words, it was presumed from what was known at the time that planet earth should have come to equilibrium and become a desolate wasteland millions of years ago. Biological evidence for evolution seemed to contradict physics. Unlike many biologists of his time, Teilhard understood the problem, and suggested a resolution to the issue. Matter-energy must be more than purely inert stuff.

Extensive research and readings about communication in nature, especially among organisms, led Teilhard to the realization that besides the emergence of consciousness and freedom, there is an increasing flow of information taking place during evolution. Besides matter and energy, there must be a noetic (cognitive, mental, intelligent) aspect to the physical universe. We experience a flow of information when we read the newspaper, talk with a friend, or watch television. Although information seems more elusive, our experience of exchanging it seems as real as our experience of exchanging matter or energy. Teilhard conceived this flow as a sort of psychic energy. In the final draft of his *Le phénomène humain,* he wrote, "No concept is more familiar to us than spiritual energy. And yet nothing remains more obscure to us scientifically."[17]

The concept of energy in evolution was a constant theme in Teilhard's private journals and essays. Because, at the time, an adequate explanation was lacking for the paradox of the two laws of thermodynamics, the first, which deals with the conservation of energy, and the second, with its dissipation, he surmised that energy consists of two aspects. He wrote, "There is no doubt that material energy and spiritual energy hold together and are prolonged by *something*. Ultimately, *somehow or other*, there must only be a single energy at play in the world."[18] He continues,

> "To think we must eat," once again. But on the other hand, so many different thoughts come out of the same piece of bread!
> The two energies—physical and psychical—spread respectively through the external and internal layers of the world behave on the whole in the same way. They are constantly associated and somehow flow into each other. But it seems impossible to establish a simple correspondence between their curves.[19]

The association of a noetic aspect to a purely material and traditional understanding of energy forced Teilhard to introduce a new model. He writes,

> We shall assume that all energy is essentially psychic. But we shall add that in each individual element this fundamental energy is divided into two distinct components: a *tangential energy* making the element interdependent with all elements of the same order in the universe as itself (that is of the same complexity and the same "centricity"); and a *radial energy* attracting the element in the direction of an ever more complex and centered state, toward what is ahead.*[20]

He adds in a footnote,

> Note by the way, that the less centered an element is (that is, the weaker its radial energy), the more its tangential energy is shown through powerful mechanical effects. Between strongly centered particles (that is, particles with a high radial energy), the tangential seems to become "interiorized" and to disappear, in the eyes of physics.[21]

However, Teilhard cautions that his model is still under development.

> Of course the considerations that follow do not presume to prove a truly satisfactory solution. Their purpose is simply to show, from one example, what line of research in my opinion should be adopted by an integrated science of nature and what type of explanation this science should pursue.[22]

"More naturalist than physicist,"[23] Teilhard introduces a model that bridges science and philosophy, and suggests a research program to investigate "the axis and arrow of evolution,"[24] as he called it. His model permits the passage of information along this axis. He calls this new "science of nature" hyperphysics. He writes,

> Take any major book written about the world by one of the great modern scientists such as Poincaré, Einstein, Jeans, and the others. It is impossible to attempt a general scientific interpretation of the universe without *seeming* to intend to explain it right to the end. But only take a closer look at it, and you will see this "hyperphysics" still is not metaphysics.[25]

Tangential energy, the energy typically studied in science, has the dominant role in pre-living entities, although the psychic energy aspect is always present, no matter how small the entity. He writes,

> It is at this preliminary phase of centrogenesis that practically the whole of time and space is *quantitatively* employed: the reason for this being precisely, perhaps, that in order to bring about the appearance of the "first improbable" the play of large numbers needs a more extensive laboratory for its experiments.[26]

In an essay written four years after he had finished *le phénomène humain* from which the above descriptions are quoted, Teilhard linked physical and psychic energies with his previous description of tangential and radial energies. He maintains, "The behaviour of these two energies (physical and psychic) is so completely different, and their phenomenal manifestations so completely irreducible, that we might believe they derive from two entirely independent ways of explaining the world." However, he continues to see a hidden connection between the two energies. He writes, "Nevertheless, since they both carry through their evolution in the same universe, in the same temporal dimension, there must surely be some hidden relationship which links them together in their development."[27]

In summary, in *The Human Phenomenon* which was completed in 1938, Teilhard stated that all energy is psychic and is composed of two aspects, radial (the axial energy of evolution) and tangential (the energy of physics). At this stage, the two aspects of energy seem to be on equal footing. Four years later in an essay entitled "Centrology,"[28] Teilhard referred to the two energies as having psychic and physical components. However, the physical aspect was not to be considered "materialized psychic energy." Although energy continues to be made up of two aspects, all energy for Teilhard is essentially psychic.

Teilhard never stopped thinking about the issue of assuming two energies to explain evolution. His private journals and later essays reveal that he was never fully satisfied with his definitions. In an essay written in 1954, one year before he died, Teilhard reveals his continued concern with this topic.[29] He distinguishes psychical or radial energy from physical or tangential, the former "escaping from entropy," the latter obeying the laws of thermodynamics. Here, the two energies are not directly transformable but are interdependent in their function and evolution. The radial aspect of energy increases with the arrangement of the tangential, and the tangential only arranges itself when prompted by the radial. Thus, the fundamental interpretation of the two energies that includes a noetic aspect is retained, and does not seem to be very different from his original analysis in 1938.

The depth of Teilhard's knowledge of classical thermodynamics is uncertain. Although he discusses and uses the formalisms of the statistics of large numbers and chance within evolutionary theory, there is no indication of his familiarity with the formalisms used in statistical mechanics. He comments in his private journals about the writings of many contemporary scientific authors. His positive review of Erwin Schrödinger's *What Is Life?* was published in 1950. Reading Norbert Wiener's *Cybernetics* in 1951 stimulated and verified his interest in information as a component in the evolutionary process. In a 1953 essay, "The Activation of Human Energy," he refers to a review by Louis de Broglie, "La Cybernétique," and concludes,

> We still persist in regarding the physical as constituting the "true" phenomenon in the universe, and the psychic as a sort of epiphenomenon. However, as suspected (if I understand them correctly) by such coolly objective minds as Louis de Broglie and Léon Brillouin, surely, if we really wish to unify the real, we should completely reverse the values—that is, we should consider the whole of thermodynamics as an unstable and ephemeral by-effect of the concentration on itself of what we call, "consciousness" or "spirit."[30]

He continues:

> An interior energy of unification (true energy) gradually emerging, under the influence of organization, from the superficial system of action and reaction that make up the physico-chemical.

In other words, there is no longer just one type of energy in the world: there are two different energies—one axial, increasing, and irreversible, and the other peripheral or tangential, constant, and reversible: and these two energies are linked together in 'arrangement', but without nevertheless being able either to form a compound or directly to be transformed into one another, because they operate at different levels.

We may well wonder whether, if we refuse to accept such a duality (which is no dualism!) in the stuff of things, it is scientifically conceivable that a universe can function, from the moment when it *reflects upon itself*.[31]

The suggestion to reconsider an axial "interior unification of energy gradually emerging" within "the whole of thermodynamics" indicates the thrust of Teilhard's long-held intuition. His proposal of a psychic aspect in nature that includes communication of information had reached a level of maturity that seems to validate what has been subsequently shown. It is interesting to consider the implications of his proposal in the physical sciences. Is it not possible that Teilhard's hyperphysics is an extension of Schrödinger's thesis that "from all we have learnt about the structure of living matter, we must be prepared to find it working in a manner that cannot be reduced to the ordinary laws of physics."[32]

Consideration of quantitative aspects of the evolution of information is more subtle. It requires familiarity with classical thermodynamics, statistical mechanics, and information theory. It turns out that Teilhard's scientific legacy regarding a proposal of radial and tangential energies, although ambiguous, seems remarkably prescient.

Between 1875 and 1876, Yale Professor Josiah Willard Gibbs developed one of the most significant relationships in science. He defined a quantity now called the Gibbs Free Energy, which represents the maximum useful work obtainable from any isolated system. The equation for the change in free energy ΔG of a system can be written,

$$\Delta G = \Delta H - T\Delta S,$$

where ΔH represents the change in calorimetric enthalpy, that is, the heat content in the system at constant pressure, T, the absolute temperature of the system, and ΔS, the change in entropy in the system. Note that ΔG is actually the sum of two energy terms, one of which is related to the entropy of the system.

Entropy is one of the most misconstrued concepts encountered in the physical and engineering sciences. In traditional thermodynamic systems, entropy relates to probability. Disordered systems with low information have high entropy, while highly ordered systems with high information content have low entropy.

Harold Morowitz and I have noticed that the organization of matter, life, and mind is related to information.[33] In a 1955 paper, "Information Theory and Statistical Mechanics," Stanford Professor E.T. Jaynes has shown that entropy is related negatively to information. Jaynes defined entropy as follows: "Entropy as a concept may be regarded as a measure of our degree of ignorance as to the state of a system."[34] Although $T\Delta S$ is an energy term, entropy itself turns out to be proportional to missing information in the micro-state of a system for an observer who knows its macroscopic parameters. In Jaynes's interpretation, the entropy function turns out to be noetic. The $T\Delta S$ term *is* psychical or cognitive because it contains a measure of information we are missing about the system. This relationship between the observer and the system characterizes the profound change in physics that occurred between the nineteenth and twentieth centuries.

Thus a modern view is that the Gibbs Free Energy has two additive components, one that is calorimetric, and one that is informatic bordering on the noetic. It is not unlike Teilhard's prescient, but often criticized, insight into "the duality of the stuff of the universe," his physical and psychical energies. The conclusion is evident. This interpretation of the Gibbs Free Energy seems to verify Teilhard's profound scientific legacy.

CONCLUSION

Teilhard was correct to consider himself first as neither theologian nor philosopher, but first as scientist. Although some rhetorical and negative implications about his scientific legacy have been raised, it seems he has left us, as a scientist, a series of insights into nature that, now more than ever, are quite relevant.

Notes

1. Professor of Chemistry and Theology, Loyola College of Maryland, Baltimore, MD 21210; Senior Fellow, Woodstock Theological Center, Washington, DC 20057.
2. Ilya Prigogine, "Time and the Unity of Knowledge," in Thomas M. King, S.J., and James F. Salmon, S.J., eds., *Teilhard and the Unity of Knowledge* (Ramsey, NJ: Paulist Press, 1983), 21.
3. Peter Medawar, "Critical Notice, Review of *The Phenomenon of Man*," *Mind* 70, no. 277 (January 1961): 99-106. I am not aware that Teilhard suffered from seizures, either from reading both his published works and his private journals or from conversations with his friends.

4. Ibid., 99.
5. Stephen J. Gould, "The Piltdown Conspiracy," *Natural History* 89, no. 8 (August, 1980): 8-28.
6. Ibid.
7. Henry Gee, "Box of bones 'clinches' identity of Piltdown palaeontology hoaxer," *Nature* 381 (23 May 1996): 261-62.
8. Pierre Teilhard de Chardin, "Le cas de l'homme de Piltdown," in Nicole and Karl Schmitz-Moormann, eds., *Pierre Teilhard de Chardin, L'Oeuvre Scientifique,* Tome I (Olten und Freiburg im Breisgau: Walter-Verlag, 1971), 208-14.
9. James Salmon, "Teilhard's Law of Complexity-Consciousness," *Revista Portuguesa de Filosofia* 61, no. 1 (2005): 185-202.
10. This talk was later published in Michael Heller, "Teilhard's Vision of the World and Modern Cosmology, *Zygon: The Journal of Religion and Science* 30, no. 1 (March 1995): 11-23, and has recently been included in Michael Heller, *Creative Tension* (Philadelphia: Templeton Foundation Press, 2003), 58-69.
11. Prigogine, "Time and the Unity of Knowledge," 23.
12. Erwin Schrödinger, *What Is Life?* (Garden City, NY: Doubleday & Co., 1956), 1.
13. Ibid.
14. Nicole and Karl Schmitz-Moormann, eds., *Pierre Teilhard de Chardin, L'Oeuvre Scientifique* (Olten und Freiburg im Breisgau: Walter-Verlag, 1971).
15. Karl Schmitz-Moormann, *Theology of Creation in an Evolutionary World* (Cleveland: Pilgrim Press, 1997), 72-94.
16. Ibid.
17. Pierre Teilhard de Chardin, *The Human Phenomenon*, trans. Sarah Appleton-Weber (Portland, OR: Sussex Academic Press, 1999), 28.
18. Ibid., 29.
19. Ibid., 30.
20. Ibid. The * refers to a footnote added by Teilhard.
21. Ibid.
22. Ibid., 29.
23. Ibid., 11.
24. Ibid., 7.
25. Ibid., 2.
26. Pierre Teilhard de Chardin, *Activation of Energy*, trans. René Hague (New York: Harcourt Brace Jovanovich, Inc., 1978), 105-6.
27. Ibid., 120.
28. Ibid., 97-127.
29. Pierre Teilhard de Chardin, *The Appearance of Man*, trans. J. M. Cohen (New York: Harper & Row, 1965), 208-73.
30. Teilhard de Chardin, *The Appearance of Man*, 393.
31. Ibid.
32. Schrödinger, *What Is Life?* 74.
33. Harold J. Morowitz, Nicole Schmitz-Moormann, and James F. Salmon, SJ, "Teilhard's Two Energies," *Zygon* (Sept. 2005): 721-23.
34. Edwin T. Jaynes, "Information Theory and Statistical Mechanics," *Physical Review* 106, no. 4 (1957): 620-30.

TEILHARD AND NATURAL SELECTION: A MISSED OPPORTUNITY?

DARYL P. DOMNING[1]

Jesuit paleontologist and mystic Pierre Teilhard de Chardin (1881-1955) is well known for his synthesis of Christian theology with evolutionary science. Taking the established facts of evolution as givens, he went on to demonstrate the congruence between Christian revelation and the evolutionary worldview, and the inadequacy in this regard of the static, pre-evolutionary worldview. In so doing, he showed how to make *constructive theological* use of evolution, rather than merely finding a *modus vivendi* between his religion and what many, then and now, have regarded as unwelcome scientific findings.

Though he would seem to have accepted not only the fact of organic evolution but the Darwinian account of natural selection as its basic mechanism, he said almost nothing about natural selection in his writings. For example, *The Phenomenon of Man*, and even the collection of essays published as *Christianity and Evolution*, make at most only passing reference to natural selection, and do not discuss how it works or emphasize its central role in Darwinian theory. The paleontologist George Gaylord Simpson, who claimed him as a friend of many years' standing, wrote that "Teilhard never grasped the concept of natural selection . . ."[2] Certainly Teilhard made no attempt at theological use of this key biological principle in developing his own thought. Rather, his interest was focused on eschatology, Christology, the Christian understanding of human nature, and the inferences for those topics that he could draw from the simple fact of evolution itself and from its large-scale *patterns*, without concern for the nuts and bolts of the evolutionary *process*.

I wish to suggest that this lack of attention to evolutionary mechanisms caused Teilhard to overlook a straightforward solution to a set of problems that are imperfectly resolved in his synthesis—indeed, the very problems that got him into trouble with church authorities: namely, evil and original sin.

Briefly, I have argued elsewhere[3] that Darwinian natural selection necessarily enforces selfish or self-centered behavior on the part of all living things, and that when organisms evolve to the level of self-conscious intelligence such as ours, this inbred tendency to self-serving behavior inevitably results in the immorally selfish choices that we call sin. This observation, which is based robustly on modern studies of evolutionary ecology and animal behavior, provides a necessary and sufficient explanation of what the Christian tradition has called original sin. I believe that had Teilhard paid more attention to natural selection and its behavioral implications, he might have achieved this same insight, and might have been able to provide a more convincing explanation of original sin than he could offer his inquisitors during his lifetime.

Why this inattention to mechanism on Teilhard's part? Several possibilities come to mind, which are not mutually exclusive.

1. It may well be, as I have just suggested, that he was simply not *interested* in evolutionary mechanisms. He was trained as, and worked as, a geologist and paleontologist like myself, and not a geneticist, ethologist, or ecologist, and consequently natural selection was not a process that he could directly observe in his own work. We paleontologists typically accept natural selection as the driving force behind the evolutionary patterns we see in the fossil record, without being able to contribute data that bear directly on how evolution works on the level of living populations, so we simply focus on what we can study.

2. It may be instead that the key evidence came along *too late* for Teilhard to know about or digest. He got his basic scientific training around the turn of the twentieth century, just when Mendelian genetics was being rediscovered, and well before biologists had built it into what is known as the Synthetic or Neo-Darwinian understanding of evolution, which combines Darwin's idea of natural selection with population genetics. This synthesis was the product of the 1930s and 1940s, and hence culminated toward the end of Teilhard's life, well after the basic outlines of his thought had

crystallized. Only after his death came the developments of sociobiology, evolutionary ecology, and behavioral studies of wild apes and other species in the 1970s and after. So in fairness to Teilhard, the implications of natural selection were less obvious in his day than in our own.

3. Then again, even if he had thought of it, he might have been reluctant to tackle the touchy theological issue of original sin by means of such a mechanistic and materialistic idea as natural selection—figuring he was in enough trouble already!

4. However, I suspect that a more important factor may have been involved. Teilhard was trained in France, years before the Neo-Darwinian Synthesis and at a time when biologists had accepted the fact of evolution, but were, in many quarters, still unconvinced that Darwin was right about selection being its primary mechanism. In particular, Continental workers, and especially the French, were more skeptical about Darwinian selection, than were most Anglo-American biologists of that day. Starting about 1888, France became the bastion of the wrongly-so-called "neo-Lamarckian" ideas, meaning belief in the inheritance of acquired characteristics as opposed to Darwinian selection. Lamarck himself, significantly, was French, whereas Darwin was British. France was also home to the vitalistic philosophy of Henri Bergson.

This French skepticism toward Darwin is well documented. Ernst Mayr,[4] himself a major architect of the evolutionary synthesis along wih Simpson and others, described France as "the only major scientific nation that did not contribute significantly" to the synthesis. The French biologist Ernest Boesiger[5] admitted that "France today (1974) is a kind of living fossil in the rejection of modern evolutionary theories: about 95 percent of all biologists and philosophers are more or less opposed to Darwinism." (Fortunately, this no longer seems to be so much the case in our own day.) Boesiger provided some analysis of the historical, philosophical, and sociological causes of this rejection; and he went on to say,[6] concerning the early twentieth century, that "All French biologists were very heavily and directly influenced by Bergson. Arguments derived directly from Bergson occur in the writings of Grassé, Cuénot, Vandel, and even Teilhard de Chardin." Another biologist, Camille Limoges,[7] did not put all the blame on Bergson, but agreed that "the spiritualist overtones of even the most rationalist of French philosophers created an intellectual environment uncongenial to a Darwinian approach." Limoges[8] concluded that from about 1903 to 1933, "there seems to have been no Darwinian biologist in France."

From our modern viewpoint, Teilhard's biology is certainly dated. The discredited notion of orthogenesis looms large in his evolutionary writings, and his stress on the psychic "inwardness" of matter, and especially of life, parallels the vitalism that long pervaded France. Yet he did not follow some of his countrymen in dismissing Darwin out of hand. A footnote in *The Phenomenon of Man*[9] addresses this issue directly:

> In various quarters I shall be accused of showing too Lamarckian a bent in the explanations which follow, of giving an exaggerated influence to the *Within* in the organic arrangement of bodies. But be pleased to remember that, in the "morphogenetic" action of instinct as here understood, an essential part is left to the Darwinian play of external forces and to chance. It is only really through strokes of chance that life proceeds, but strokes of chance which are recognized and grasped—that is to say, psychically selected. Properly understood the "anti-chance" of the Neo-Lamarckian is not the mere negation of Darwinian chance. On the contrary, it appears as its utilisation. There is a functional complementariness between the two factors; we could call it "symbiosis."
>
> It may be added that if we give its proper place to the essential distinction (still too often ignored) between a biology of small units and a biology of big complexes—in the same way as there is a physics of the infinitesimal and another of the immense—we appreciate the advisability of distinguishing two major zones of the organic world, and treating them differently. On the one hand, is the Lamarckian zone of very big complexes (above all, man) in which anti-chance can be seen to dominate; on the other hand, the Darwinian zone of small complexes, lower forms of life, in which anti-chance is so swamped by chance that it can only be appreciated by reasoning and conjecture, that is to say, indirectly.

So (if I read him correctly), Teilhard was trying to bridge these contrary views by recognizing that evolution on the human, cultural level is "Lamarckian," but freely conceding evolution on the lower, most basic levels to Darwinian mechanisms. In reserving a role for the "Within" while admitting that this is not empirically observable on these lower levels, he avoids a philosophical infringement on the domain of natural science. The point on which I would fault him, however, is his thinking of "anti-chance" factors in evolution too narrowly, as being only, or most importantly, the action of this mysterious, vaguely-described psychic "Within." To us Neo-Darwinians, natural selection plays the necessary and sufficient anti-chance role in evolution, all the way up to the dawn of culture. What Teilhard failed to realize was that a rigorous insistence on this mechanistic principle would not exclude the spiritual dimension; on the contrary, it would clarify some problems to which spiritual factors by themselves gave no satisfactory answer (such as evil and original sin).

In short, Teilhard's background was not conducive to enthusiasm for the Neo-Darwinian synthesis that was developing during his mature years, and given that a mechanistic emphasis on selection was a natural position for atheistic materialists to adopt, it is not surprising that he seemed to keep this concept at arm's length. Had it not been for this Gallic disinclination toward Neo-Darwinism, together with the suppression of his theologizing by church authorities, he might have examined natural selection more closely, and perhaps he might have put it to more constructive use in solving the "Problem of Evil" with which he struggled. Instead, it took more than thirty years after Teilhard's death for Catholic theologians such as John Haught, Denis Edwards, and others to become fully at ease with the mechanistic aspects of Neo-Darwinian theory, and to see that they are not necessarily incompatible with Christian belief, but actually complementary to it.

Although the views of these contemporary "evolutionary theologians" differ in detail concerning the theological inferences to be drawn, they agree in broadly accepting the scientific consensus about how evolution itself operates. My own view[10] of the theological implications is straightforward: it is an incontrovertible fact of science that the origin of our present material world involved an immensely long and still-continuing process of organic evolution. The only way known to science by which complex organisms like ourselves could have been brought forth from the simplest "living" arrangements of matter is through Darwinian natural selection acting on genetic variation. This variation arises ultimately from random copying errors or "mutations" in the genetic material (errors that in most cases harm the organism and thus qualify as a form of "physical evil"). Such a process necessarily enforced on all evolving organisms, and encoded into their genomes, behavior patterns that are ordered to self-preservation and self-reproduction. In "higher" animals, including ourselves, these self-centered, or "selfish," survival mechanisms became reinforced by learned, cultural behaviors. In self-consciously intelligent (and therefore morally responsible) agents such as humans, this heritage of genetic and cultural self-ishness inevitably takes the form of the universal inclination to moral evil (deliberately selfish behavior) that Christians have called "original sin." In bringing forth moral agents from a material universe, therefore, the Creator evidently had no alternative to creating ones that would be congenitally inclined to sin. If, however, the goal of this Creator is moral agents who reject sin and behave unselfishly—as Christian theologians agree—then the idea of God becoming incarnate in order to reveal to us an alternative approach to life (one that offers otherwise-unattainable salvation from the Darwinian rat-race) becomes logically intelligible.

In short, the Creator's decision to create moral agents out of matter and through a material process inescapably entailed for them the constraints inherent in matter—in particular, the need to compete in order to survive and evolve—and their consequent congenital selfishness. There was no way to avoid the tension between this limitation of any material creation, on the one hand, and the destiny God willed for us on the spiritual plane. This tension could only be resolved by making us conscious of the need to put aside the selfish survival mechanisms that made us what we are, and taking the new path toward what we are to become.

Teilhard grasped much of this in general outline, but failed to complete the chain of logic: he did not see the evolutionary continuity between the unavoidable physical "evil" (but occasional, indispensable benefit) of errors in copying the genetic material, combined with the unavoidable "evil" of the struggle for survival, and on the other hand the moral evil produced by the selfishness that is our Darwinian legacy. Moral evil has literally evolved out of physical "evil," and it could not have been otherwise. Only by grasping this truth can the philosophical "Problem of Evil" and the riddle of theodicy be solved. Teilhard intuited that, in an evolutionary universe,

> The problem (the intellectual problem) of evil disappears. In this picture, physical suffering and moral transgressions are inevitably introduced into the world not because of some deficiency in the creative act but by the very structure of participated being: in other words they are introduced as the *statistically inevitable by-product* of the unification of the multiple. In consequence they contradict neither the power of God nor his goodness. Is the game worth the candle? Everything depends on the *final* value and beatitude of the universe—a point on which we may well trust ourselves to God's wisdom.

> [Footnote] In a general way, this amounts to saying that the problem of evil, insoluble in the case of a static universe (i.e. a "cosmos"), no longer arises in

the case of a (multiple) evolutive universe (i.e. a cosmogenesis). It is strange that so simple a truth should still be so little perceived and stated.[11]

In order, however, to actually "derive the equation" and lay out all the steps in the argument summarized above, Teilhard would have had to attend to the messy details of evolution, not just its grand outlines, because here, truly, both God and the devil are in the details. He would have had to see something supremely *constructive* in the nuts and bolts of the process—not just the regrettable entropy that leads to degeneration (but also yields all the beneficial mutations that occur), not just the destructive mayhem of natural selection (but also the progress that can come about in no other way).

The difficulty in perceiving this is the great stumbling block for those who would walk the path between evolution and theology, in either direction. Special creationists and atheistic evolutionists alike are unable to reconcile the sufferings implicit in the Darwinian process with a God both good and omnipotent. Both make the mistake of thinking the Creator had other options besides putting us through the travail of entropy, mutation, and selection; but science reveals no other alternative in a material universe ruled by known laws. If only they would take the science at face value, and then notice that the tension between evolutionary selfishness and salvific selflessness is just what the Bible portrays throughout salvation history—for example, in Romans 7:22-23: "My inner self agrees with the law of God, but I see in my body's members [read: in the biologically inherited sources of my behavior] another law at war with the law of my mind; this makes me the prisoner of the law of sin in my members."

Evolutionary theology in the Christian community today both embraces Darwin and traces its descent through Teilhard's pioneering efforts. It has yet to succeed, though, in winning over the adherents of creationism, including the latter's most recent reincarnation as "Intelligent Design" (ID). It is worth examining why this is so. Obviously, fundamentalists who adhere to Genesis 1-3 as literal history will always reject evolution out of hand. But numerous Christians and others who are not committed to biblical literalism nonetheless recoil, if not from the fact of evolution, then at least from the mechanism Darwin proposed to explain it. A good God, they feel, would simply not have created by the cruel means of mutation and natural selection; hence, God is either cruel or nonexistent, and a universe governed by cruel chance makes our existence meaningless. These understandable existential concerns, and not alleged flaws in evolutionary science, are the true roots of the endless creation-evolution controversy: many well-meaning people look at the picture of the world presented by evolutionists, and honestly can see no hope of reconciling it with their natural desire for meaning and hope in this world, much less God and an afterlife.[12]

A notable example of this discomfort with evolution among even non-fundamentalist Christians is the affinity for ID felt by many conservative Roman Catholics—right up to the top of the hierarchy. In a seminar on "Creation and Evolution" that Pope Benedict XVI held with some of his former theology students in 2006, most of the participants (including the pope but especially Cardinal Christoph Schönborn of Vienna) expressed some degree of reluctance to accept the clear consensus of science about how evolution works.[13] This is plainly a reflection of the Neo-Scholastic philosophy these senior churchmen learned in their seminary days—in particular, the ancient Aristotelian notion of unchanging "essences" of things, including living things. This essentialist view, which almost precludes a grasp of the modern evolutionary paradigm, leads them to entertain as logical possibilities only the polar opposites of atheistic materialism and divine intervention in natural processes (today's ID). It is, in short, the static view of the cosmos that Teilhard criticized in the quotation above.

But Teilhard, still viewed askance in Rome, was scarcely mentioned by the seminar participants. Worse, they do not even seem aware of the growing body of Catholic literature on evolutionary theology. This new school of thought presents a detailed version of noninterventionist theistic evolution, and envisions a truly autonomous creation, without inherent "purpose" discernible by empirical science, yet nonetheless accomplishing the purposes of its Creator. Among Pope Benedict's circle, alas, this idea simply does not compute: the appearance of life, humanity, and an unstated amount of organic change besides, *must* have been due to God's direct intervention. As a result, their reaction to the attacks on religion of atheists like Richard Dawkins is to move toward ID, an idea that is two centuries out of date.

Such outmoded thinking survives, I repeat, because the alternative *seems* to be rejection of God and religion. Although essentialist natural philosophy (like biblical literalism) largely rules out *a priori* any significant degree of evolution, adherents of this philosophy might be more willing to reconsider this position if they became familiar with the demonstrations that evolutionary theology does not threaten the essentials of their faith. Teilhard certainly felt this way, and the field has come still farther in this direction in the half-century since his death. It is time for the Christian community and its leaders to take a careful look at this new way of thinking about God's creation.

Notes

1. Professor of Anatomy, College of Medicine, Howard University, Washington, DC 20059.

2. G. G. Simpson, *Concessions to the Improbable: An Unconventional Autobiography* (New Haven and London: Yale University Press, 1978), 137.

3. Daryl P. Domning. "Evolution, evil and original sin: putting the puzzle together," *America* 185, no. 15 (2001): 14-21; D. P. Domning and M. K. Hellwig, *Original Selfishness; Original Sin and Evil in the Light of Evolution* (Aldershot, UK: Ashgate, 2006).

4. E. Mayr and W. B. Provine, eds., *The Evolutionary Synthesis: Perspectives on the Unification of Biology* (Cambridge: Harvard University Press, 1980), 309.

5. E. Boesiger, "Evolutionary Biology in France at the Time of the Evolutionary Synthesis," in Mayr and Provine, *The Evolutionary Synthesis*, 309-21, at 309.

6. Ibid., 314.

7. C. Limoges, "A Second Glance at Evolutionary Biology in France," 322-28, in Mayr and Provine, *The Evolutionary Synthesis*, 322-28, at 326.

8. Ibid., 324.

9. Pierre Teilhard de Chardin, *The Phenomenon of Man*, trans. Bernard Wall (New York: Harper & Row, 1965), 149-50 n.

10. Domning and Hellwig.

11. Pierre Teilhard de Chardin, *Christianity and Evolution* (New York: Harcourt Brace & Co., 1971), 196; emphasis in original.

12. See, for example, R. T. Pennock, "Naturalism, creationism and the meaning of life: the case of Philip Johnson revisited." *Creation/Evolution* 16, no. 2 (1997): 10-30.

13. S. O. Horn and S. Wiedenhofer, compilers, *Creation and Evolution: A Conference with Pope Benedict XVI in Castel Gandolfo* (San Francisco: Ignatius Press, 2008); reviewed by D. P. Domning, Reports of the *National Center for Science Education*, 28, no. 3 (2008): 25-27.

TEILHARD'S SCIENCE
OF THE BIOSPHERE

INTRODUCTION

Since the dawn of the theory of evolution, life on Earth has been characterized by continual and irreversible change due in part to non-deterministic mechanisms that give rise to new species and forms. Some evidence even suggests that life has gradually but surely been evolving towards greater complexification and diversification. Although a continual and irreversible evolution in time is well established, the mechanisms of evolution are still a matter of investigation, as is the question as to whether there is evidence for a direction towards greater complexity in evolution. In this paper, I review the work of Teilhard and others who, like him, find it necessary to study evolution on the macrocosmic scale in order to engage these questions.

NATURAL SELECTION AND THE PROBLEM OF CHANCE

The mechanisms of evolution accepted by the large majority of scientists are based on the theory of natural selection proposed in the second half of the nineteenth century by Charles Robert Darwin and Alfred Russell Wallace.[2] Darwin and Wallace noted that in spite of the tendency of the number of individuals in a species to increase in number according to a geometrical ratio, this number actually remains quite constant. From this they deduced that life struggles for survival.[3] They also noted that individuals of a species vary appreciably and that these variations are inheritable. Thus they proposed the theory of natural selection:

> Since there is a struggle for existence among individuals, and since these indi-
> viduals are not all alike, some of the variations among them will be
> advantageous in the struggle for survival, others unfavourable. Consequently,
> a higher proportion of individuals with favourable variations will on the
> average survive; a higher proportion of those with unfavourable variations will
> die or fail to reproduce themselves. And since a great deal of variation is trans-
> mitted by heredity, these effects will in large measure accumulate from
> generation to generation. Thus natural selection will act constantly to improve
> and to maintain the adjustment of animals and plants to their surroundings
> and their way of life.[4]

The modern synthesis, Darwin's theory as revised in the first half of the twentieth century, harmonizes the concepts of natural selection and Mendel's discovery of genetics with chromosomal theory and population genetics. This was considered, at least during the 1960s, the only approach that could explain the mechanisms of evolution. As a matter of fact, because of the findings of molecular biology, that is, the discovery of the double helix structure of DNA and the theory of mutations, many of these mechanisms have been confirmed.[5] As a consequence, many scientists find that this legitimizes the belief that the cosmic landscape is governed by impersonal evolutionary mechanisms and devoid of a general plan.

In his book *Variations of Plants and Animals under Domestication*,[6] Darwin compares natural selection to an architect who is asked to use the stones at the foot of a landslide to build a house. The shape and position of the stones are the result of chance, of the composition of the rocks, of the various agents acting on the rocks, and of the hits received by the falling stones. However, the architect is not using the stones randomly. Instead, he tries to make best use of them, placing them in the most suitable positions. In this example, two different chains of causation operate. Stone diversity represents the variability of the individuals of a species; the architect represents natural selection, the ordering factor on this variability. In the theory of natural selection, then, it is impossible to find a continuing chain of deterministic causes. From these aspects come all the causal interpretations of nature and evolution that have strongly influenced natural philosophy from Darwin to Monod[7] and to Dawkins.[8] Nature becomes the field of action for mechanisms strongly based on chance.[9]

THEORIES OF EVOLUTION: COMPLEXITY AND BIOSPHERE THEORY

The theory of natural selection considers changes in the frequency of the genes, generation after generation, at the level of the population. An alternate approach is to apply the science of complexity and to look at the biosphere as a whole in order to understand fully the evolutive mechanisms, especially those that are hidden at the population level. In this approach to evolution, called Biosphere Theory,[10] living things are described not only by the quality and quantity of their components but also by the interrelationships of component parts.[11] Information such as this is lost whenever an object is studied by separating it from its context. Biosphere Theory, then, is more holistic, since it takes into account more than the micro-level.

Austrian geologist Eduard Suess first proposed the term, biosphere, adding this envelope of living beings to the well-known envelopes surrounding our globe: the atmosphere, the lithosphere, and the hydrosphere. His was one of the first attempts to view our planet globally, considering not only its components but also their interconnections and interrelationships. However, the idea of the biosphere can be traced to English geologist James Hutton and to Italian geologist Antonio Stoppani, founder of modern Italian geology. Later it was developed by Russian geochemist Vladimir Vernadsky[12] and French Jesuit paleontologist Pierre Teilhard de Chardin.[13] Hutton suggested establishing the discipline of geophysiology, a field intended to study the Earth as a single organism. Hutton noted that geophysiology could be useful as a science for the Earth, just as physiology is helpful to the study of animals and plants.

During the same period, Stoppani noted that while Earth's geological history is a history of continual change, some of Earth's physical parameters, such as seawater salinity, are stable. Aware of the effect that living beings have on geological activity, he developed the idea that, like the atmosphere, the envelope of living beings can affect geological phenomena. Therefore, he attempted to develop a theory that synthesized evolutionary processes with forces that maintain the biosphere's steady state, defining the biosphere from the perspective of stability.[14]

It became clear that life is responsible for the dynamic mechanisms of homeostasis that are able to maintain the stability of the parameters allowing its own survival. This global perspective was a completely new way of thinking about the relationship between living and nonliving things. Despite its novel approach, Biosphere Theory had no immediate resonance. However, by the early

1920s, the idea returned with two distinct interpretations proposed by Russian geochemist Vladimir Vernadsky and French paleontologist Pierre Teilhard de Chardin.

Vernadsky and the Biosphere as a Thermodynamic Machine

According to Vernadsky, the biosphere is not limited to the living envelope surrounding Earth, but extends to all the nonliving components that are linked to and related to the continuing activity of life. Vernadsky viewed the biosphere as a kind of energy converter, a gigantic thermodynamic machine,[15] linking Earth and Sun,[16] transforming solar energy into forms useful to the terrestrial globe. The presence of life provides a more organic vision of the relation between life and the rest of matter, and differentiates it from other known celestial bodies.

According to Vernadsky, the traditional vision of the science of life is incomplete. Neither vitalism nor mechanicism is useful when viewing life at the level of the biosphere. Instead, a scientific and empirical description of the mechanisms at work in the biosphere as a whole, where life is not reducible to its physical and chemical components, is needed. Likewise, a purely chemical and physical treatment of the components of Earth is insufficient. When life is observed and studied in its totality, mechanisms related to chance become less evident while order and regularities become more evident. Living beings populating Earth are seen as the result of a complex cosmic process, characterized both by order and necessity. Nothing is due purely to chance.

The new science of the biosphere clearly emerges in Vernadsky's approach. He described the movement of the chemical elements in the biosphere, their cycles, and the ways that cosmic energy is processed. He also tried to investigate models to explain these mechanisms, proposing instead a new field of science, geochemistry of the biosphere. His books and papers were published outside the Soviet Union, and slowly became the basis for the science of the biosphere, at least from the viewpoint of physics and chemistry. In the early 1920s, while teaching geochemistry at the Sorbonne, Vernadsky met Teilhard and his friend, philosopher Édouard Le Roy. Starting from different premises and impacted by different cultural and philosophical milieus, these three found that they had reached similar conclusions. Undoubtedly, these thinkers, who during that time also proposed the concept of the noosphere, influenced each other profoundly.

TEILHARD DE CHARDIN AND THE
BIOSPHERE AS A WHOLE EVOLVING OBJECT

Like Vernadsky, Teilhard developed a theory of the biosphere side by side with his theory of biological complexity. Because the reductionist approach refused to investigate the general tendencies of evolution and to describe them with general laws, Teilhard looked for a different approach to evolution, one that was general and global, in order to discover those hidden mechanisms that are responsible for the general movement of evolution. In fact, he attempted to establish a new branch of science called geobiology, devoted to the study of the evolution of living beings in their environmental context on a large scale and over a long period of time.[17] His scientific research program would not only include the Darwinian mechanisms of evolution, but also search for the general laws characterizing the evolution of matter and of life that might demonstrate the mechanisms involved in the rise of the thought. The result was the science of biological complexity which he attempted to define in 1926.

> I would be strongly tempted to introduce at the origin of its branches, its rami-
> fications, biological mechanisms of a special order whose subject would be not
> individuals but the more or less important parts of the Biosphere. In all
> sciences, it seems to me that we give in too readily to the illusion that all
> phenomena can be represented on the microscale, or explainable by their
> constituent elements alone. But it is only in geometry that figures keep their
> properties as they become smaller. The natural groups of living things ought
> to have properties which are missing when living things are taken in isolation.
> I call for a biology of the Biosphere—just as we are beginning to have a
> chemistry of the lithosphere.[18]

The field of geobiology relies on two assumptions: first, that all the living beings taken as a whole form a single system bound to the surface of Earth where the elements are organically interdependent; and, second, that this organic system is physically inseparable from Earth. Geobiologists investigate the internal functioning of the biosphere and, at the same time, determine the functional and structural place it occupies within the system of the other terrestrial envelopes, always aiming to discover the laws that permit a continual movement towards complexity, life, and consciousness. Towards the end of his stay in China, Teilhard and his collaborators were able to apply geobiological methods to many animal groups on a continental scale and to reproduce without distortion evolutionary patterns.[19]

The result of Teilhard's paleontological research was the discovery within the fossil record, seen over a long period of time and on a continental scale, of parallelisms and canalizations that were, in his view, evidence that evolution was mainly a moving towards complexity and consciousness.[20] He describes his insight using a landscape metaphor. Like a river that traces its course through a landscape of hills and valleys, life experiences many forces. The interaction of these forces is responsible for the phenomenon of co-evolution. Not only does the river's flow respond to the landscape, the river's very act of flowing changes the landscape. The river is not going everywhere, submitting only to the rules of chance, but it is moving towards, according, at least, to the law of gravity. He cautions, however, that evidence for this "moving towards" can be seen only at the level of the biosphere.[21] On this level rather than on the microscopic level, evolution can be characterized more by convergence than by dispersion.

Two recent paleontologists, Mark McMenamin[22] and Simon Conway Morris,[23] also support parallelism. Both claim that evolution is characterized by convergence. They note how at many times and in many places similar structures have evolved independently. One of the most famous examples of convergent evolution is that of the saber–tooth tiger. This mammal is characterized by giant canines, a very peculiar morphological evolution of the tooth structure. Yet, in spite of their peculiarity, giant canines evolved independently in both marsupial and placental mammals.

THE BIOSPHERE AS A CONTROL SYSTEM

James Lovelock[24] and Lynn Margulis have recently reworked biosphero-centric theory.[25] English scientist James Lovelock[26] proposed a theory to explain the stability of the biosphere that is curiously reminiscent of Stoppani's theory and a development of the theory proposed by Vernadsky and Teilhard. For Lovelock, the biosphere resembles an organism rather than a machine because even though its components are in constant flux, it is able to adjust to external changes and to actively maintain the parameters suitable for life. Moreover, it uses external energy to maintain some of these parameters far from thermody-namic equilibrium.[27] For instance, despite fluctuations in solar radiation, the parameters necessary for life's survival, such as atmospheric temperature, oxygen and carbon dioxide levels in the atmosphere, and seawater salinity remain rela-tively constant. In Lovelock's view, life is no longer seen as laboriously attempting to adapt to a continually changing environment. On the contrary, at the global level, living things taken as a whole actively maintain an environment suitable for survival. Just as a mammal is able to adjust its metabolism in order to respond to an external change in temperature and thus stabilize its internal temperature, so the biosphere is able to respond to outside forces in order to stabilize those parameters that allow life to survive. Thus, its behavior is like that of an organism. Lovelock calls this particular interpretation of biosphere activity the Gaia hypothesis.

Biospheric stability is a powerful new concept for evolution. In fact, the maintenance of dynamic stability becomes the main task of the biosphere. From this perspective, evolution is no longer a matter of competition and survival of the fittest alone. Rather, co-operation and symbiosis aid in preserving stability and nurturing life. Furthermore, the links between humanity and other species are links based not only on generation and dependence, but also on cooperation and symbiosis.[28]

According to the Gaia hypothesis, living and nonliving beings are related at the planetary level by negative feedback that maintains Earth's stability. Feedback is present in a chain of reactions in which the final product influences one or more of the previous passages. For instance, consider a chain reaction where A produces B, B produces C, C produces D, and D is able to interact with one of the previous steps in the chain, for instance from A to B. If the feedback is positive, the production of D will increase the production of B from A. This will increase the production of C from B and of D from C. And the increased production of D will again increase the production of B. Soon, we will have an overproduction of D and an exhaustion of A, and the system will collapse.

On the contrary, if the feedback is negative, the production of D will lower the production of B from A. In this case, whenever D's production is lowered, B's is increased and vice versa. This will cause a fluctuation about a stability parameter and avoid any collapse. Negative feedback encourages system stability. After Lovelock proposed his hypothesis, many investigations were carried out in order to determine the chains of negative feedback responsible for the stability of the parameters. Here, I present a simple example from the study of the stability in carbon dioxide content in the atmosphere to illustrate the kind of research program used by the Gaia hypothesis.

Carbon dioxide is a molecule that is produced both by respiration and by geological processes and, when diffused in the atmosphere, has the peculiar characteristic of allowing the passage of incoming solar energy while blocking the escape of heat. However, an excess of carbon dioxide causes the atmosphere to act like a greenhouse with a resultant rise in temperature. Despite this fact, the level of carbon dioxide and the temperature of the atmosphere have remained quite constant over both geological and historical time. According to the Gaia hypothesis, the reason for this is negative feedback involved in the carbon dioxide cycle. When the level of carbon dioxide in the atmosphere rises, the temperature also rises. But this causes the temperature in the temperate zones to rise both on the ground and in the oceans. The diffusion of warmer air throughout the temperate zone causes, in turn, a rise in the quantity of biomass in the biosphere, both green plankton in the waters and terrestrial plants. As a consequence of the increase in photosynthesis, carbon dioxide is removed and oxygen is produced. Since removing carbon dioxide implies a diminution in the greenhouse effect, the temperature drops due to negative feedback.

The biosphere is normally very resilient, able to return to a steady state after experiencing external or internal perturbations. However, Teilhard notes that the biosphere, like every complex object, is subject to threshold effects, that is, to continual and slow changes that can sometimes give rise to rapid and unforeseeable events of a catastrophic level. This is one of the applications where René Thom's catastrophe theory might be applied to link mass extinction with disequilibria.[29] According to catastrophe theory, for a system near the boundaries of the steady state, a small perturbation can have catastrophic effects. Thus, many present–day changes in the steady state parameters of the biosphere could drive the biosphere past a critical threshold.

Symbiosis is a set of ecological interactions between organisms due to the protracted physical associations of one or more members of different species. Symbiotic partnerships may be loosely or exceedingly tightly integrated on the behavioral, the metabolic (trophic), the gene product, or the genetic level. These relationships are not causal. However, they are significant to the wellbeing or the lack of wellbeing of one or both of the participants.

According to a proposal by Lynn Margulis,[30] symbiosis is one of the most important and diffused mechanisms of evolution. It is the mechanism that allowed cells to pass the threshold from prokaryotic and eukaryotic. It is also the main mechanism that allows life to survive in extreme environments. The colonization of an environment as hostile to life as that of the hydrothermal vents is possible, due to symbiosis between chemotrophic bacteria, some of which are endocellular symbiotic organisms, and their autotrophic host animals.

CONCLUSION

Two divergent attitudes regarding the process of evolution coexist in today's world. The first considers evolutionary mechanisms as strongly nondeterministic and views humanity as one of the possibilities arising from chance events. The second looks to the mechanisms for hints of a "moving towards" and for the scientific laws explaining them. In this view, humankind is the probable result of these laws of evolution. Although Teilhard knew nothing about complexity theory as it is practiced today, he pioneered this second view. His evidence for direction in the universe did not come primarily from theological considerations. Instead, it arose from his work as a paleontologist. He found that, rather than being characterized by dispersion and random diversification, the patterns embedded in the fossils that he discovered display canalizations and parallelisms. However, he did not limit himself to describing these patterns. Rather, he suggested that the mechanisms responsible for these patterns be investigated. However, in order to develop this approach, it was necessary to transcend the reductionist methods practiced by followers of the modern synthesis. He needed to develop a more holistic approach. It is for this reason that Teilhard suggested developing the science of geobiology, a science of the evolution of the biosphere. As more paleontological evidence for evolution is discovered, it might well be that Teilhard's hypothesis for direction in evolution will be better substantiated.

Notes

1. Professor of Biology, Università di Pisa; Dipartimento di Chimica e Biotecnologie agrarie, Pisa, Italy.
2. As summarised by J. Huxley, *Evolution: The Modern Synthesis* (London: Allen and Unwin, 1942).
3. This deduction was derived from the work of Thomas R. Malthus, *An Essay on the Principle of Population* (1798; Oxford: Oxford University Press, 1993).
4. Huxley, *Evolution*, 14.
5. E. Mayr and W. B. Provine, eds., *The Evolutionary Synthesis: Perspectives on the Unification of Biology* (Cambridge: Harvard University Press, 1980).
6. Charles R. Darwin, *Variations of Plants and Animals Under Domestication* (London: Murray, 1868). This metaphor is summarized in St. George Mivart, *On the genesis of species* (London: MacMillan, 1871), 254-55.
7. J. Monod, *Le Hasard et la nécessite, essai sur la philosophie naturelle de la biologie moderne* (Paris: Le Seuil, 1970).
8. Richard Dawkins, *The Blind Watchmaker* (London: Longman, 1986).
9. This is clearly stated in the second half of the twentieth century by J. Monod in his revision of Darwinism made on the basis of molecular biology.
10. C. H. Waddington, *Tools for Thought* (London: Paladin, 1977).

11. A synthesis of the theory is presented in Ludovico Galleni, "Is Biosphere Doing Theology?" *Zygon: The Journal of Religion and Science* 36 (2001): 33-48.

12. J. Grinewald, "A History of the Idea of the Biopshere," in P. Bunyard and E. Goldsmith, eds., *Gaia: The Thesis, the Mechanisms and the Implications,* (Wadebridge: Quintrell, 1988).

13. Ludovico Galleni, "How does the Teilhardian vision of evolution compare with contemporary theories?" *Zygon: The Journal of Religion and Science* 30 (1995): 23-43.

14. A. Stoppani, *Acqua ed Aria, ossia la purezza del mare e dell'atmosfera fin dai primordi del mondo animato* (Milano: Hoepli, 1882).

15. M. Lamotte, *Théorie actuelle de l'évolution* (Paris: Hachette, 1994).

16. Vladimir Vernadsky, "The Biosphere and the Noosphere," *American Scientist* 33 (1945): 1-12.

17. Ludovico Galleni, "How does the Teilhardian vision of evolution compare with contemporary theories?" 29.

18. The original French text is, "Je serais fort tenté de faire intervenir, aux naissances de branches, aux fourches, des causes biologiques, d'un ordre spécial, dont le sujet serait, non pas les individus, mais des fractions plus ou moins importantes de la Biosphère. En toutes sciences, il me semble que nous cédons beaucoup trop à l'illusion que tous les phénomènes sont représentables en petit, ou explicable par les seuls éléments. Mais il n'y a qu'en géométrie que les figures gardent leurs propriétés en diminuant ! Les blocs naturels des vivants doivent avoir des propriétés qui manquent aux vivants pris isolément—J'appelle de mes vœux une Biologie de la Biosphère—comme il commence à y avoir une Chimie de la Lithosphère." Pierre Teilhard de Chardin, "Lettres inédites à un savant de ses amis," *Christus* 54 (1967): 238-58, at 251.

19. For a detailed reconstruction of the scientific research program of Teilhard de Chardin see L. Galleni and M. C. Groessens-Van Dyck, "Lettres d'un Paléontologue: Neuf lettres inédites de Pierre Teilhard de Chardin à Marcellin Boule," *Revue des Questions Scientifiques* 172 (2001): 3-104.

20. Pierre Teilhard de Chardin, *Le phénomène humain* (Paris: Seuil, 1955).

21. Pierre Teilhard de Chardin, *The Vision of the Past*, trans. J. M. Cohen (New York: Harper & Row, Publishers, 1966), 272.

22. Mark McMenamin, *The Garden of Ediacara* (New York: Columbia University Press, 1998).

23. Simon Conway Morris, *The Crucible of Creation* (Oxford: Oxford University Press, 1998).

24. James Lovelock, "Geophysiology: The Science of Gaia," in S. H. Schneider and P. J. Boston, eds., *Scientists on Gaia* (Cambridge, MA: MIT Press, 1991), 3-10.

25. L. Margulis, "Symbiogenesis and Symbioticisms," in L. Margulis and R. Fester, eds., *Symbiosis as a Source of Evolutionary Innovation* (Cambridge: MIT Press, 1991), 1-14.

26. James Lovelock, *Gaia: a New Look at Life on Earth* (Oxford: Oxford University Press, 1979); James Lovelock, *The Ages of Gaia: A Biography of Our Living Earth* (London: W. W. Norton, 1988).

27. The term, far from thermodynamic equilibrium, means that concentrations of some components of the atmosphere, mainly oxygen and methane, are in excess with respect to the chemical equilibrium concentration.

28. Margulis, "Symbiogenesis and Symbioticisms," 1-14.

29. V. Benci and L. Galleni, *Stability and Instability in Evolution*, J. theor. Biol. (1998): 541-49.

30. Margulis, "Symbiogenesis and Symbioticisms," 1-14.

GEOLOGY AND GRACE:
TEILHARD'S LIFE AND ACHIEVEMENTS[1]

JAMES W. SKEHAN, S.J.[2]

Marie Joseph Pierre Teilhard de Chardin, better known today by his family name, Teilhard de Chardin, was born May 1, 1881 in Auvergne, a province in central France that is distinguished by the presence of numerous young volcanoes. The family château, Sarcenat, is located a few miles from the provincial capital, Clermont-Ferrand. Prior to 1955, Teilhard was known in limited academic circles in France, China, and the United States for his geological and paleontological expertise. In even more limited religious circles, he was known for ideas that were labeled controversial and even suspect. In the past half-century, however, the writings of this Jesuit priest, geologist, and mystic have become progressively more widely known, and are no longer under an ecclesiastical cloud of disapproval. In fact, as Teilhard's works became more widely studied, they met with approval by Cardinal De Lubac (1967) and Cardinal Agostino Casaroli writing in the name of Pope John Paul II.[3] Since their appearance in 1955 in French and in 1959 in English, Teilhard's writings, founded as they were, in part, on a modern scientific vision, have reached an ever-widening audience, serving as a source of authentic inspiration.

In this paper I focus on two aspects of this remarkable man: Teilhard as professional geoscientist, and Teilhard as mystic in action. However, I will first explore his early life and activities in the hopes of uncovering those influential "seeds" that were to flower in his later life.

TEILHARD'S EARLY LIFE

Teilhard's mother, Berthe-Adèle de Dompierre d'Hornoy, was a devout Catholic who read the classical writings of the Christian mystics and transmitted her love of the Sacred Heart of Jesus to her son by word and example. As Teilhard wrote in *The Heart of Matter*: "At the age when other children, I imagine, experience their first "feeling" for a person, or for art, or for religion, I was affectionate, good, and even pious: by that I mean that under the influence of my mother, I was devoted to the Child Jesus."[4]

Teilhard's father, Emmanuel Teilhard de Chardin, was a trained archivist-historian, an accomplished amateur naturalist, and an outdoorsman. His own curiosity about and love for the cratered terrain led him to take his children on walking tours of the area. These natural history treks included an examination of deposits formed from hot ashes and molten lava that had erupted in the not-so-distant past. Those ancient events, which produced the cratered volcanic landscape of Teilhard's "front yard," may well have become a source for the images that continued to inspire him throughout his life.

Reflecting on his childhood interests, he recalled

> I was just like any other child [which of course he was not—fortunately!]. I was interested specially in mineralogy and biological observation. I used to love to follow the course of the clouds, and I knew the stars by their names. . . . To my father I owe a certain balance, on which all the rest is built, along with a taste for the exact sciences.[5]

Another important influence on the youthful Teilhard occurred when he was almost eleven years old. As was customary for boys at that age, Teilhard was sent off to be educated by the Jesuit fathers at a boys' boarding school north of Lyons, the École Libre de Notre-Dame de Mongré at Villafranche-sur-Saône, one of the leading French educational institutions for the teaching of the natural sciences. Teilhard has been characterized as "an exemplary, though rather taciturn, even self-absorbed pupil,"[6] who won many of the prizes annually. One of his teachers revealed that he had "learned the secret of his [Teilhard's] seeming indifference."[7] Teilhard's mind was transported "far away from us . . . [by] a jealous and absorbing passion—stones."[8]

Both in the short- and long-term, Teilhard's mother and father, as well as the Jesuit fathers at Mongré, influenced dominant aspects of Teilhard's personality and aspirations. They helped him at an early age to grow toward

---

realizing his potential. In 1901, Teilhard wrote to his parents: "At the moment when [the Society of Jesus in France] is being so severely persecuted . . . I shall never forget all you have done to assist my vocation."[9] Thanks to the influence of these early mentors, Teilhard would subsequently, through the broad spectrum of published scientific research and spirituality, influence his colleagues and the world to a degree that can only be described as monumental.

TEILHARD: JESUIT SCHOLASTIC

A new period in Teilhard's life dawned on March 20, 1899, when, not quite eighteen years old, he began his life as a Jesuit, having been accepted as a novice in the Jesuit house in Aix-en-Provence. This year was doubly significant for Teilhard because Pope Leo XIII consecrated the whole of humanity to the Sacred Heart of Jesus, a devotion that was central to Teilhard's spirituality as well as to that of the whole Jesuit order.

The Jesuit novitiate is a two-year period in which the novice becomes familiar with and is energized by the *Spiritual Exercises* of Ignatius of Loyola, the founder of the Jesuits.[10] This formative period in a young Jesuit's life includes a thirty day retreat during which he prayerfully follows the graduated, devotional, mainly Scripture-based reflections modeled on the "exercises" written by his sainted Founder. Ignatius wrote these exercises when he was undergoing his own conversion experience as he transitioned from a previously dissolute lifestyle to "lighting the fire of dedication and love for his Lord and Savior." Ignatius' adopted name, taken from the Latin root for fire, *ignis*, fired Teilhard's imagination, and inspired the youthful Teilhard whose perspective and mission was dominated by the Ignatian charism. It is likely that Teilhard's own memories of the once fiery volcanoes that were so much a part of his boyhood experience in the mountains of Auvergne may have heightened his attraction to the Ignatian charism. Teilhard took his first vows as a Jesuit on March 25, 1901.

The next phase of Teilhard's Jesuit life included the study of language and literature, notably Latin and Greek, which he obviously enjoyed and in which he excelled in creative ways. These led to his first academic degree from the University of Caen, just as the French government passed laws restricting the activities of religious orders. As a result, Jesuit communities from Laval and elsewhere in France hastily fled France. Teilhard and fellow Jesuit scholastics soon found themselves established on the English Isle of Jersey where they continued their studies in philosophy.

Even before beginning his doctoral studies, Teilhard demonstrated his ability both to focus his energies on a significant geological project and to carry out paleontological and related geological investigations in the field. Along with two Jesuit companions, August Valensin and Pierre Charles, he pursued the study of the complex geology and paleontology of the Isle of Jersey. His results and a map of its geological structure were published in a professional journal in 1920 after Teilhard had mustered out of the French military. Teilhard had prudently deferred publication of his earlier observations on the geology of Jersey until after he had revisited the island to check on the perceived validity of his fledgling, but masterful, observations on the geological relationships of this intricate assemblage of ancient, mainly older than 600 million year old, igneous rocks.

During this period, Teilhard befriended a fellow Jesuit scholastic, Ernest Gherzi, who became for him a scientific colleague. Gherzi was a tall, goateed man of immense good humor, who obviously enjoyed telling how he "saved Teilhard's life" when they were engaged in geological mapping along the chalk cliffs of the English coast while Teilhard was in Hastings for theological studies. Recounting the story in mock seriousness, he reported that, while they were mapping, it was his role to stand back from the cliff where Teilhard was studying the rock formation and collecting fossils and to "save Teilhard's life" by shouting a warning whenever there was danger of a loose block separating from the cliff and falling on the unsuspecting geologist below.

Later, when Teilhard was carrying out his geological and paleontological work in Tientsin and Peking, Gherzi served as a distinguished and famous meteorologist at the Zi-ka-wei Observatory in Shanghai. George Barbour records that, sometime between 1928 and 1929, Father Gherzi was approached by the Director of the China Geological Survey for advice on the appointment to the position of Honorary working Advisor to the Director. Gherzi advised him to appoint Teilhard de Chardin to that important and prestigious post, which he did in 1929. Barbour suggests that Teilhard probably never knew the source of the recommendation for that appointment.[11]

TEILHARD: SCIENCE TEACHER AND RESEARCHER

After his studies in Jersey, Teilhard began his regency, teaching physics and chemistry for three years in the Jesuit Collège de la Sainte-Famille in Cairo, Egypt. In their free time, Teilhard and his companions made many geological excursions into the desert. Teilhard approached this work in a very professional manner. His experience with mapping the complex geology of Jersey had prepared him well for reading the history locked up in the rock formations of northeastern Egypt. When he and his companions returned home with "fantastic fossils," Teilhard studied them and published the results, including descriptions of marine forms which were of special interest to him. One of the specimens found by Teilhard was later named *Teilhardi* after him.[12] Since Teilhard's initial discovery of *Teilhardi*, two additional species have been identified as *Teilhardina americana* and *Teilhardina belgica*. The newly discovered primate genus, *Teilhardina asiatica*, is a tribute to the growing esteem in which Teilhard is held.[13]

Teilhard's expeditions to the region around Cairo and other parts of Egypt are enthusiastically recounted in "Letters from Egypt,"[14] a collection of letters addressed to his father and mother. His father must have been delighted to see how much the fieldtrips that he conducted for Teilhard as a youth in Clermont had inspired his early career.[15]

While in Egypt, Teilhard became acquainted with a number of professional geologists in the region, some of whom took an interest in Teilhard's ability as a geologist and paleontologist. His experience in Egypt had a profound and broadening impact. He recalls, "The East flowed over me in a first wave of exoticism. I gazed at it and drank it eagerly."[16]

THEOLOGICAL STUDIES AND PRIESTHOOD

On Teilhard's return from Egypt, he returned to the study of theology in Hastings, a Medieval English Channel port with seaside cliffs of rock formations rich in fossils. Here, a new field of geological investigation opened up for him, the study of the cliffs of white chalk studded with flint concretions and shells of the Cretaceous age at Sussex Downs near Hastings. Again, he was reunited with his field companion Ernest Gherzi.

Teilhard's class focused on a passage from St. Paul concerning Christ, "All things hold together in Him."[17] This led him to read with great interest both the letters of St. Paul, especially the cosmic hymns contained therein, and the Gospel of St. John, which emphasized the primacy of Christ in whom all creation is grounded. These scripture passages provided a fundamental integrating theme for Teilhard's life and for his writings. Many years later, he recalled how the God who dwells in Nature was never far from his thoughts.

He remembered so vividly

> the extraordinary solidity and intensity I found then in the English countryside, particularly at sunset when the Sussex woods were charged with all that "fossil" Life which I was then hunting for, from cliff to quarry, in the Wealden clay. There were moments, indeed, when it seemed to me that a sort of universal being was about to take shape suddenly in Nature before my very eyes.[18]

Theological studies led to Teilhard's ordination to the priesthood on August 24, 1911. On that otherwise joyful occasion, Teilhard's parents and four brothers wore black as a sign of mourning for his sister, Françoise Teilhard de Chardin, who died that same year in Shanghai.[19] Ursula King insightfully recalls a passage from "The Priest" that Teilhard wrote some years later during World War I that must have served as a theme to strengthen him and others repeatedly in this time of stress and sorrow: "I shall tell those who suffer and mourn that the most direct ways of using our lives is to allow God, when it pleases him so to do, to grow within us, and, through death, to replace us by himself."[20]

STRETCHER BEARER THROUGHOUT WORLD WAR I

In December 1914, Teilhard joined the French army and chose to serve as a medical orderly or stretcher-bearer, which inevitably meant that he would serve mainly at or near the front lines of battle. It has generally been claimed that his regiment was composed of Zouaves and Moroccan Tirailleurs, but Ursula King[21] has recently verified that he served with distinction in an Algerian regiment. For his excellent service he was named Chevalier de la Légion d'Honneur.

Between 1916 and 1919, Teilhard authored eighteen memorable religious essays that contain many of the themes that he would elaborate on at various stages of his life. For instance, "The Priest," a prayerful meditative essay, is often compared with "Mass on the World" which Teilhard completed in 1923 while on a geological expedition in the Ordos Desert of China. These essays were transmitted from time to time for safe keeping to his cousin and confidant, Marguerite Teillard-Chambon. They were eventually assembled in a magnificent volume, *Writings in Time of War*.[22] Commenting on Teilhard's first essay, "Cosmic Life," Marguerite notes that it represents "in embryo all that was later to be developed in his thought."[23]

BRIGHT SKIES AND STORM CLOUDS GATHERING

Teilhard was mustered out of the French Army in 1919 and, shortly after receiving the Ph.D. degree in geology and paleontology, "was appointed to the chair of Geology left vacant by the death of Professor Boussac. This was a position in which he would inevitably rise to the upper echelons in French academic circles."[24]

Since the war, Teilhard "had realized that humankind formed a single whole, a large cosmic reality that far transcended individuals and groups . . . like a dynamic, living organism . . . a network whose threads stretched over the face of the whole earth."[25] "For a time Teilhard called the thinking Earth the anthroposphere, but in 1924," either alone or in conversation with Édouard LeRoy and Vladimir I. Vernadsky, he invented the concept of the noosphere. "Noosphere was to become one of Teilhard's key ideas."[26]

TEILHARD: MATURE JESUIT GEOLOGIST AND MYSTIC

In 1923, Teilhard was sent by the Paris Museum to join Jesuit Émile Licent, Director of the Natural History Museum in Tientsin, China. He and Licent set out on a four-month expedition that was so successful that Teilhard decided to extend his stay into 1924 to allow him to undertake another expedition with Father Licent the following spring in the high Mongolian plateau and along the fringe of the Gobi desert. The manuscript of Teilhard's "Mass on the World" bears the notation "Ordos, 1923." This suggests that on occasion while on the expedition in the Ordos desert, Teilhard prayed his famous prayer of which what follows are but the introductory paragraphs:

> Since once again, Lord—though this time not in the forests of the Aisne [in France] but in the steppes of Asia—I have neither bread, nor wine, nor altar, I will raise myself beyond these symbols, up to the pure majesty of the real itself; I, your priest, will make the whole earth my altar and on it will offer you all the labors and sufferings of the world. Over there, on the horizon, the sun has just touched with light the outermost fringe of the eastern sky. Once again, beneath this moving sheet of fire, the living surface of the earth wakes and trembles, and once again begins its fearful travail. I will place on my paten, O God, the harvest to be won by this renewal of labor. Into my chalice I shall pour all the sap which is to be pressed out this day from the earth's fruits. My paten and my chalice are the depths of a soul laid widely open to all the forces which in a moment will rise up from every corner of the earth and converge upon the Spirit.[27]

CROWNING YEARS OF SCIENTIFIC ACHIEVEMENT AND MYSTICISM

Teilhard's potentially distinguished route to fame in academic circles took a most unexpected turn when, at the urging of a block of French bishops, the Jesuit General sent Teilhard into exile from France. This was a time when any one who dared to speak or write on religious topics would be closely scrutinized by the guardians of "Catholic orthodoxy."[28]

Between 1926 and 1935, Teilhard immersed himself in the challenging task of understanding the geology of China and the surrounding countries of southeastern Asia in collaboration with his Chinese and expatriate European and American colleagues. In addition, he was simultaneously absorbed in developing his approach to an "action-mysticism" that motivated him to an extraordinary degree in his efforts to link his thinking and his scientific work to their long term culmination in "Christ-Omega." He found in George Barbour a soul mate geologist with whom, around a campfire in the evenings after a day of fieldwork, he often discussed his latest ideas about spirituality.

In 1929, the Director of the Geological Survey of China appointed Teilhard to the position of Honorary Advisor to the Director, automatically elevating him to a position of influence in China. This position provided him with the means to carry out significant studies in geology and paleontology. While the position was termed Honorary Advisor, Teilhard was, in fact, very influential in planning major programs of field and laboratory research in geology and paleontology throughout China.

Between the years 1929 and 1935, Teilhard personally participated yearly in several months of field expeditions. Prior to his heart attack on June 1, 1947 and the ensuing period of failing health, he had made a number of visits to important human paleontological sites in southeastern Asia and in Africa that produced an important body of knowledge in both of these related fields.

In the summer of 1929, Teilhard joined his collaborator, George Barbour, on an expedition first along the Yangtze River (South-central China) to the Red River Basin in Szechwan, then across the Tsinling Range from the Yellow River into the Han Basin (South–central China but north of the Yangtze).

Teilhard's influence on the practice of research continued to spread after his appointment as Honorary Advisor to the Director of the Geological Survey of China. Many of the Chinese geologists and paleontologists had been trained in Europe and appreciated the high standards of research that Teilhard maintained in his own work at both the continental and local scale on fundamental aspects of stratigraphy.

The ten volumes of Teilhard's scientific research and an accompanying collection of high quality geological maps, many of them in color, attest to Teilhard's efforts to establish the most rigorous control possible on stratigraphic correlations and relatively precise age–dating methods.[29] This was of particular concern for preparing maps of the various stratigraphic layers and the related determination of the ages of life forms. Maps of subdivisions of Pleistocene deposits over large parts of southeastern Asia, particularly those of Early and Late Pleistocene, are of special interest because such rock formations might be the sites of human fossils.

The geological traverses, each requiring work extending over a period of several months, were in part planned by Teilhard and carried out personally by him and his Chinese and expatriate colleagues. These China expeditions were planned so as to provide reconnaissance over a period of several years on all major parts of China, especially along the principal rivers, as well as detailed information on specific localities such as the famous Chóu-Kóu-Tien site. This is the site where the famous human fossil skull, *Sinanthropos pekinensis*, "Peking man," was discovered.

CHÓU-KÓU-TIEN AND PEKING MAN

With the discovery first of a single, and later of two humanoid or possibly human teeth in 1929 at the Chóu-Kóu-Tien site, Davidson Black, a Canadian and Chair of neurology, embryology and anatomy at the Peiping Union Medical College, spearheaded the effort to establish the Cenozoic Laboratory for exhaustive research on this site. The Laboratory was to be a collaborative research unit under the Chinese Geological Survey supported by the Rockefeller Foundation. Teilhard, one of Black's closest friends and collaborators, served as advisor and collaborator working in Peking at the Lockhart Hall laboratory and at the famous cave site, Chóu-Kóu-Tien. On Black's sudden and untimely death in 1934, Teilhard was asked to serve as Acting Director of the Cenozoic Laboratory until the new Director should arrive from Frankfurt.

Between expeditions, Teilhard visited Peking where he met a number of scientists from various countries. These contacts expanded his horizon and made it attractive and enormously fruitful for him to stay on indefinitely in China, despite the sense that he was a man in exile. It was during this period that he apparently came to see the vast sweep of geology in Asia in a broader perspective than was previously possible. As a result, Teilhard dreamed of coming to understand the tectonic construction of the eastern Asiatic continent, including the vast region of China. It became clear that the accomplishment of this dream would be substantially aided by undertaking lengthy traverses over some of the most difficult terrain in the habitable parts of the earth.

George B. Barbour, who had worked at the Sang-han-ho diggings as early as 1925, was a most astute geomorphologist and stratigrapher, who had taught at Yenching University since 1920, and was arguably Teilhard's most beloved and respected colleague after Black. Barbour was very skillful "in analyzing successive stages of the geology of a region, at finding in it clues to the periods of erosion and of fills, and of connecting these with orogenic or climatic events."[30] Amadeus Grabau, an American, a former professor at Columbia University, a stratigrapher, and a gregarious host of scientists, taught at the Pei-ta, or National University of Peking (father of all of the institutions for natural history, including *Paleontologia Sinica*). He it was who assisted V. K. Ting, who established the Chinese Geological Society and the Museum of Natural History in Peking, and Wen-hao Wong, his colleague, who later succeeded Ting as Director of that organization.[31]

TEILHARD'S STATURE AS A "BRIDGE-BUILDER" AND GEOLOGIST

Teilhard's relationships with the Chinese were consistent with his spirituality. This was particularly important because in 1929, nationalism was on the rise and scientific expeditions began to meet increasing resistance from Chinese authorities. Teilhard notes, "The Chinese have become so suspicious of research by foreigners that every non-Chinese *organization* (even though established in China, like the Licent museum) is looked at askance. *Individual* foreigners on the other hand (like me) are welcome."[32] Even the Geological Survey of China was affected to the point of feeling that it had to take rigorous precautions in dealing with foreign expeditions.

In connection with this growing nationalist feeling on the part of the Chinese, an interesting and instructive letter by Teilhard[33] shows his appreciation for the Chinese people, an attitude that might well serve today to alleviate international and interdenominational tensions if Teilhard's words were to be heeded:

> The end of my stay in Peking has been interesting and busy. I have been to see Sven Hedin [a Swedish scientist]. We had three hours of friendly and even intimate conversation. Hedin is a "most fascinating man" who is obviously lavish with his charm. . . .

When he was getting ready to go to Turkestan in 1926, Hedin came up against Chinese touchiness about rights in scientific material, and he was the first to accept the conditions they insisted on. . . . He was criticized at the time, I know, and disowned by even his best European friends, who accused him of going over to the Chinese.

Just then I met him, and urged him to trust the Chinese and work with them. He is still touchingly grateful to me, as though my words had kept him going during the long months that preceded his success, which is now complete. He now has the full confidence of even the most anti-foreign Chinese, and every single one of those he took with him is now his devoted friend.[34]

Teilhard's early biographer, Claude Cuénot, notes, "The reaction of the Chinese to Teilhard's enlightened attitude to cooperation between East and West was to invite him to exercise general supervision over the Geological Survey."[35] Teilhard's approach to interpersonal and intercultural cooperation is similar to the enlightened approach of Matteo Ricci, the first Jesuit allowed entrance to China in 1583. A mathematician and astronomer, Fr. Ricci was elevated to the rank of Mandarin, and was eventually invited by the Emperor to serve as the Imperial Astronomer. This paved the way for two other Jesuit astronomers to follow in his footsteps as imperial astronomers. Joseph F. MacDonnell, S.J., attributes Ricci's success "to his personal qualities, his complete adaptation to Chinese customs and to his authoritative knowledge of the sciences."[36] Such examples of sensitivity to cultural diversity, so necessary to fruitful working relationships between and among members of the human family, might well be cultivated today, as we attempt to work in a spirit of peace and harmony to "grow" and "build" the Earth.

TEILHARD'S MYSTICISM

Clearly Teilhard's spirituality motivated him to an extraordinary degree, allowing him to accomplish his geological research in the harsh climate conditions and terrain of China, and at the same time to write the sublime compositions that comprise his "new mysticism," a mysticism of action. The essay, "Super-Humanity, Super-Christ, Super-Charity," written in 1943, sums up succinctly a number of the concepts or themes at the heart of Teilhard's "evolutionary" spirituality. These must have been strong sources of motivation giving force to his extraordinary accomplishments in science and spirituality over the years as his thought matured. Teilhard is preoccupied with our "psychological need . . . to love human progress before [we] can dedicate ourselves to it completely." He underscores the point that "the source of a universal love . . . can only come from Christianity, which alone can teach us how to love deeply . . . a universe whose very evolution has been impregnated with love."

> Because everything in the universe is in fact ultimately moving towards Christ-Omega; because cosmogenesis, moving in its totality through anthropogenesis, ultimately shows itself to be a Christogenesis; because of this, I say, it follows that the real is charged with a divine presence in the entirety of its tangible layers. As the mystics knew and felt, everything becomes physically and literally lovable in God; and conversely, God can be possessed and loved in everything around us. . . . I repeat, if the whole movement of the world is in the service of a Christogenesis (which is another way of saying that Christ is attainable in his fullness only at the end and summit of cosmic evolution), *then clearly we can draw near to him and possess him only in and through the effort to bring all to fulfillment and synthesis in him* [emphasis added]. And this is the reason that life's general ascent towards higher consciousness as well as the whole of human endeavor enters organically and by right into the preoccupations and aspirations of charity (divine love).[37]

Teilhard goes on to explain the core of the action-mysticism which underlies his entire thought about the relationship of the Incarnation and, implicitly, the mystery of the Eucharist to all of the spheres of cosmic evolution:

> We have seen that Christ, by reason of his position as Omega of the world, represents a focus towards whom and in whom everything converges. In other words, he appears as One in whom all reality . . . establishes union and contact in the only direction possible: the line of centres. What can this mean except that every action, as soon as it is oriented towards him, takes on, without any change in itself, the psychic character of a centre-to centre relationship, that is to say, of an act of love. . . . At first the Christian aspired only to be able to love . . . *while* acting. Now he [or she] is aware of being able to love in acting, that is to say . . . unite . . . directly to the divine Centre through action itself, no matter what form such action takes. In him all activity is, if I may use the expression, "amorized." . . . There are [those] today . . . among whom the lived conjunction of the two ideas of Incarnation and evolution has led to the creation of a synthesis of the personal and the universal. For the first time in history [humans] have become capable not only of understanding and serving, but of *loving evolution*.[38]

In his lifelong attempt at a synthesis of his progressively evolving thought and spirituality, Teilhard's "new mysticism"[39] is focused simultaneously on love of Christ and on love of the earth (as part of God's creation). Teilhard wanted his twofold whole-hearted and simultaneous love of the God-man and of the earth to be the center of, and to encapsulate, his spirituality. In a letter dated April 15, 1916, Teilhard reflects on this love as follows:

> I have been trying to discover what there could be that is divine and predestined within matter of the cosmos. . . . cannot the object . . . of our human love be transfigured, transferred into the . . . divine? . . . I want to love Christ with all my strength in the very act of loving the universe. . . . Besides a communion with God and a communion with the earth, is there not also a communion with God in and through the earth?[40]

Because Teilhard's language is sometimes both poetic and abstract, his theology may be difficult to extract at times. One also wonders about the source of some of his ideas and themes. Personally, I have become increasingly convinced that some of Teilhard's fundamental themes and insights are found either explicitly or implicitly, and not surprisingly, in the writings of St. Ignatius, one of the greatest mystics of all time,[41] founder of the Jesuit Order. One of the great spiritual classics, *The Spiritual Exercises of St. Ignatius,* is not so much a book to be read as it is a prolonged series of meditations to be engaged in by the maturing Christian. The aim of its practices is "to find God in all things." This theme pervades Teilhard's writings and finds expression in a variety of forms.

Teilhard was one of the most receptive of Ignatius's many followers. His experiences in prayer "set him on fire" with an intense desire to accomplish great things for Jesus. This motivated and spurred him on to his truly monumental accomplishments both in geology and paleontology and in his writings on spirituality. Intimate union, the fruit of his deep prayer, fueled the fire of his love and his desire "ever to excel."

"Finding God in all things," a key phrase from the Exercises, summarizes Teilhard's mysticism, a mysticism rooted in the deep desire to live a life of accomplishing great things for Christ-Omega. The *Spiritual Exercises* of Ignatius of Loyola, and the biblical readings referred to in it, are the ground and driving force at the heart of Teilhard's motivation. However, his mysticism was fresh and new, departing in some ways from a long tradition.

From as long ago as the Middle Ages and continuing into our own day there
is a valid Christian tradition of passive spirituality that still flourishes, known
as "apophatic" or as a mysticism of unknowing. The venerable and traditional
mysticism of unknowing is traced at least as far as to a 14th century classic, the
anonymously authored *Cloud of Unknowing*.[42]

Teilhard, on the other hand, wrote about and practiced another kind of
mysticism, one with its primary roots in Ignatius's *Spiritual Exercises,* and
correctly characterized as a mysticism of action, a "katophatic" mysticism, if you
will.[43] He boldly sums up his struggle and his approach to what might appear
to be a paradox in one of his most succinct formulations: "There is a communion
with God, and a communion with earth, and a communion with God through
earth." And, in order to be able to articulate this approach to his satisfaction,
like Jacob, he too "fought with the angel until day was come." [44]

TEILHARD'S VIEW OF THE UNIVERSE

Throughout his life, Teilhard sought to articulate his view of how we might
participate in cosmic evolution through the sacrament of the Eucharist. He
began to summarize that spirituality in his essay, "The Priest." There Teilhard
had written that, because he had neither bread nor wine nor altar, he was taking
the whole universe as the matter of his sacrifice.[45] "The Mass on the World"
begins with almost identical words:

> Since over again, Lord—though this time not in the forest of the Aisne but
> in the steppes of Asia—I have neither bread, nor wine, nor altar, I will raise
> myself beyond these symbols, up to the pure majesty of the real itself; I, your
> priest, will make the whole earth my altar and on it I will offer you all the
> labors and sufferings of the world.[46]

The lyrical essay is simply signed "Ordos," the name for the region where
he was carrying out his research at the time.

In a recent encyclical on the Eucharist, *Ecclesia de Eucharistia*, Pope John
Paul II refers to the cosmic character of the Eucharist in a way that is similar
to Teilhard's "The Mass on the World."

> When I think of the Eucharist, and look at my life as a priest, as a Bishop and
> as the Successor of Peter, I naturally recall the many times and places in which
> I was able to celebrate it. I remember the parish church of Niegowic, where I
> had my first pastoral assignment, the collegiate church of Saint Florian in

Krakow, Wawel Cathedral, Saint Peter's Basilica and so many basilicas and churches in Rome and throughout the world. I have been able to celebrate Holy Mass in chapels built along mountain paths, on lake shores and seacoasts; I have celebrated it on altars built in stadiums and in city squares. . . .

This varied scenario of celebrations of the Eucharist has given me a powerful experience of its universal and, so to speak, cosmic character. Yes, cosmic! Because even when it is celebrated on a humble altar of a country church, the Eucharist is always in some way celebrated on the altar of the world. It unites heaven and earth. It embraces and permeates all creation. The Son of God became man in order to restore all creation, one supreme act of praise, to the One who made it from nothing. He, the Eternal High Priest who by the blood of his Cross entered the eternal sanctuary, thus gives back to the Creator and Father all creation redeemed. He does so through the priestly ministry of the Church, to the glory of the Most Holy Trinity. Truly this is the *mysterium fidei* which is accomplished in the Eucharist: the world which came forth from the hands of God the Creator now returns to him redeemed by Christ.[47]

Cardinal Joseph Ratzinger (now Pope Benedict XVI), in one of his books on the liturgy, praised Teilhard's Mass as follows:

Teilhard went on to give a new meaning to Christian worship: the transubstantiated Host is the anticipation of the transformation and divinization of matter in the Christological "fullness." In his view, the Eucharist provides the movement of the cosmos with its direction; it anticipates its goal and at the same time urges it on.[48]

Though a cosmic understanding of the Mass is found in some of the early Church writers, it was not part of recent theology until it was developed by Teilhard.[49]

Notes

1. Published in similar form as James W. Skehan, S.J., "Geology and Grace: Teilhard's Life and Achievements," *Teilhard Studies* 53 (Fall 2006).

2. Emeritus Professor of Geology and Geophysics, Director Emeritus Weston Observatory, Boston College, Weston, MA, 02193.

3. James W. Skehan, *Praying with Teilhard de Chardin* (Winona, MN: St. Mary's Press, 2001), 64.

4. Ursula King, *Spirit of Fire: The Life and Vision of Teilhard de Chardin* (Maryknoll, NY: Orbis Books, 1996), 4.

5. Claude Cuénot, *Teilhard de Chardin: A Biographical Study* (Baltimore: Helicon Press, Inc., 1965), 3.

6. Ursula King, *Spirit of Fire*, 10.
7. Ibid.
8. Cuénot, *Teilhard de Chardin*, 4.
9. Ibid., 6.
10. See, for instance, David L. Fleming, S.J., *The Spiritual Exercises of St. Ignatius: A Literal Translation and a Contemporary Reading* (St. Louis: The Institute of Jesuit Sources, 1978).
11. George B. Barbour, *In the Field with Teilhard de Chardin* (New York: Herder and Herder, 1965).
12. Ursula King, *Spirit of Fire*, 25.
13. The web site for Teilhardina is http://www.sinofossa.org/mammal/teilhardina.
14. Pierre Teilhard de Chardin, *Letters from Egypt, 1905-1908*, trans. Mary Ilford (New York: Herder and Herder, 1965).
15. Ursula King (*Spirit of Fire*, 25) notes that Teilhard's letters during this period were distant in tone and expressed little of the tremendous emotional impact that these years made on him. She notes also that his letters expressed a far greater interest in nature than in society. These included letters to his parents which remained formal and descriptive. "Only his essays, written years later, give strong expression to his memorable experiences and reflect something of the haunting and lasting appeal that a large Eastern country had on the life of his mind."
16. Jeanne Mortier and Marie-Louise Aboux, eds., *Teilhard de Chardin Album* (New York: Harper & Row Publishers, 1966), 36.
17. Col 1:17b.
18. Pierre Teilhard de Chardin, *The Heart of Matter* (New York: Harcourt Brace Jovanovich, 1978), 25-26.
19. Ursula King, *Spirit of Fire*, 35.
20. Mortier and Aboux, *Teilhard de Chardin Album*, 44.
21. Personal communication, 2005.
22. Skehan, *Praying with Teilhard*, 26.
23. Ibid., 13.
24. Ibid., 27.
25. Ursula King, *Spirit of Fire*, 87.
26. Ibid., 88.
27. Pierre Teilhard de Chardin, *Hymn of the Universe*, trans. Simon Bartholomew (New York: Harper & Row, Publisher, 1961), 11.
28. Skehan, *Praying with Teilhard*, 27.
29. Nicole and Karl Schmitz-Moormann, eds., *Pierre Teilhard de Chardin, L'Oeuvre Scientifique* (Olten und Freiburg im Breisgau: Walter-Verlag, 1971).
30. Cuénot, *Teilhard de Chardin*, 75.
31 Ibid., 72.
32. Ibid., 76. The letter was written 2 April 1929.
33. Pierre Teilhard de Chardin, *Letters from a Traveller*, trans. Bernard Wall (New York: Harper & Row, Publishers, 1962), 153-55.
34. Cuénot, *Teilhard de Chardin*, 76.
35. Ibid., 77.
36. Joseph MacDonnell, S.J., *Jesuit Geometers* (St. Louis, MO: The Institute of Jesuit Sources, St. Louis University, 1989); Joseph MacDonnell, S.J., *Jesuit Family Album: Sketches of*

Chivalry from the Early Society (Fairfield, CT: The Clavius Group, Fairfield University, 1997).

37. Pierre Teilhard de Chardin, *Science and Christ*, trans. René Hague (New York: Harper & Row, Publishers, 1968), 168-69.

38. Christopher F. Mooney, S.J., *Teilhard de Chardin and the Mystery of Christ* (New York: Harper & Row, 1964), 162.

39. James W. Skehan, S.J., "Exploring Teilhard's 'New Mysticism': Building the Cosmos," *Journal of Ecotheology* 10, no. 1, (2005): 11-34.

40. Quoted in Mooney, *Teilhard and the Mystery of Christ*, 28-29.

41. Harvey D. Egan, S.J., *What are they saying about Mysticism?* (New York: Paulist Press, 1982); Harvey D. Egan, S.J., *Ignatius Loyola the Mystic* (Wilmington: Michael Glazier, 1987).

42. James W. Skehan, S.J., "Toward a Spirituality of Scientific Research," in Patrick Byrne, ed., *Science and Religion: What We Have Learned From One Another* (Scranton: Scranton University Press, 2005), 199.

43. Ibid.

44. Pierre Teilhard de Chardin, *Writings in Time of War*, trans. René Hague (New York: Harper & Row, 1967), 14.

45. Ibid., 205.

46. Teilhard, *Heart of Matter*, 119.

47. Pope John Paul II, Papal Encyclical, *Ecclesia de Eucharistia*, no. 8, (*Origins* 32, no. 46 [May 1, 2003]: 409ff. Pope John Paul II directly quotes a passage from Teilhard's Mass in Pope John Paul II, *Gift and Mystery, on the Fiftieth Anniversary of My Priesthood* (New York: Doubleday Dell Publishing Co., 1996), 73.

48. Joseph Cardinal Ratzinger, *The Spirit of the Liturgy* (Ft. Collins, CO: Ignatius Press, 2000), 18.

49. Thomas M. King, *Teilhard's Mass: Approaches to The Mass on the World* (New York: Paulist Press, 2005), 22.

GENETICS AND THE
FUTURE OF HUMANITY

RONALD COLE-TURNER[1]

As well as anyone in his generation, Jesuit paleontologist Pierre Teilhard de Chardin recognized the fateful juxtaposition of two features of our contemporary situation. The first feature goes back to the mid-eighteenth century and is associated most prominently with the work of Charles Darwin. It is the discovery of the historicity of the cosmos, of planet earth, of life upon this planet and perhaps elsewhere, of the human species only late in time, and more recently of something that might be called civilization. None of these phenomena is eternal or static. The second feature, only in its infancy when Teilhard wrote more than fifty years ago, is the growth of technology, or more precisely, the acceleration of its rate of growth and the proliferation of its forms. Through technology's exponentially expanding capacities, human technologists are acquiring ever more power to transform and modify nature. Taken together, these two features of our situation are quickly bringing us to the point where technology can affect the evolution and historic transformations of some of these phenomena. Technology is already rapidly affecting human culture, and soon it will have the potential to modify human nature itself.

Of these two features of our age, Teilhard could see the first with clarity but the second only in anticipation, although with remarkable prescience. The fact of evolutionary process, however, is central to his thought. The change of consciousness of which he speaks is precisely a changed view of the nature of things, not as static and ordered but as dynamic. "To our clearer vision the universe is no longer an Order but a Process. The cosmos has become a Cosmogenesis."[2] Anthropology has become anthropogenesis, a process of evolutionary emergence. For Teilhard, anthropogenesis is not limited to the past. Teilhard criticizes evolutionary biologists who "still believe that the human species, having attained the level of *Homo sapiens*, has reached an upper organic limit beyond which it cannot develop, so that anthropogenesis is only of retrospective interest in the past."[3] Teilhard regards this as the "wholly illogical and arbitrary idea of arrested hominisation."[4] Why should human evolution not continue? It is in this context that Teilhard speaks of the "ultra-human."[5]

For Teilhard, the fact of human evolution meant not only that the human species emerged over the eons from previous forms of life, but also that a vast expanse of time might lie ahead. Will our species become extinct or simply languish on an evolutionary plateau, surviving but as a "living fossil"? No, Teilhard argued; on the contrary, "the human social phenomenon affords evidence that the evolution of Life on earth, far from having come to a stop, is on the contrary now entering a new phase."[6] Through human beings, through their new consciousness and emerging powers, evolution of life is generally infused with new possibilities. Nowhere are these new possibilities more awesome than when they rebound on human beings themselves, either to transform consciousness or the biological nature that is its material substrate.

According to Teilhard, "from the time of Man the evolutionary mechanism undergoes a radical change."[7] On the one hand, human beings may act "noospherically," by which today we might think of information technology, most notably the internet, a global web of networked processors not unlike a single brain. But Teilhard also anticipates another area of technology, even less developed in his time than were computers and global communications—that of genetic modification. In an essay first published in 1948, Teilhard writes that the human now "feels himself to be on the verge of acquiring the power of physico-chemical control of the operations of heredity and morphogenesis in the depths of his own being. So we may say that since by a sort of chain-reaction consciousness, itself born of complexity, finds itself in a position to bring about 'artificially' a further increase of complexity in its material dwelling...."[8] While Teilhard cannot foresee the revolution in molecular genetics that is about to occur, much less the powers of genetic engineering that are only now taking hold, he can anticipate that "the terrestrial evolution of Life, following its main axis of hominisation, is not only completely altering the scale of its creations but is also entering an 'explosive' phase of an entirely new kind."[9]

Teilhard recognizes that many of his contemporaries lacked faith in progress. "For all his discoveries and inventions, twentieth century man is a sad creation."[10] Optimism gives way to pessimism, not because evolution is rejected, but because on scientific grounds, there seems to be no way to avoid the prospect that the future of humanity is not continued evolution but sheer extinction. Why should our species not "simply vanish, one sort being replaced by another"?[11] If there is an answer, it lies in the unique quality of humanity as the species that has "entered the realm of Thought."[12] What Teilhard has in view is clearly not a technological paradise of abundance and pleasure, a "bourgeois" paradise rooted in "pagan materialism," nor should the "ultra-human" be "some form of threadbare millennium."[13] On the contrary, "it is upon its point (or superstructure) of spiritual concentration, and not on its basis (or infra-structure) of material arrangement, that the equilibrium of Mankind biologically depends."[14] By themselves, evolution and technology only arouse our pessimism. They bring change but no direction, and they leave us asking: "towards what summit, or what abyss?"[15] If there is truly a future for humanity as a species, it depends upon such "spiritual concentration" which, for Teilhard as a Christian intellectual, is identical with the core of Christian belief in God incarnate in Christ. Pessimism and despair are countered by eschatological expectation of the full and final meaning of Christ. For "the ultra-human perfection which neo-humanism envisages for Evolution will coincide in concrete terms with the crowning of the Incarnation awaited by all Christians."[16] The two ideas—evolution's future and God's promise—converge in their meaning and in their certainty. "For such a Christian the eventual biological success of Man on Earth is not merely a probability but a certainty: since Christ (and in Him virtually the World) is already risen."[17]

Not everyone shares this religious certainty, and many who assent to its theological basis (Christ is risen) do not agree that this truth bears any connection whatsoever to the future of evolution. On the contrary, they claim that the incarnation fixes the theological definition of human nature in the precise form of humanity assumed historically in Jesus of Nazareth. His genome, which we all share, is the full and final expression of humanity as assumed by God into the eternal fellowship of the triune life.[18] Still others, who share with Teilhard both the theology and the view that humanity is an emergent species, are apprehensive nevertheless about any human role in human "improvement." The classic statement of this objection is C. S. Lewis's *Abolition of Man.*

First written in 1943, at about the same time as Teilhard's essays, *Abolition* argues precisely the opposite of Teilhard: "if any one age really attains, by eugenics and scientific education, the power to make its descendants what it pleases, all men who live after it are the patients of that power. They are weaker, not stronger: for though we may have put wonderful machines in their hands we have pre-ordained how they are to use them."[19] In summary, his warning is that "Each new power won *by* man is a power *over* man as well. Each advance leaves him weaker as well as stronger. In every victory, besides being the general who triumphs, he is also the prisoner who follows the triumphal car."[20]

The difference between Teilhard and Lewis could not be more striking, and it is a difference that continues to this day to divide Christians who reflect on technological modifications of human nature. The basis for the difference appears at first glance to lie in different assessments of the moral state of human agents, whether developers or consumers of transformative technologies. Are we fallen beings whose actions are more likely to plunge us further into fallenness than to lift us to a free and virtuous humanity? Lewis fears what we will do to each other, while Teilhard is more optimistic about our respect for moral limits. But surely this difference in their theological anthropology alone does not go far enough in explaining the eschatology, because in both cases eschatology is primarily the work of God, not of human beings. Whatever their differences on the moral state of humans (between Teilhard and Lewis but also between all who line up behind one position or the other), these are insufficient to explain the differences in attitude toward technological modification. Also at play is a different view of God or more precisely of providence, God's role in determining the end. Will God direct the outcome, using whatever contributions might be made by human technology and restraining human folly, while assuring the general shape of its pathway and determining its final state? Or is God merely offering us salvation while allowing us to create our own hell, whether individually or collectively, with human folly unrestrained? Or is there some third option?

Teilhard's theological certainty aside, it might be asked whether there is some other basis for confidence, if not exactly in the future of evolution, then at least in the view that evolution has a direction and that there may be such a thing as evolutionary progress after all. Recently, Simon Conway Morris has argued that the surprising amount of convergence in evolution (independent origins of similar adaptive solutions) provides a basis for re-thinking the questions of direction and progress. Conway Morris concludes:

> we need [not] imagine that the appearance of humans is the culmination of all evolutionary history. Yet, when within the animals we see the emergence of larger and more complex brains, sophisticated vocalizations, echolocation, electrical perception, advanced social systems including eusociality, viviparity, warm-bloodedness, and agriculture—all of which are convergent—then to me that sounds like progress.[21]

Nevertheless, Conway Morris cites Lewis with approval. He warns against genetic determinism and the false confidence it gives in biotechnology. In particular he cautions against the juxtaposition of biotechnology with the view that nature is without intrinsic value, and that evolution lacks intrinsic directionality, which must be respected.

> these myths of genetic determinism, set in a dreary world of reductionism, are being used to drive new agendas, most notably in eugenics. At present it is the natural world, which, according to some, should be treated as a sort of genetic play-dough. Now vanished is the notion that the world we have been given might have its own integrity and values. Rather the prevailing view of scientism is that the biosphere is infinitely malleable.[22]

The irony here is that while Conway Morris shares with Teilhard the conviction that there is a direction in evolution, one that might even be called toward "hominisation,"[23] he agrees with Lewis, not Teilhard, about the role of biotechnology in the service of evolutionary progress.

Almost as if he is paraphrasing Lewis, Conway Morris observes that science "gives us tools that treat the world as endlessly malleable, ostensibly for the common good but as often as not for the enrichment of the few and the impoverishment of the many."[24] Religion rightly criticizes this tendency, and thus is sometimes seen as anti-science. More fundamental, however, is that Conway Morris's "directionality" in evolution is not an inevitable progression toward a Teilhardian Omega point. "Hominisation" may be sabotaged by individual human beings and their new kit of tools and its future might by-pass us altogether, precisely because hominisation is not unique to our species but convergent. If there is a future to hominisation,[25] it may or may not include us. While in Conway Morris there might be the sort of directionality and purpose that a theologian could label as "providence," it is not the sort of providence that requires our participation, depends upon our survival, or precludes our self-withdrawal.

Whatever the future of evolution might be, whether good or ill, our technological intrusion into its processes raises new concerns of a profound sort, not merely about the future of our lives as individuals or of our social and national institutions, but of human life itself, perhaps even beyond. At these levels of generality and finality, the depth of concern registers itself on an eschatological scale, perhaps not literally reaching the ultimate finality of a theological heaven and hell, but pointing us in that direction and attaining a kind of penultimate state. If technology does not usher in the true and final heaven or the ultimate annihilation, it may be the next best (or worst) thing. As such, technological futures invite theological exploration under the doctrine of eschatology, the doctrine of the end. A recent journalistic survey of trans-human and post-human technological scenarios, for instance, includes a chapter on techno-heaven and one on techno-hell, not with hosts of angels and legions of demons, but with ubiquitous computers and swarming nanobots.[26] Among the prophets of the new technological heaven are Hans Moravec[27] and Ray Kurzweil,[28] while hell is foretold by Bill Joy.[29]

These scenarios depend upon a full range of emerging technologies, while our attention here is somewhat limited to consideration of new genetic technologies that are being applied to human beings or are soon to be ready for human use. At the core of our focus is the notion of human germline modification, often called "designer children." A recent study defines germline modification this way:

> Human Germline Genetic Modification [HGGM] refers to techniques that would attempt to create a permanent inheritable (i.e. passed from one generation to the next) genetic change in offspring and future descendants by altering the genetic makeup of the human germline, meaning eggs, sperm, the cells that give rise to eggs and sperm, or early human embryos.[30]

Germline modification is possible in other species, including mammals and even primates. Accepted standards of safety, however, require that the techniques currently used in other animals be refined considerably before the human germline modification can be considered safe enough to approve even on an experimental basis. Some doubt whether sufficient safety will ever be achieved so that legitimate approval will be given. Others point to recent developments to suggest that, in time, the technology of genetic modification will be safe.

Before describing some of the technical strategies that might be used to achieve human germline modification, it is useful to reflect for a moment on the social context of these technologies. The most immediate and obvious reason to use germline modification is to allow couples at risk for a genetic disease to start a pregnancy while avoiding the risk. But in the majority of such cases, the risk can be avoided using an existing technique known as preimplantation genetic diagnosis (PGD). This technique depends upon *in vitro* fertilization (IVF), which is used to create multiple embryos that are allowed to develop to about eight cells each. One cell from each embryo is removed and tested for genes related to disease, allowing for the selection of healthy embryos for implantation.

In some respects, PGD is seen as a moral improvement on genetic tests run during pregnancy, for instance by using amniocentesis. But PGD requires the testing and the destruction of embryos, which is opposed by some. For them, germline modification—though far more complex and risky at the moment— is in principle morally superior to PGD, because rather than destroying unhealthy embryos, it allows the creation of a healthy embryo in the first place. For instance, Catholic teaching forbids IVF and PGD, but leaves the door open for human germline modification. The Catholic Catechism teaches that "one must hold as licit procedures carried out on the human embryo which respect the life and integrity of the embryo and do not involve disproportionate risks for it, but are directed toward its healing, the improvement of its condition or health, or its individual survival."[31]

The technical possibility of human germline modification is still some decades in the future, but recent advances have brought it closer. Advances in gene modification are critical, and new techniques of homologous recombination allow precise gene targeting. Well-publicized work in cloning or nuclear transfer also opens new possibilities, as do advances in human embryonic stem cells. One possible strategy for human germline modification combines these techniques. In humans, it is possible to modify embryonic stem cells with precise homologous recombination.[32] In mice, at least, it is possible to create eggs and sperm from mouse embryonic stem cells.[33] If human eggs or sperm could be created from genetically modified stem cells, and if these modified eggs or sperm could be used to create an embryo, the result would be genetically modified embryos. Or it might be possible to modify human embryonic stem cells, and then use nuclear transfer, transferring the nucleus of one of the modified cells into a human enucleated egg. In either case, human germline modification would result. Other more futuristic techniques are also being considered, such as the insertion of an artificial chromosome with multiple genes into a fertilized egg.

Germline modification to avoid disease enjoys some religious and moral support. No one, however, thinks that germline modification will be limited to the avoidance of disease. A far more enticing use will be to enhance various traits, some of which might be related to health and some that clearly go beyond any concern related to health. It may be morally acceptable to use germline modification to enhance the immune system of future generations or to enhance resistance to cancer, but enhance cognitive or athletic ability? Yet it is precisely these more grandiose forms of enhancement (assuming they will someday be possible) that are central to the dreams and the nightmares of technology in the service of eschatology.

If we are to reflect on the potential for genetic technologies to modify our humanity, we must note in passing the other areas of technology that will also play a significant role in human self-modification and transformation. Beyond biotechnology, these extend to nanotechnology, information technology, and cognitive science. A recent report describes the range of fields as "nano-bio-info-cogno" (NBIC), which includes the "provinces of science and technology, each of which is currently progressing at a rapid rate: (a) nanoscience and nanotechnology; (b) biotechnology and biomedicine, including genetic engineering; (c) information technology, including advanced computing and communications; (d) cognitive science, including cognitive neuroscience."[34] From these fields of research, not taken alone but through their convergence, dramatic transformations are forecast:

> Examples of payoffs may include improving work efficiency and learning, enhancing individual sensory and cognitive capabilities, revolutionary changes in healthcare, improving both individual and group creativity, highly effective communication techniques including brain-to-brain interaction, perfecting human-machine interfaces including neuromorphic engineering, sustainable and "intelligent" environments including neuro-ergonomics, enhancing human capabilities for defense purposes, reaching sustainable development using NBIC tools, and ameliorating the physical and cognitive decline that is common to the aging mind.[35]

What is most remarkable about this statement is that it is not the fantasy of an individual techno-enthusiast, but the consensus view from a group study funded by the US government through the National Science Foundation and the Department of Commerce.

The critical claim here is not just that each of these areas is expanding rapidly, or even that each has a major potential to affect the capacities or performance abilities of human beings, but that the four areas are undergoing what should be called "convergence," which suggests that we are now faced with technological convergence on top of evolutionary convergence. Technological convergence is cultural, not biological or genetic, but, nonetheless, it shares certain features with Conway Morris's view of convergence in evolution. It bears perhaps even greater similarities to Teilhard's view of the technology of the future. The report suggests that

> Convergence of diverse technologies is based on *material unity at the nanoscale and on technology integration from that scale.* The building blocks of matter that are fundamental to all sciences originate at the nanoscale. Revolutionary advances at the interfaces between previously separate fields of science and technology are ready to create key *transforming tools* for NBIC technologies. Developments in systems approaches, mathematics, and computation in conjunction with NBIC allow us for the first time to understand the natural world, human society, and scientific research as *closely coupled complex, hierarchical systems.* At this moment in the evolution of technical achievement, *improvement of human performance through integration of technologies* becomes possible.[36]

So defined, the convergent "evolution of technical achievement," while profoundly different from convergent evolution in biology, shares some parallels with its biological counterpart, parallels at least of a metaphoric or linguistic sort. Technology solves problems, and so does evolution, at least if Conway Morris is right about adaptation and life's "solution." Both are radically decentralized; that is to say, there is no central problem-solving authority guiding either. Independent fields of research (parallel to independent lines of descent) come to similar solutions, in part because of the constraints imposed by physics and chemistry (the nano-scale), in part because of the selective pressures of the environment, ecological or human. Complex "solutions" are the cumulative result of many small solutions and of many more useless attempts that are discarded. A direction or tendency can be observed in retrospect and, with great caution, tentatively projected into the future. Even so, there is a fundamental difference between these two uses of the word "convergence." As Conway Morris applies it to evolution, it refers to similar solutions independently evolved; as the NBIC report applies it to technology, it refers to the merging of techniques, leveraging the power of each to a higher level.

Quite remarkably, however, the report exhibits an unapologetic Teilhardian hopefulness about the future, not Lewis's (or Conway Morris's) apprehension of technologies of control gone out of control. The report asserts "converging technologies could achieve a tremendous improvement in human abilities, societal outcomes, the nation's productivity, and the quality of life."[37] In a key summary, the report presents this optimistic view of the future:

> People may possess entirely new capabilities for relations with each other, with machines, and with the institutions of civilization. In some areas of human life, old customs and ethics will persist, but it is difficult to predict which realms of action and experience these will be. Perhaps wholly new ethical principles will govern in areas of radical technological advance, such as the acceptance of brain implants, the role of robots in human society, and the ambiguity of death in an era of increasing experimentation with cloning. Human identity and dignity must be preserved. In the same way in which machines were built to surpass human physical powers in the industrial revolution, computers can surpass human memory and computational speed for intended actions. The ultimate control will remain with humans and human society. With proper attention to safeguards, ethical issues, and societal needs, quality of life could increase significantly.[38]

Ethics, according to this report, will be needed and will indeed be found adequate to new demands of convergent technology, guiding technology and technologist and the end-consumer of technology alike to the path of human improvement. "It may be possible to develop a predictive science of society and to apply advanced corrective actions, based on the convergence ideas of NBIC. Human culture and human physiology may undergo rapid evolution, intertwining like the twin strands of DNA, hopefully guided by analytic science as well as traditional wisdom."[39] Let us hope so.

Standing upon "analytic science" and upon his own not-too-traditional version of "traditional wisdom," Teilhard grounds his hope scientifically *and* theologically in the God of cosmogenesis and hominisation. These processes are sure and certain for Teilhard because they are founded on Christ in God.

But at precisely this point, a theological question must be posed. Does the Christian God of creation, the God of Jesus Christ, guarantee the future of history or the future of evolution? Is that the meaning of providence, to secure its outcome even if it means that God overrides human folly? Does "Christ died for our sins" mean that God cancels the grip of sin on history, including the future of our technological transformations of nature? Or must we not acknowledge that the future is at risk even for God, that God does not control the precise form of the future, that sin is forgiven but its wounds remain, and that hell is always a real option for free mortals? In that case, God should then be said to draw the world toward its future rather than control each step in that process, inviting but not demanding.

Such a view is consistent with Christian theological positions known as *kenotic*, which see God as self-limiting, thereby sharing the determination of the cosmic future with the cosmos itself. While this view tends toward deism, it stops decidedly short, for it does not rule out all divine influence on the present or in the determination of the future.

> One could not give credit to a God who created an open-ended universe and then merely *hoped* for a final consummation that would be to "his" liking. God must also "draw the world unto himself" through some sort of causal activity. The tradition has called this influence providence.[40]

Tradition, we should add, has debated the scope and specificity of this providence. Well before theology's encounter with contemporary science, some theologians have endorsed a view of providence that is based on self-limited power.

Today, with contemporary science as a clarifying constraint upon theology, we can think of providence at play particularly in the responses of free and conscious creatures. "Certainly by the point that minds emerge, some influence on their creativity and comprehension could be postulated.... Moreover, to the extent that sentient beings of all sorts—hence most of the animal kingdom—evidence an openness and a creative striving that anticipates the virtually unconstrained creativity of mind, could there not also be some space for response to actual divine influence, even of the most limited or constrained kind, here as well?"[41] Whatever this may look like among non-humans, among our own kind, this "actual divine influence" may be seen as the theological counterpart to ethics. And if so, then ethics is far nobler than we often think. It is more than our effort to sort out good and bad options. Ethics is our response to providence and our openness to its transforming work in our own lives. It is our consent to God's continuing creation of the future. It is our tuning in, as it were, to God's welcoming call of the cosmos to its future, a call or a prompting which is self-limited, but for that reason all the more God-like in its form of power.

In this connection, we can appreciate Teilhard's forceful rejection of the idea, which he identifies as existentialist, that the future is sheer void until we decide what to make of it. The notion that the future is a "substance into which we may cut as we please, as expediency dictates and in any direction, is positively and *scientifically* incorrect."[42] Like Teilhard, Hans Jonas also warns us of the dangers of seeing nature as a valueless void that greets us with no limits, no goods to be preserved, no values to be respected. "Since nothing is sanctioned by nature and therefore everything is permitted to us, we have full freedom for creative play that is guided by nothing but the whim of the playing impulse and makes no claim other than to master the rules of the game, that is, the claim of technical competences."[43] We are not permitted to determine the future by whim or fancy because the future, not in detail but in its general form, is directed toward its end, its divinely chosen *telos* or all-embracing purpose. Careful and reflective attention to the end or purpose of our acts is a necessary condition for any ethics, and theological ethics begins with discerning and acquiescing to the purposes of God in creation.

The danger of a future made worse by technology is real and not merely hypothetical because, although we are not *permitted* to reject God's purpose for creation, we are free to do so. We are not constrained by nature or God, and with the growing influence of technology at our disposal, we are not so limited in our powers. We are free to refuse to acknowledge God's purposes, but we may yet be given the grace to consent, to put ourselves and our technology in the service of the creator. In that case, we have good reason to hope for the future, not because of the wonders of technology *per se*, but because of the potential of technology in service, as new modes of divine creation. Consent begins with acknowledging value and purpose in nature, perhaps only seen now in a small way by the natural sciences, but central to the theological doctrine of creation, as coming from God, evolving to the delight of God, and returning to its source for the endless glory of God.

Our intellectual challenge is to see these two claims—the scientific and the theological—as mutually illuminating and inspiring. Our moral challenge is to surrender every self-indulgent impulse and technological fantasy of human control to this greater purpose, even if only vaguely grasped. Our ecclesial challenge is to form communities that can form character, confronting our selfishness and sustaining our vision. Our pedagogical challenge is to teach, not with dispassionate neutrality about the intellectual puzzles of science and religion, but in order to form intellectual, moral, and spiritual traits of character that hold technological possibility and theological piety in balance. In these ways it is to agree with Teilhard that

> Life, and most particularly the extreme point of Life represented by Mankind, is not simply a *state*. It is on the contrary . . . a vast, directed movement, bound up with the very structure of the Cosmogenesis. It has a "thread" which cannot be suppressed, and which must continue to show itself, in no way impaired, but respected, utilized and expressed, until (and at this point more than ever) it reaches the highest, most conscious forms of its development.[44]

Of course, while consent to God's purposes or ends is necessary for a robust Christian ethics, teleological consent alone is not sufficient. Attention to ends by themselves can lead to casual acceptance of immoral means, which violate fundamental principles. Furthermore, ethics requires that we attend to the human moral agent, to the formation of virtues or habits of character, and to the culmination of these virtues in faith, hope, and above all, love. Good ends and right means must flow from a heart open to being made holy, at least in the Christian vision of the moral life. But it is a clear vision of the end of our actions, a telos of our technology, that is most painfully lacking today. In this void, all things are permitted. With technology in our hands, all things are becoming possible. To hope in ethics, as the authors of the NBIC report do, is to take on more than they probably imagine. Hope cannot be an arbitrarily optimistic and theologically groundless choice, perhaps motivated sincerely by the need to silence our shudders over the advent of techno-hell, but with no real basis for salvation. The only real hope is the kind that is created within us, given together with a rigorous faith and a self-transcending love.

Notes

1. H. Parker Sharp Professor of Theology and Ethics, Pittsburgh Theological Seminary, Pittsburgh, PA 15206.
2. Pierre Teilhard de Chardin, *The Future of Man*, trans. Norman Denny (New York: Harper & Row, 1964), 274.
3. Ibid.
4. Ibid.
5. Ibid., 280.
6. Ibid., 204.
7. Ibid., 205.
8. Ibid.
9. Ibid.
10. Ibid., 313.
11. Ibid.
12. Ibid., 316.
13. Ibid., 317.
14. Ibid.
15. Ibid., 260.
16. Ibid., 280.
17. Ibid., 246-47.
18. Nigel M. de S. Cameron and Amy Michelle DeBaets, "Germline gene modification and the human condition *coram Deo*," in Ronald Cole-Turner, ed., *Design and Destiny: Jewish and Christian Perspectives on Human Germline Modification* (Cambridge, MA: MIT Press, 2008): 93-118.
19. C. S. Lewis, *The Abolition of Man* (1947; New York: Collier Books, 1962), 70.
20. Ibid., 71.
21. Simon Conway Morris, *Life's Solution: Inevitable Humans in a Lonely Universe* (Cambridge: Cambridge University Press, 2003), 307.
22. Ibid., 325.
23. Ibid., 274.
24. Ibid., 329.
25. Ibid., 274.
26. Joel Garreau, *Radical Evolution* (New York: Doubleday, 2004).
27. Hans Moravec, *Robot: Mere Machine to Transcendent Mind* (New York: Oxford University Press, 1999).
28. Ray Kurzweil, *The Singularity Is Near: When Humans Transcend Biology* (New York: Viking, 2005); see also www.kurzweilai.net.
29. Bill Joy, "Why the Future Doesn't Need Us," *Wired* 8, no. 4 (April 2004); available at http://www.wired.com/wired/archive/8.04/joy_pr.html.
30. Susanna Baruch, et al., *Human Germline Genetic Modification: Issues and Options for Policymakers* (Washington: Genetics and Public Policy Center, 2005), 9.
31. *The Catechism of the Catholic Church*, English translation (Washington: United States Catholic Conference, 1994, 1997), N2275, 549.
32. Thomas P. Zwaka and James A. Thomson, "Homologous recombination in human embryonic stem cells," *Nature Biotechnology* 21 (March 2003): 319-21.
33. H. Kubota, M. R. Avarbock, and R. L. Brinster, "Growth factors essential for self-renewal

and expansion of mouse spermatogonial stem cells," *Proceedings of the Natural Academy of Science U S A* 101 (23 November 2004): 16489-94; M. Kanatsu-Shinohara, S. Toyokuni, and T. Shinohara, "Genetic Selection of Mouse Male Germline Stem Cells in Vitro: Offspring from Single Stem Cells," *Biology Reproduction* 72 (2005): 236-40.

34. Mihail C. Roco and William Sims Bainbridge, eds., *Converging Technologies for Improving Human Performance: Nanotechnology, Biotechnology, Information Technology and Cognitive Science* (Arlington, VA: National Science Foundation, 2002), ix; available at http://www.wtec.org/ConvergingTechnologies/Report/NBIC_report.pdf.

35. Roco and Bainbridge, *Converging Technologies*, ix.

36. Ibid.

37. Ibid.

38. Ibid., 22.

39. Ibid.

40. Philip Clayton, "Panentheism Today: A Constructive Systematic Evaluation," in Philip Clayton and Arthur Peacocke, eds., *In Whom We Live and Move and Have Our Being: Panentheistic Reflections on God's Presence in a Scientific World* (Grand Rapids, Michigan: Eerdmans, 2004), 264.

41. Ibid.

42. Teilhard de Chardin, *The Future of Man*, 236.

43. Hans Jonas, *The Imperative of Responsibility: In Search of an Ethics for the Technological Age* (Chicago: University of Chicago Press, 1984), 33.

44. Teilhard de Chardin, *The Future of Man*, 236.

The day will come when
after harnessing
the ether,
the winds,
the tides,
gravitation,
we shall harness for God
the energies of love.
And, on that day,
for the second time
in the history of the world,
humanity will have discovered fire.

—Pierre Teilhard de Chardin,
Toward the Future, 87

INDEX

A

Abolition of Man (1947), 228

Abraham (founding patriarch of Israelites), 63-64

Academy Goncourt, Paris (est. 1900) (French literary organization), 72

Academy of Natural Science, Philadelphia, 72

acoustics, 99, 119, 121

Acropolis, Athens, 95

"The Activation of Human Energy" (1953), 183

Aczel, Amir D. (b. 1950) (Israeli mathematician, scientist), 84-85n

Adam (Biblical patriarch, 1st man), 4, 61-62, 67n, 70, 75, 78, 82; see Eve

aesthetics, xiv, 94, 96, 127-30

Africa, 75, 214

agriculture, 47, 229

Aisne, France, 213, 220

Aix-en-Provence, France, 209

alienation, 34, 46

American Teilhard Association, ix, 7n, 51n

analogia entis (Lt. analogy of being), 129

angels, 22, 92-93, 101, 220, 230

animals, 41, 57, 80, 154, 168, 176, 179, 188, 191, 198-99, 201, 204, 229-30, kingdom, 18, 235; suffering, 60, 65n

anthropology, 226, 228

apes, 107, 176, 189

Appleton-Weber, Sarah, 116n

Aquinas, Thomas, O.P., St. (c. 1225-1274) (Italian Dominican, scholastic theologian), 81-82, 87, 165

Aristotle (384-322 B.C.) (Greek philosopher), 80, 165

art, xi, 34, 41, 92, 95, 97-101, 119, 127-32, 134, 208; artists, 47, 94, 96-101, 130, 132, 179

asceticism, 9; Teilhard, 26

Asia, 10, 37, 91, 213-15, 220

Ateneo de Manila University, Philippines, ix

atheists, xii, xv, 193; materialistic, 191, 194

atmosphere, 15, 21, 61, 131, 199, 202-04, 206n

atom, 7, 13, 16, 38, 40, 44, 95-96, 120, 154, 179

Atran, Scott (b. 1952) (American anthropologist), 56-57

Augustine of Hippo, St. (c. 354-450) (Romanized Berber, Bishop of Hippo Regius, theologian), 74

Auvergne, France, 3, 9, 71, 85n, 207, 209

B

Balthasar, Hans Ur von, Cardinal (1905-1988) (Swiss theologian), xiv, 129-32, 134n

Baltimore, Maryland, 177, 185n

Bampton Lectures, Oxford University (1996), 28n

baptism (Christian sacrament), 37

Barbour, George, S.J. (Jesuit geomorphologist, stratigrapher), 210, 214, 216

Barbour, Ian Graeme (b. 1923) (American theologian), 25, 30n, 84, 163

Barthélemy-Madaule, Madeleine, 84

Beatrice, Folco Portinari (1266-1290) (Florentine friend of Dante), 100

beauty, x, 24, 49, 91, 121-22, 127-28, 131, 133, 143, 170; Balthasar on, 129, 131; Divine, xiv, 22-24, 94-96, 131-32; feminine, 95-96, 100; moral, 96; music, 94; nature, xiii, 11-12, 14, 26, 94, 96; redemption by, 128, 132; souls, 95; Teilhard on, xiii, 23-24, 91-101, 131

Bégouën, Simone, 72

behavior, 155, 160-61, 166, 188-89, 191-93, 203-04

Behe, Michael (b. 1952) (American biochemist), xii, 169, 171n

Being and Time (1962), 170-71n

Benedict XVI, Pope (b. 1927) (265th pope, German theologian), 194, 221

Berger, Peter (b. 1929) (sociologist), 66n

Bergson, Henri-Louis (1859-1941) (French philosopher), 12, 79, 83-84, 189

246 | Rediscovering Teilhard's Fire

Resistance, French, 77
Resurrection of Jesus Christ, 9, 117n, 138, 142-43, 168
Ricci, Matteo, S.J. (1552-1610) (Italian Jesuit, missionary, Chinese *literati*), 217
Ricoeur, Paul (b. 1913-2005) (French philosopher), 61, 67n, 128, 133
Ridley, Matthew White (b. 1958) (British journalist, zoologist), 59
rituals, 34, 38, 44, 99
Rockefeller Foundation, 215
rocks, 3, 5, 12, 35, 58, 198, 210-11, 215
Romans, Pauline epistle, 193
Rome, 69-76, 80-81, 194, 221; see Church, Catholic
Rue, Loyal (American theologian, Luther College, Iowa), 56
Ruse, Michael (b. 1940) (British biology philosopher), 66n
Russo, François, 75
Ryan, John, xiv

S

sacred, 18, 37, 56, 130
The Sacred Canopy (1990), 66
Sacred Heart (title for Christ), 23, 112, 208; consecration of human race, 209; see Jesus Christ
Sacred Scripture, xii, 39, 209, 211
Saint Florian Collegiate Church, Krakow (est. 1185), 220
Saint Peter Basilica, Vatican City (built c. 326, rebuilt 1506-1626), 220
Salmon, James, S.J., x, xiv, 185n
salvation, 37, 39, 44, 115, 192-93, 228, 237
Sang-han-ho, China, 216
Sarcenat, Auvergne (Teilhard family chateau), 207
satisfaction, 60, 66n
Schleiermacher, Friedrich (1768-1834) (German Reformed minister, theologian), 67n, 105
Schaab, Gloria, S.S.J., xiv
Schmitz-Moormann, Karl, 179-80, 186n
scholasticism, 78-80, 84, 194
Schönborn, Christoph Maria, O.P., Cardinal (b. 1945) (Archbishop of Vienna), 194
Schrödinger, Erwin (1887-1961) (Austrain physicist), 178, 183-84
scientism, xii, 229

Scotus, John Duns, O.F.M. (c. 1266-1308) (Scottish Franciscan theologian, philosopher), 165
secularism, 4-5, 34, 37, 39, 109
sentience, 57-58
sexuality, 20, 26, 151
sin, 54, 60, 73, 82, 114, 141, 188, 192-93, 235
Shanghai, China, 210, 212
Sinanthropus pekinensis (discovered 1929-1930), 72; see Peking man
Sisters of St. Joseph, Philadelphia (est. 1858), x
Skehan, James, S.J., xiv, 31n, 221
skull, 176, 215
Sloyan, Gerard, 66n
Smith, Huston Cummings (b. 1919) (American religious studies scholar), 30n
socialization, 107-08, 150-51
social thought, xi, xv
Society of Jesus, see Jesuits
sociologists, 66n
Socrates (c. 469-399 B.C.) (Greek philosopher), 99-100
Solage, Bruno de, Mgr., 77
Sophia Lecture, Washington Theological Union (2004), 65n
Sorbonne University, Paris (est. 12th c.), 30n, 71-72, 75, 200
soul, 10, 21, 23, 46, 49, 71, 93-97, 99-100, 113, 115, 117, 168, 213; creation of, 74; human, 147; modern, 110; pantheistic, 12; religious, 9; soul mates, 214
soul-making, 19
Soul of the World (Teilhard's term for God), 10, 92, 94
South Africa, 75
South America, 75
Soviet Union, 200
species, 33, 44, 60, 80, 87n, 91, 151, 158, 189, 197-98, 203-05, 211, 225-30
speculation, 41, 50
Spirit of Fire: The Life and Vision of Teilhard de Chardin (1996), 28n
The Spirit of One Earth: Reflections on Teilhard de Chardin and Global Spirituality (1989), 28n
Spiritual Exercises, 209, 219-20
spirituality, xii-xiii, 6, 9-12, 15, 17-18, 21, 24-27, 33-34, 36-41, 43-44, 46-48, 50, 60, 62, 92-93, 119, 209, 214, 216-17, 219-20